SHELLEY & REVOLUTIONARY IRELAND | PAUL O'BRIEN

From Susan,   24/9/07.

Paul O'Brien

Shelley &
Revolutionary
Ireland

PAUL O'BRIEN

REDWORDS
LONDON AND DUBLIN

Shelley & Revolutionary Ireland by Paul O'Brien

Published in 2002 by

REDWORDS

1 Bloomsbury Street, London WC1B 3QE

and 47 Synge Street, Dublin 8

Copyright © Paul O'Brien

www.redwords.org.uk

ISBN paperback: 1 872208 19 3

ISBN hardback: 1 872208 20 7

Design and production by Roger Huddle

Printed by The Bath Press, Bath

Shelley & Revolutionary Ireland
CONTENTS

        Footnotes appear at the end of each chapter

Redwords and Paul O'Brien would like to
thank the following for their help and
support in making this book possible.

John Charlton

Clare Fermont

Paul Foot

Mike Gonzalez

Marnie Holborow

Roger Huddle

Conor Kostic

Mary Phillips

Mary Ryder

Pauline Ryder

Colm Ryder

Dara Ryder

and Dave Waller

For my Father
Peter O'Brien (1918-1980)

Preface
PAUL FOOT

SHELLEY went to Ireland twice, in 1812, when he was 19, and in 1813. These excursions are routinely patronised by Shelley's many biographers. The trips to Ireland, and what Shelley wrote about Ireland at the time, are almost unanimously written off as the passing spasms of a young fanatic. Much fun is had by the more scornful and world-weary biographers with Shelley's desperate and in many cases futile attempts to spread his message among the Irish, and with his sense of having achieved nothing through his visit or by his pamphlets. Others derive from this failure the curious conclusion that Shelley in Ireland, as earlier in England and later in Italy, was as useless and ineffectual in politics as he was brilliant in verse.

Paul O'Brien, a socialist, a Shelleyan and a Dubliner, in what is the first full-length book about Shelley in Ireland, presents a quite different picture. By 1812, the young Shelley accurately identified Ireland as the nerve centre of the British oppression he had already come to detest.

The rebellion of 1798, the enforced Union of Ireland with Britain in 1800 and the revolt led by Robert Emmet, crushed in 1803, had all combined to expose the British government's brutality, cynicism and contempt for the Irish people. By 1812, what was left of Irish resistance was regrouping round the two demands of Catholic emancipation and repeal of the union.

Even before he went to Ireland, Shelley wrote his *Address to the Irish People*. As soon as he encountered the full horror of Irish poverty and destitution, and started to meet republicans, Shelley wrote another pamphlet with a new and quite different title and message: *Proposals for an Association*. In language much more specific and direct he urged all those who opposed oppression in Ireland to come together, to meet and agitate for repeal and emancipation. He also wrote a *Declaration of Rights*, a political testament. His decisive breach with the passive politics of what he later called the fireside revolutionaries infuriated and frightened Shelley's mentor, William Godwin, who wrote in desperation: 'Shelley, you are preparing a scene of blood!'

Paul O'Brien analyses these pamphlets in the context of Shelley's experiences in Ireland at the time. His book effectively rewrites the received story, and reveals the young Shelley not as some madcap adventurer but as a serious reformer and revolutionary with a genuine aim to stir the Irish masses to revolt. The book rescues two characters in particular from the condescension of history. Harriet Westbrook, Shelley's first wife, is usually underplayed by official Shelley historians, most of whom are keen to move on to the more exciting relationship between Shelley and his second wife Mary, the author of *Frankenstein*. Paul O'Brien paints a quite different picture of Harriet. Even more interesting is the emergence from the shadows of Dan Healy, the 'servant' who served some months in prison for posting up Shelley's provocative posters in Devon. He has been traditionally portrayed at best as sinister at worst as imbecilic, but here we discover that Shelley found him in Ireland and took to him and employed him not least for his revolutionary opinions.

There are plenty of books about Shelley in England, and Shelley in

Italy but this is the first about Shelley on Ireland. It is not confined to the pamphlets and visits of 1812 and 1813. Paul O'Brien is a lover of all Irish literature, especially the literature that flowed from the revolutionary events leading up to Irish independence in 1921. He finds and discloses how the genius of Shelley inspired the best of Irish writers. Yeats, O'Casey, Shaw, Joyce were all disciples of the young firebrand who was attracted first to Ireland before any of them had written a word. For all lovers of Irish republicans and revolutionaries this book digs up all sorts of treasures, and deserves pride of place on the shelves of anyone who, like Shelley, recognises that the important history of Ireland is a history of challenge and resistance.

All changed, changed utterly:
A terrible beauty is born [1]

THESE dramatic lines of W B Yeats on the 1916 Easter Rising in Dublin could just as easily describe the impact of the French Revolution on Shelley and his contemporaries. Yeats's 'terrible beauty' captures both the fear and the excitement of a revolution that transformed the world at the turn of the 19th century. One such consequence was to break down the barrier between poetry and the external world. The poet now spoke not just for himself, but for all mankind – their cry became his cry. But, if the poet was to speak for the masses, it was on condition that he not only shared their hopes for a better world, but identified with their suffering as well. This was the inspiration for Shelley's journey to Ireland in 1812, where he hoped to add his own 'little stock of usefulness' to the struggle for Catholic emancipation and repeal of the Union.

That we should start with Yeats is appropriate, for when he wrote that 'Shelley shaped his life' he did not exaggerate. Shelley touched the imagination of many Irish writers – the Young Ireland poets of 1848, Bernard

Shaw, James Joyce, Sean O'Casey, Charlie Donnelly and many more. In Irish politics there has always been a current inspired by the example and lyricism of Shelley. O'Casey always described himself as a 'Shelleyan Communist' and James Larkin, perhaps the finest orator produced by the Irish labour movement, found inspiration in the words of Shelley and Keats to sustain and inspire the downtrodden.

Yeats in his essay *The Philosophy of Shelley's Poetry* writes of going to a learned scholar, to ask the meaning of Shelley's poem *Prometheus Unbound*, and being told 'that it was Godwin's *Political Justice* put into rhyme, and that Shelley was a crude revolutionist'.[2] Yeats was writing in the 1890s, when the Shelley industry was in full swing, excising 'every trace of political or social thought from Shelley's work'.[3] A generation of Shelley lovers grew up for whom 'lies were more beautiful than truth'. No wonder his great revolutionary poems – *Queen Mab, Revolt of Islam* and *The Mask of Anarchy* – disappeared from the selected works and anthologies and all we were left with was Matthew Arnold's parody of the real Shelley:

> The Shelley of actual life is a vision of beauty and radiance, indeed,
> but availing nothing, effecting nothing. And in poetry no less than
> in life, he is a beautiful and ineffectual angel, beating in the void his
> luminous wings in vain.[4]

Bernard Shaw, in a brilliant but now forgotten essay, *Shaming the Devil about Shelley*, written on the 100th anniversary of Shelley's birth in 1892, tried in vain to put an end to the bogus Shelley being peddled by Arnold and his friends:

> In politics Shelley was a republican, a leveller, a radical of the most
> extreme type. He was even an Anarchist of the old-fashioned
> Godwinian School… In Religion, Shelley was an atheist… I now
> venture to suggest that in future the bogus Shelley be buried and
> done with. I make all allowances for the fact that we are passing
> through an epidemic of cowardice on the part of literary men and
> politicians which will certainly make us appear to the historians of
> 1992 the most dastardly crew that has ever disgraced the platform
> and the press.[5]

Fortunately it took less than a 100 years for the 'bogus Shelley to be buried and done with'. In 1950, Kenneth Cameron's *The Young Shelley* was among the first to restore the political ideas without which Shelley's poetry loses so much of its magic and meaning. Richard Holmes followed this in 1974 with his wonderful biography, *Shelley the Pursuit*, which opens with the statement: 'There will always be Shelley lovers, but this book is not for them'—the best recommendation possible. Paul Foot's *Red Shelley* (1980) is a powerful polemic, which in his own words, 'attempts to take Shelley out of the academic prison in which he has been firmly trapped for over half a century'.[6] One other book is worth mentioning; written in 1872 and now largely forgotten, Denis Florence MacCarthy's *Shelley's Early Life*. MacCarthy, a poet and a supporter of the Young Ireland Movement was one of the first to expose the lies and deceptions of Shelley's earlier biographers who tried to repackage him for the Victorian age. His book was also the first extensive and realistic account of Shelley's intervention in Irish politics, and a starting point for anyone interested in Shelley's early life.

For a while it was fashionable in literary circles to divide Shelley's life and work into his juvenile and mature periods. His agitation and writing on Ireland were always relegated to his juvenile period and dismissed, as Mary Shelley, for the worst of reasons, was later to write of *Queen Mab*:

> It is doubtful whether he would himself have admitted it into a collection of his works... and the change his opinions underwent would have prevented him from putting forth the speculations of his boyhood days.[7]

Shelley, in later life, had doubts about *Queen Mab*, not because it went too far in denouncing religion, but because it did not go far enough. So it was with Ireland. The two months he spent in Dublin provided Shelley with the most 'intensive period of practical political education that he experienced in his life',[8] yet, as MacCarthy noted as early as 1842, his interest in Irish affairs is constantly diminished by friend and foe alike.[9]

The Shelley industry has generated an output beyond count, but to my knowledge no one has seen fit to publish Shelley's writings on

Ireland in one volume, or indeed a comprehensive critique of them. This book has two functions – primarily to collect together for the first time Shelley's pamphlets, poems and letters concerning Ireland and, secondly, to present, in a thematic way, his lifelong interest in Ireland and his influence on Irish affairs down through the years.

Shelley quite astutely wrote in the *Notes on Hellas* that 'circumstances make men what they are'.[10] However, historical development is more complicated than Shelley imagined. Karl Marx put forward in 1852 a more rounded view: 'Men make their own history, but not just as they please. They do not choose the circumstances for themselves, but have to work upon circumstances as they find them, under conditions handed down from the past'.[11] For Shelley and his contemporaries it was the historical circumstances handed down by the French Revolution and the reaction in England and Ireland that made them what they were.

For Shelley, born in 1792, the French Revolution was a tradition, not a personal experience. But he was formed by the events in France, just as the first generation of Romantics – Wordsworth, Coleridge and Southey – were transformed by the reality of the revolution. Shelley experienced it at second hand, through the books of Godwin and Paine, Condorcet and Volney, but his radicalism grew out of a living contact with the brutality of the industrial world at the beginning of the 19th century. As Kenneth Cameron reminds us: 'Shelley – became what he was, not so much because he read as because he lived'.[12]

Beethoven, like Shelley, was inspired by the French Revolution and gave eloquent voice to it. The final movement of his choral symphony is an *Ode to Joy*,[13] which was addressed to all mankind, just as Shelley's *Prometheus Unbound* spoke to the world about justice and freedom:

The loathsome mask has fallen, the man remains

Sceptreless, free, uncircumscribed, but man

Equal, unclassed, tribeless and nationless,

Exempt from awe, worship, degree, the king

Over himself; just, gentle, wise. [14]

Poetry, like music or art, at its best propels us into a world beyond our immediate experience – a world of 'what ought to be or might be'.

Unfortunately, poetry today is less popular than in the past, but it retains all of its power and vitality, and it is still possible to read *Ode to the West Wind, Prometheus Unbound* and *The Mask of Anarchy* in the way that Shelley intended – one that awakens our sense both of wonder and outrage at the world around us.

NOTES

1   W B Yeats, *Collected Poems* (London, 1950), 'Easter 1916', lines 15-16, p203.

2   W B Yeats, *Selected Criticism* (London, 1964), p53.

3   P Foot, *Red Shelley* (London, 1980), p10.

4   M Arnold, *The Essential Matthew Arnold* (London, 1949), p405.

5   G B Shaw, *Pen Portraits and Reviews* (London, 1949), p236.

6   Foot, *Red Shelley*, p13.

7   M Shelley, 'Note on *Queen Mab*' in *Shelley Poetical Works* (London, 1991), p835.

8   R Holmes, *Shelley the Pursuit* (London, 1974), p117.

9   See *Dublin Evening Post*, 24/11/1842.

10 P B Shelley, *Shelley Poetical Works*, (Oxford, 1991) 'Hellas', Notes, p479.

11 K Marx, *The Eighteenth Brumaire of Louis Bonaparte* (London, 1926), p23.

12 K Cameron, *The Young Shelley*, (New York, 1950) p158.

13 *Ode to Joy* was written by the German Romantic poet Johann Schiller in 1797 and set to music by Beethoven between 1815 and 1824 as the final movement of his Ninth Symphony.

14 *Poems*, 'Prometheus Unbound', act 3, scene 4, lines 193-97, p204.

CHAPTER 1

The Irishman's Song

PERCY Bysshe Shelley, with his wife Harriet and her sister Eliza, departed the miserable port of Whitehaven in Cumbria at midnight on 3 February 1812. By the next morning they were in the Isle of Man, and after a stopover of five or six days they finally boarded ship for Dublin. The crossing was rough. A storm drove the ship far up along the coast into the north of Ireland, and after an arduous coach journey they finally reached Dublin on the evening of 12 February, exhausted, but determined to succeed. They came to Ireland on business of political importance – to campaign for the repeal of the Union between Ireland and Britain, and to play their part in the fight for Catholic emancipation.

Shelley had put together a collection of poems to celebrate the cause of liberty, and with all the certainty of youth believed that the time had come to put his political principles into practice. The idea of visiting Ireland was first mentioned on 10 December 1811.[1] It seemed the most obvious place to have his poems published and begin his career as a political activist. In the months prior to their departure the Shelley household was a hive of intellectual activity. All were engaged in the study of Irish history in preparation for the trip. Their enthusiasm is evident from a letter Harriet sent to their friend Elizabeth Hitchener a few days before their departure:

> You must come to us in Ireland. I am Irish, I claim kindred with them; I have done with the English, I have witnessed too much of John Bull and I am ashamed of him.[2]

Shelley was busy preparing a pamphlet on Catholic Emancipation, which eventually became *An Address to the Irish People*, for distribution in Dublin. He outlined his plans in a letter a week before their departure:

> All is prepared. I have been busily engaged in an address to the Irish which will be printed as Paine's works were, and pasted on the walls of Dublin…it is intended to familiarise to uneducated apprehensions ideas of liberty, benevolence peace and toleration. It is secretly intended also as a preliminary to other pamphlets to shake Catholicism at its basis.[3]

By the end of January they were ready to embark, not just for Ireland, but also on a journey of discovery and commitment that was to last until Shelley's tragic death in 1822. He travelled as an outcast from his family and his class. In Ireland he came face to face with the misery, degradation and despair of the new industrial working class and it was this experience more than anything else that transformed his youthful sympathy for the poor and the oppressed into the anger, indignation and compassion of his adult life.

A few months earlier, in August 1811, Sir Timothy Shelley learned that his son, Percy Bysshe Shelley, had eloped with the 16 year old Harriet Westbrook, whom he contemptuously referred to as 'an inn-keepers daughter'. He was determined that Shelley should be punished. To add to the disgrace of his recent expulsion from Oxford, Shelley had now married 'below' him. After all, Sir Timothy was a man of substance, heir to a baronetcy, a member of parliament, and squire of a large estate in Sussex.[4] Perhaps this was a lapse of memory on Sir Timothy's part? His own father, Bysshe Shelley, from whom Shelley inherited his unfortunate middle name, had acquired the family fortune and instigated a family tradition, by eloping with the 16 year old daughter of a wealthy clergyman, whose estates he inherited on her death. This left him well placed to remarry, again eloping with the daughter of a wealthy aristocratic family, possessed of extensive estates in the Home Counties. In the fullness of time Mr Bysshe Shelley, as he was until 1806, used his acquired wealth to buy a baronetcy, purchase a seat in parliament for his son and build a stately home befitting a man of his station. Shelley's failure as a fortune-hunter cost him his allowance of £200 per year.

Percy Bysshe Shelley was born at Field Place, Horsham, Sussex, on Saturday, 4 August 1792. Contrary to popular belief, he was not born into an old aristocratic family, but into a nouveau riche country family, regarded as outsiders by some in the area. We know little of Shelley's early life. His parents, who outlived him, surprisingly left no written remembrance of his childhood. Shelley grew up in a family dominated by girls, with four sisters and only one brother, who was born when Shelley was 14. He had a private tutor until the age of 10, when he was packed off to Syon House Academy, a barbarous place even by the standards of the day. At Syon House, at the age of 11 or 12, though isolated from the momentous events in the outside world, Shelley came to feel that the world was a hostile place that had to be confronted. Thomas Medwin, his cousin, recorded this early memoir of his feelings:

> When he heard of, or read of, some flagrant act of injustice,
> oppression or cruelty, then indeed the sharpest marks of horror and
> indignation were visible in his countenance.[5]

At the age of 12, he moved to Eton College, where he remained until he was almost 18. For a boy who hated sport, the playing fields of Eton held little attraction. Shelley did not fit into the atmosphere of a school designed to train the sons of the aristocracy for the tasks of empire and conformity. Shelley remembered his early years at Eton with a loathing that affected his later attitudes to authority and social conventions. He refused to accept the 'fag' system, whereby younger boys are forced to act as servants for the senior boys. For this act of rebellion he became an object of scorn for the school bullies – 'he was the scoff, the butt, the victim, of the whole school'. But his tormentors never succeeded in breaking his spirit. In time he was even to win their respect:

> Hogg records that he was dignified by the title 'the Eton Atheist', a title reserved for those who had successfully opposed the school authorities. The implication was sociological rather than theological; but it implied recognition.[6]

Instead of conforming, Shelley developed an avid interest in literature, politics and ideas of any sort. Encouraged by Dr James Lind, he turned to serious reading, and made his first contact with William Godwin's *Enquiry Concerning Political Justice,* which was to be so influential in his political development. Shelley spent his life denouncing king, priest and statesman or privilege of any sort. Almost all his narrative poems feature a king or tyrant to be challenged or overthrown. He had a special hatred for George III:

> An old, mad, blind, despised, and dying king, –
> Princes, the dregs of their dull race, who flow
> Through public scorn, – mud from a muddy spring, –
> Rulers who neither see, nor feel, nor know,
> But leechlike to their fainting country cling,
> Till they drop, blind in blood, without a blow.[7]

The irony was that his mentor Dr Lind, a kindly man of liberal ideas in politics and science, was not a master at Eton College, but the royal physician to George III at nearby Windsor Castle. Shelley was later to portray him as a humanitarian in his poem, *The Revolt of Islam.*

Shelley, in his last term at Eton, published his gothic novel *Zastrozzi,* for which he received the remarkable sum of £40, more than he was to earn from any future work. He was genuinely interested in mystery and the occult, and his second book published a year later, *St Irvyne* or *The Rosicrucian,* was in the same vein. He was also writing poetry and in the autumn of 1810, in collaboration with his sister Elizabeth, he published *Original Poetry* by 'Victor' (Shelley) and 'Cazire' (Elizabeth). He also completed, with his cousin, Thomas Medwin, his long poem *The Wandering Jew;* an attack on religion that was later to find expression in a more complete way in *Queen Mab.* His writings from this period are a combination of gothic horror and romantic trivia. Yet, within a year, we have Shelley, Whig-reformer, atheist, republican and Godwinian egalitarian. This was not an instant conversion, but the genesis of his later radicalism is to be found in this early work. In *Henry and Louisa* (1809), his first attempt at a major poem, he is voicing anti-war and republican sentiments. The opening lines were an attack on the futility of the war with France:

> Where are the Heroes? Sunk in death they lie.
> What toiled they for? Titles and wealth and fame.
> But the wide heaven is now their canopy,
> And legal murderers their loftiest name.[8]

This poem, according to Kenneth Cameron, was 'the predecessor of the now lost *Poetical Essay on the Existing State of Things*' [9] which Shelley published in 1811 to raise funds for the Irish journalist Peter Finnerty, who was jailed for seditious libel. One other poem is of interest, *The Irishman's Song*, written in October 1809 as a protest against repression in Ireland, which concluded that the Irish, inspired by the spirit of dead revolutionaries, would fight to regain their freedom. Stylistically there is little to recommend it and it shows scant indication of Shelley's potential lyrical qualities:

> Ah! where are the heroes! triumphant in death,
> Convulsed they recline on the blood sprinkled heath,
> Or the yelling ghosts ride on the blast that sweeps by,
> And 'my countrymen! vengeance!' incessantly cry.[10]

But even at 17 the anger that brought him to Ireland three years later in support of the agitation for Catholic emancipation and repeal of the Union is evident. Shelley completed his second novel *St Irvyne* in the summer of 1810. *St Irvyne* is little read today, but it provides additional evidence of Shelley's early interest in Irish affairs. The influence of Tom Moore's *Irish Melodies* is clearly evident in the character if its hero:

> Fitzeustace is an Irishman, and so very moral, and so adverse to every species of gaiete de coeur, that you need be under no apprehensions...recline on the sofa and I will play you some of those Irish tunes you admire so much.[11]

Shelley can be faulted for casting as his moral hero an upper class Irishman in the image of Tom Moore acceptable in the drawing rooms of London society, but, set against the caricature of Irish people prevalent in the literature of the time, Fitzeustace emerges as a rounded and likeable character.[12]

These now forgotten novels and poems are clearly the work of the young apprentice. Those who are unsympathetic to the ideas that Shelley was struggling to develop will see nothing but faults. The sympathetic reader will find the embryo of his views on society, religion, politics and sex, and the fledgling lyrical poet, if they care to look.

Shelley arrived at Oxford in October 1810, his literary apprenticeship complete. He had now progressed to journeyman, with the opportunity and the means to test his skill. His father, who travelled with him, introduced him to Slatter's, the Oxford publisher and bookseller: 'My son here has a literary turn: he is already an author, and do pray indulge him in his printing freaks'.[13] This was an indulgence, that Sir Timothy was shortly to have much cause to regret.

The Shelley's were large landowners in Sussex and therefore naturally aligned themselves with the largest landowner in the county, the Duke of Norfolk. The duke was a supporter of the radical Whigs, so the Shelley family's political connections, according to Leigh Hunt, 'belonged to a small party in the House of Commons itself belonging to another party. They were Whig aristocrats, voting in the interests of the Duke of Norfolk'.[14]

Though an advocate of reform, the Duke of Norfolk was the leading boroughmonger of his day, controlling 15 seats in the House of Commons. Sir Timothy Shelley was in the pocket of the duke, who owned his parliamentary seat of Shoreham-on-Sea, with its 15 electors. The Duke of Norfolk, whose first wife was Irish, came from a Catholic family and had to renounce his faith in order to legally enter politics. He belonged to the left wing of the Whigs, supporting Fox and Sheridan. In the early years they were advocates for the French Revolution, supporters of reform, champions of the Irish cause, and in favour of Catholic emancipation. But by the end of the 1790s the radical Whigs were a spent force. After the defeat of the Reform Bill in 1797 they withdrew from parliament until 1800, content to tend to their businesses and their country estates. No doubt, in the seclusion of their country houses, radical and republican ideas were still discussed, and there the young Shelley was introduced to the world of politics. The Duke of Norfolk had recommended to Shelley, 'the study of politics as the proper career for a young man of ability and of your station in life'.[15] He was invited to Norfolk House where he was offered the parliamentary seat for Horsham,[16] which was in the gift of the duke. Shelley rejected the offer, because he considered this to be an attempt to 'shackle his mind, and introduce him into life as a mere follower of the duke'.[17]

The influence of the Duke of Norfolk on the young Shelley should not be underestimated. It is most likely that it was the duke who first interested him in Irish politics. He supported Catholic emancipation in the debates in the House of Lords in 1808 and 1810, and refused the Order of the Garter in February 1812, the month of Shelley's departure for Ireland, because of the Prince Regent's turncoat tactics on Ireland. In contrast, his father, Sir Timothy Shelley, though a supporter of the duke, voted against Catholic emancipation on five occasions. Shelley's allowance of £200 a year was eventually restored through the duke's intervention and it was to him that Shelley turned when he needed money to finance his trip to Dublin, though we have no evidence that he received any.

The end of the landowning aristocratic reformer neatly coincides with the end of the 18th century. The industrial revolution had created two new mutually antagonistic classes, bourgeoisie and proletariat, which transformed the political landscape. But the ruling coalition of merchants and landowners was not about to go quietly. The rotten borough system ensured their control of parliament, and they opposed every attempt at reform. But if the rising capitalist class was disenfranchised, the new working class was suppressed by force.

> We can now see something of the truly catastrophic nature of the industrial revolution; as well as some of the reasons why the English working class took form in those years. The people were subjected

simultaneously to an intensification of two intolerable forms of relationship: those of economic exploitation and of political oppression.[18]

The Combination Acts of 1799 and 1800 proscribed trade unions. Military barracks were built all over the country. By 1812 there were more troops maintaining order in England than fighting the war in Spain, and the industrial areas were treated almost as a conquered country. Shelley writes angrily of their presence: 'I have beheld scenes of misery – The manufacturers [workers] are reduced to starvation. My friends the military are gone to Nottingham – Curses light on them for their motives, if they destroy one of its famine-wasted inhabitants'.[19] Political demonstrations were broken up by force. Those voicing opposition faced jail or transportation. What terrified the radical Whigs was the 'sans-culottes' and 'the men of no property'. The nightmare of every ruling class, 'the mob' were demanding 'The Rights of Man' – not 'the mob' in the sense that we understand it today, but rather in the sense that James Connolly, the Irish socialist, described it:

In the course of its upward march the mob has transformed and humanised the world…with one sweep of its grimy, toil-worn hand swept the rack, the thumbscrew, the wheel, the boots of burning oil, the torturer's vice and the stake into the oblivion of history, and they who today would seek to view those arguments of kings, nobles, and ecclesiastics must seek them in the lumber room of the museum… Against all this achievement of the mob, its enemies have but one instance of the abuse of power – the French reign of terror – and they suppress the fact that this classic instance of mob fury lasted but eight months, whereas the cold-blooded cruelty of the ruling classes which provoked it had endured for a thousand years. All hail, then, to the mob, the incarnation of progress![20]

Despite the oppression, strikes, riots and machine wrecking kept the ruling class in a state of terror. Their instinct for self preservation was more important than reform. They saw 'the mob' behind every attempt at change. When Sir Francis Burdett, an Independent Whig, tried to introduce a bill of reform in 1809 the Whigs refused to support him, and later, when he made a searing attack on the government over its decision to hold a secret inquiry into the disastrous Walcheren navy expedition,[21] they supported the government in having him committed to the Tower of London. The Whigs were repudiating their radical past with all the zeal of the convert. In the drawing rooms of the great houses we can be sure that Burdett's plans were discussed. Disgusted with the fireside reformers as represented by his father and the Duke of Norfolk, Shelley now made a decisive break with the Whigs. He became an admirer of Burdett and took another step along the political road that was to make him so despised during his life. Shelley was engaging with the real world, relating to those who were prepared to take action in pursuit of their political goals. In a public declaration of his support for Burdett, he dedicated his poem *The Wandering Jew* as follows:

> To Sir Francis Burdett, Bart.MP, in consideration of the active virtues by which both his public and private life is so eminently distinguished, the following poem is inscribed by the author.[22]

New voices were emerging that broadened his horizon – pamphlets by the score, written in a language and style accessible to workers, newspapers that found a mass audience, Cobbett's *Political Register*, Leigh and John Hunt's the *Examiner*, Eaton's *Politics for the People*. Their very names indicate the readers they were trying to reach.[23]

His friend Thomas Hogg claimed that 'a newspaper never found its way to his rooms the whole period of his residence at Oxford'.[24] This assertion was accepted by later writers to create the image of Shelley as an 'ineffectual angel'. Nothing could be further from the truth. Shelley threw himself into the newspaper controversies of the day, writing letters to the editor, disagreeing or congratulating them on their opinions, and always supporting the freedom of the press. His first political campaign was in support of Peter Finnerty, the Irish journalist jailed for libelling Castlereagh.

The trial of Peter Finnerty in February 1811, in London, had its origins in the 1798 rebellion in Ireland. Shelley was a professed admirer of the United Irishmen, and the events and personalities of 1798 were important in his political and intellectual development. Castlereagh was sent to Ireland in 1797, as chief secretary, to crush the United Irishmen. His brutality made him the most hated man in Ireland, a reputation that was to follow him to England. Shelley developed an abiding hatred for Castlereagh, venomously expressed in the *Mask of Anarchy:*

I met murder on the way –
He had a mask like Castlereagh –
Very smooth he looked, yet grim;
Seven bloodhounds followed him:

All were fat; and well they might
Be in admirable plight,
For one by one, and two by two,
He tossed them human hearts to chew,
Which from his wide cloak he drew.[25]

In Ulster, Castlereagh instigated a ferocious and bloody crackdown, which led to the arrest and torture of 500 members, including nearly all the leadership, of the United Irishmen. Their newspaper, the *Northern Star,* was suppressed and their printshop destroyed. Fifty members of the United Irishmen were executed in 1797, amongst them William Orr from Carrickfergus, who was convicted on the word of two informers, each of whom received £100 for their services. Lord Castlereagh assisted the prosecution, sat on the grand jury and dined each evening with the judge. As the charge was brought under the Insurrection Act, John Philpot Curran, who defended Orr, was precluded from making any speech for the defence.

After the closure of the *Northern Star*, its replacement, the *Press,* in Dublin, was always a likely candidate for suppression: 'Even its founders christened it "The Newgate" and laid bets on its viability'.[26] Within a few months the administration duly obliged. Peter Finnerty, the editor, was a man of fearless courage who could not be corrupted or intimidated. He was indicted for an article, which appeared in the *Press*, denouncing the actions of Castlereagh and the illegality of the trial of William Orr. Its author, Deane Swift, grandson of

Jonathan Swift, did not mince his words:

> The death of Mr Orr the nation has pronounced one of the most
> sanguinary and savage acts that have disgraced the laws. In perjury,
> did you not hear, my lord, the verdict was given? Perjury
> accompanied with terror, as terror has marked every step, of your
> government.[27]

Finnerty used the trial to establish the truth about Orr. Curran, defending him, described Orr's trial with a brutal frankness which went beyond advocacy, and in one of the great speeches of the time conveyed the public's horror and indignation at the government's actions:

> It is not with respect to Mr Orr or Mr Finnerty, that your verdict is
> now sought. You are called upon, on your oaths, to say, that the
> government is wise and merciful – the people prosperous and
> happy; that military law ought to be continued; that the
> constitution could not be with safety restored to Ireland; and that
> statements of a contrary import by your advocates, in either
> country, are libellous and false.[28]

Curran may have succeeded in putting the government in the dock, but he could not save Finnerty. He was found guilty of sedition, imprisoned for two years and sentenced to stand for an hour in the pillory in Green Street in Dublin. The pillory was intended to humiliate him; instead it became a celebration. Arthur O'Connor and Lord Edward Fitzgerald, of the United Irishmen, stood on each side and a large crowd cheered him throughout the hour. A few weeks later, the *Press* was suppressed and its printing press smashed up by the militia. Their printer, John Stockdale, was sentenced to six months and left penniless as a result.

The defeat of the United Irishmen and the Act of Union in 1800 meant there was no room in Ireland for a radical journalist like Finnerty. Curran obtained a position for him in London with the Whig *Morning Chronicle.* There he joined the United Irishmen's network, which had been reinforced by the arrival of the political exiles following the 1798 rebellion. Finnerty was one of many activists who tried to revive the movement with their English sympathisers. The English radicals had plans for some sort of action in London, with the expectation that this would spark off a larger movement in the provinces. However, before they could implement their plans, one of the leaders, Colonel Despard,[29] along with his associates, was seized in London in November 1802 and executed for high treason. At the same time in Ireland, Robert Emmet was planning an armed revolt and there is some evidence to suggest that Despard and Emmet tried to coordinate their activities.[30] Finnerty was implicated in the Despard conspiracy and left for Dublin to evade possible arrest. There he became involved in the preparations for Emmet's insurrection in 1803, before eventually returning to London. He remained active in revolutionary circles and continued his outspoken attacks on the establishment. The issue that led to his prosecution in February 1811 was his report in the *Morning Chronicle* of the disastrous Walcheren expedition, which resulted in 20,000 British deaths. Leigh Hunt, in a long article in the *Examiner,* of 24 February, wrote:

> The immediate cause of Mr Finnerty's present misfortune is well known to the public. He had accompanied the expedition to Walcheren at the request of Sir Home Popham, in order to write an account of it for publication, but was forced to return home by an order to that effect by Lord Castlereagh… He vented his feelings in a letter to Lord Castlereagh, which was published in the *Morning Chronicle,* and in which he plainly accused the Viscount of an intention to harass and destroy him, – reminding his Lordship at the same time of the tyrannous and horrible cruelties practised upon the people of Ireland during the noble lord's administration in that country. In consequence of this letter, the Attorney-General was directed to file an information for libel against Mr Finnerty.

Finnerty allowed the judgement to go by default, but sought in mitigation to justify the libel. Appearing before Lord Ellenborough produced over 50 affidavits charging Castlereagh with sanctioning torture in Ireland:

Finnerty: I have an affidavit from Mr O'Connor.
Ellenborough: Who is Mr O'Connor?
Finnerty: A gentleman transported by Lord Castlereagh without any warrant.

Ellenborough: Reject this.

Finnerty: Here is an affidavit from Mr Clare.

Ellenborough: Who is Mr Clare?

Finnerty: The affidavit shows that various kinds of torture, whippings, picketings, half hangings were practised under the walls of Dublin Castle and that Lord Castlereagh must have known.

Ellenborough: Can this be endured… Have you any inoffensive affidavits?

Finnerty: My lords, at the trial of X you asked why he had no proof. I have written not a syllable which I cannot prove. I offer proof that Lord Castlereagh is the basest individual who ever prostituted high office.

Ellenborough: We cannot hear you offer fresh libels to which Lord Castlereagh will have no opportunity to reply.

Finnerty: Will you hear my affidavits? I am curious to know what your lordship means by mitigation.

Ellenborough: Not to the purport of those you have offered.

Finnerty: I will state the purport and ask your lordship to rule on them. Here is one from Mr Hughes who says Lord Castlereagh saw him with his back raw from the scourge and his shirt a mass of blood.

Ellenborough: This is contumacious to the Court.

Finnerty: Here is Mr Dixon's affidavit to say that he saw three peasants whipped and tortured without trial.

Ellenborough: What does that prove?

Finnerty: He says it was with Lord Castlereagh's privity and sanction.[31]

Finnerty was sentenced to 18 months in Lincoln jail. Francis Burdett and the *Examiner* launched an appeal to sustain Finnerty in prison, and various support groups were formed across Britain and Ireland. Shelley, now clearly identified with the Burdett/Hunt group, was eager to play his part. The *Oxford Herald* supported the campaign and announced in the issue of 23 February 1811:

Liberty of the Press. – The friends of the Liberty of the Press are informed, that a subscription on behalf of Mr Finnerty is opened at the office of the *Oxford Herald*.

The following week, the announcement was repeated and in addition to the four subscribers from the previous week, listed the name, 'Mr P B Shelley. 1£. 1s. 1d'. In the same paper for 9 March the following advertisement appeared:

Literature

Just published, Price Two Shillings,

A POETICAL ESSAY

on the

Existing State of Things.

AND FAMINE AT HER BIDDING WIDE

THE WRETCHED LAND TILL IN THE PUBLIC WAY,

PROMISCUOUS WHERE THE DEAD AND DYING LAY,

DOGS FED ON HUMAN BONES AND IN THE OPEN LIGHT OF DAY.

Curse of Kehama.

By a

GENTLEMAN of the University of Oxford.

For assisting to maintain in Prison

Mr Peter Finnerty,

Imprisoned for a libel.

London: Sold by B Crosby and Co

And all other booksellers.

1811.

Though it was extensively advertised, no copy of Shelley's poem has ever come to light. In addition to the *Oxford Herald*, advertisements appeared in the *Courier* on 11 and 15 March, the *Morning Chronicle* on 15 and 21 March and in the *Times* on 10 and 11 April. Shelley raised nearly £100, which was presented to Finnerty, as reported in the *Dublin Weekly Messenger* of 7 March 1812. How the money was raised and whether the poem exists as a separate or original work is still uncertain. As regards the money, we can be in no doubt as to the amount. Shelley was in Dublin at the time of the *Dublin Weekly Messenger* article. If the announcement was false, his enemies would have seized on this to discredit him. Although Finnerty was still in jail, he was in contact with the paper, and it is inconceivable that such a statement would go unchallenged if correct. But whether the money was raised exclusively from this poem or not we cannot be sure.

The existence of the poem as an unknown work is more problematic. Richard Holmes says that 'of the poem itself we know nothing, but what appears to be an earlier version occurs in the *Esdaile MS Notebook*'.[32] Holmes was referring to the 1811 poem, *A Tale of Society as it is.*[33] The Oxford publisher Slatter, in a letter, said of Shelley's book of poems, *The Posthumous Fragments of Margaret Nicholson,* which he published in November 1810, that Shelley 'directed the profits to be applied to Peter Finnerty'.[34] To have received almost £100 for a single poem, more than Shelley received for any publication in his lifetime, without any copy surviving seems unlikely.[35] The most probable explanation is that the money was raised from a number of sources. We have evidence for *Margaret Nicholson* and *The Poetical Essay*, and possibly it included the royalties from his novel *St Irvyne* which was published two months earlier.

There can be little doubt that the advertisement announced a poem by Shelley. He had used the pseudonym 'a Gentleman of the University of Oxford' for *St Irvyne*. Although we cannot be sure that the poem deals with Ireland, the quotation from Southey's *The Curse of Kehama* indicates that it does – 'the wretched land' is probably a reference to the terrible conditions in the period after the rebellion of 1798.

In the same issue of the *Oxford Herald* in which the advertisement for his *Poetical Essay* appeared, a report referred to the recent trial and acquittal of the brothers Leigh and John Hunt over an article in the *Examiner* attacking the systematic use of flogging in the British army. On 2 March Shelley wrote to Hunt at the *Examiner* to congratulate him on his acquittal and propose a plan of action:

The ultimate intention of my aim is to induce a meeting of such enlightened unprejudiced members of the community, whose independent principles expose them to evils which might thus become alleviated; and to form a methodical society, which should be organised so as to resist the coalition of the enemies of liberty, which at present renders any expression of opinion on matters of policy dangerous to individuals. It has been for want of societies of this nature, that corruption has attained the height at which we now behold it; nor can any of us bear in mind the very great influence, which some years since was gained by Illuminism without considering that a society of equal extent might establish rational liberty on as firm a basis as that which would have supported the visionary schemes of a completely-equalised community.[36]

Enclosed with his letter were 'an address to the public' and a 'proposal for a meeting', which were not published and are now lost. Hunt did not reply, but he must have been shaken by Shelley's proposition. Shelley went far beyond Hunt's proposal for a union between Burdett's reformers and the left Whigs. The Illuminists, whom Shelley referred to, were a secret Jacobin society dedicated to worldwide revolution. Their doctrine was one of militant egalitarianism, opposition to private property, religion and marriage. They were a conspiratorial underground movement dating back to a Spanish sect of the same name. Shelley became acquainted with their ideas during his first term at Oxford through Abbé Agustin Barruel's *Histoire du Jacobinisme*. The influence of Illuminism on the United Irishmen was noted in 1798: 'The proposals for it [the United Irishmen] are couched in the style and exact terms of the hierophants of Illuminism. They recommend the formation of an association or, as it is styled, a beneficent conspiracy to serve the people'.[37]

Shelley's political ideas were moving beyond reform, to the necessity for 'a completely-equalised' form of society. In one form or another this central idea was to be the basis of Shelley's political ideology for the rest of his life. A year later, in Dublin, Shelley issued his *Address to the Irish People* and his *Proposals for an Association*, which were clearly based on the ideas set out in the letter to Hunt. Shelley had moved beyond the political gossip of the big house, and the reformists grouped around Hunt and Burdett. He was now relating to the movement from below. Tom O'Brien, a Dublin poet in the 1930s confronted by a similar situation, explained why he volunteered to fight with the International Brigades in Spain. He wrote in his notebook:

I have written poems in words
Now I shall write one in action
I shall go and do the things
I wrote and thought about.[38]

Shelley never saw a contradiction between words and actions. We do not have to share his desire for freedom or his thirst for action to enjoy his poetry, but if we deny it, we deny everything about him:

The thirst for action, and the impassioned thought
Prolong my being. If I wake no more
My life more actual living will contain
Than some grey veteran's of the world's cold school.[39]

Shelley's mind was alive with ideas, not just politics, but also religion, science and ethics. After the 1810 Christmas vacation Shelley and his college friend Thomas Hogg decided to publish a summary of their ideas on the existence of god. On 9 February 1811 the following advertisement appeared in the *Oxford Herald*:

Speedily will be published
To be had of the booksellers of London and Oxford,
THE NECESSITY OF ATHEISM

This was a dangerous project – nobody had dared to openly publish such views before for fear of prosecution. It was on display for less than half an hour in Slatter's window in Oxford, when a passing cleric and fellow of an Oxford College walked in and read the little pamphlet. He demanded that all copies were burnt, though one was retained as evidence for the college authorities. But, in a reckless challenge to religious authority, Shelley had posted a copy to all the bishops and heads of college. By the time the post was opened, Shelley's future at Oxford was sealed. His support for Peter Finnerty had already exposed him as a dangerous radical in conservative Oxford. The pamphlet was unsigned, and he might have survived after a short suspension if he had apologised, or recanted his beliefs. But this was not a passing whim – his atheism was essential to everything he believed in. He was summoned to the master's lodgings and asked if he was the author of the pamphlet. He was expelled for refusing to answer, or, in the bureaucratic language of the time, for 'contumacy in refusing to answer certain questions put to him'. Hogg, in solidarity with Shelley, also refused to answer and was expelled.

Shelley was five months short of his 19 birthday when he departed Oxford on 26 March 1811. Hogg was to write of Shelley's expulsion:

> The scene was changed from the quiet seclusion of academic groves and gardens…to the stormy ocean of that vast and shoreless world, to the utmost violence of which he was, at an early age, suddenly and unnaturally abandoned.[40]

Hogg showed great loyalty in standing by his friend, but he had no idea of the path that Shelley was going down. Shelley chose a life that was to be a constant battle against the 'stormy ocean'. Therefore, it is ironic that in the end the stormy ocean off the coast of Italy claimed his life, but his words and thoughts still live to defy the waves, almost 200 years later.

NOTES

1   F L Jones,(ed), *The Letters of Percy Bysshe Shelley*, (Oxford, 1964), vol 1, p201. This is the first reference of their intention to visit Ireland, but with summer 1812 as the intended date.

2   Ibid, p247.

3   Ibid, p162.

4   A distant relative, Francis Shelley, was married to Richard Fitzwilliam, who succeeded as the Fifth Viscount Fitzwilliam of Merrion in 1704, and lived in Mount Merrion House, County Dublin. She entered a Catholic convent after her separation from her husband and died in 1771. It is unlikely that Shelley was aware of this Irish connection. See *Dublin Historical Record,* vol 51, no 2 Autumn 1998.

5   T Medwin, *The life of Percy Bysshe Shelley* (London, 1913), p18.

6   R Holmes, *Shelley the Pursuit* (London, 1974), p30.

7   P B Shelley, 'England in 1819', *Poetical Works of Shelley* (Oxford, 1991) lines 1-6, p574.

8   Shelley, *The Esdaile Notebook* – a volume of early poems (London, 1964), p131, lines 1-4.

9   Ibid, p260.

10   *Poetical Works of Shelley,* op cit, lines 13-16, p849. Written at the same time as *Henry and Louisa* probably after Shelley read Godwin's *Political Justice* for the first time. Line 13 is almost identical to line 1 of *Henry and Louisa.*

11   Shelley, *St Irvyne,* (London, 1822), pp209, 217.

12   See Harvey and Pry, 'John O'Keeffe as an Irish playwright within the Theatrical, Social and Economic context of his time'; also *Eire-Ireland* (St Paul, 1987), vol 22, no 1, Spring 1987, p19.

13   R Holmes, *Shelley,* op cit, p36.

14   L Hunt, *The Autobiography of Leigh Hunt* (London, 1903), vol 2, p28.

15   Dr Anster, *North British Review,* (November 1847), p229.

16   Horsham was the first constituency in Britain to elect a Roman Catholic to the House of Commons after the Catholic Emancipation Act of 1829.

17   T Medwin, op cit, vol 2, p156.

18   E P Thompson, 'Variety within the Working Class', in *The Industrial Revolution in Britain* (Massachusetts, 1970), p74.

19   *Letters,* op cit, p213.

20   J Connolly, *Collected Works* (Dublin, 1988), vol 2, p410. See also W Godwin, *Enquiry Concerning Political Justice* (London, 1976), p87 for similar formulation.

21   In 1811, during the Peninsular War, a sea-borne expedition was sent to Walcheren in Holland to relieve French pressure on the Duke of Wellington's army. Over 20,000 were killed in that disastrous engagement.

22   Shelley, *The Complete Poetical Works* (Boston, 1901), p575.

23   For details see E P Thompson, *The Making of the English Working Class* (London, 1964), p834.

24   T Hogg, *Life of Shelley* (London, 1906), vol 1 of two, p167.

25   *Poetical Works of Shelley,* op cit, lines, 5-13, p338.

26   L Hale, *John Philpot Curran* (London, 1958), p154.

27 Ibid, p156.

28 '98 Centenary Cttee. Publications no1, *The Storey of William Orr* (Dublin, 1898), p26.

29 Edward Despard (1751-1803) born in Ireland, he was arrested in November 1802 and charged with conspiracy to assassinate the king and seize the Tower of London and the Bank of England. There was little evidence for this conspiracy but he was hanged with six associates in 1803. For an account of Despard's conspiracy see Linebaugh and Rediken, *The Many Headed Hydra*, (Boston 2000), pp248-286.

30 See S Redmond, *Partners in Revolt* (Dublin, 1998), p17; also M Elliot, *Partners in Revolution* (London, 1982), p293.

31 L Hale, op cit, p159.

32 R Holmes, op cit, p51.

33 Shelley, *Esdaile*, op cit, p62.

34 R Montgomery, *Oxford or Alma Mater* (London, 1833), p442. Over £2,000 was raised for Finnerty. His trial and imprisonment was one of the issues that helped bring down the government in 1812.

35 See *Complete Poetical Works of Shelley,* (Boston, 1901), pp589-90 for details.

36 *Letters,* op cit, p54.

37 R Clifford, 'Application of Barruel's Memoirs of Jacobinism to the secret Societies of Ireland and Great Britain' in Abbé Barruel, *Memoirs Illustrating the History of Jacobinism* (London, 1798), vol 4, appendix 1, pp1-2.

38 H G Klaus (ed), *Strong Words Brave Deeds* (Dublin, 1994), p11. Tom O'Brien, a Dublin poet, volunteered to fight in Spain in 1937 because he felt it was not enough to simply go on writing in a world facing imminent disaster.

39 Shelley, 'To Harriet' in *Esdaile,* op cit, lines 64-67, p85.

40 T Hogg, *Life of Shelley*, op cit, p172.

CHAPTER TWO

Political Justice

I beheld in short, that I had duties to perform

AS he boarded the stagecoach for London in March 1811, Shelley turned his back on Oxford, his life as a 'votary of romance', and the gothic world of his imagination. In politics he had outgrown Whig reformism. His republican and atheistic ideals were beginning to coalesce around a greater vision, where the fight for reforms were not just goals in themselves, but part of a bigger plan, the transformation of society itself.

He was introduced to the ideas of Hunt and Cobbett by the radical newspapers and he became aware of the working class movement that was gathering momentum across the country. He was reading extensively – 'David Hume and Gibbon, Voltaire and Condorcet, Paine and Franklin, Rousseau, Godwin and even the political economist Adam Smith'.[1] His politics were developing around the republicanism of Tom Paine and the anarchism of William Godwin. If Tom Paine's *The Rights of Man* was the most influential book in the formation of British radical thought, then William Godwin's *Political Justice* was a close second.

Published in 1793, it caught the incoming tide of political opinion. During the treason trials of 1794 Godwin only escaped prosecution because of Pitt's sneer 'that a three-guinea book would do little harm among the working class'.[2] But the authorities are nearly always sheltered from the realities of the world. *Political Justice* reached a wide layer of workers and activists, through circulating libraries, reading clubs, cheap pamphlets, pirate editions and lectures, which popularised Godwin's ideas.[3] He risked prosecution with his open letter to the *Morning Chronicle*, which gave encouragement to members of the radical societies and affected the popular demand for the release of those charged. Godwin was now at the height of his fame. *Political Justice*, caused a sensation when it was published. Hazlitt wrote:

> No one was more talked of, more looked up to, more sought after, and wherever liberty, truth and justice was the theme, his name was not far off… no work in our time gave such a blow to the philosophical mind of the country as the celebrated *Enquiry concerning Political Justice*…'Throw away your books of chemistry' said Wordsworth… 'and read Godwin on necessity'.[4]

Southey, reflecting on his youth, declared, 'I read and almost worshipped Godwin,' and Coleridge sang his praises: 'Mighty eagle, thou that soarest'. Thomas Russell, of the United Irishmen, pronounced *Political Justice* to be a 'masterly work' and Samuel Neilson said 'he admired it more that any other book'.[5]

Unfortunately for Godwin and his radical friends, the English enlightenment was short lived. England and France were at war. Government repression and the advent of the 'terror' in France turned most of the intellectual community against the revolution and against Godwin. By the turn of the century his reputation had, in Hazlitt's words, 'sunk below the horizon'. The attack on Godwin was misplaced. He was opposed to violence in any form. He cautioned against revolution and spoke out against the radical agitators in London. But 'he stood condemned as the pre-eminent English philosophical disciple of Rousseau and Helvétius, who were by now accepted as the bloody forerunners of the terror'.[6] He stood alone as an isolated intellectual, when all others had gone over to the side of reaction. Bending under this pressure he toned down his ideas in later editions of his book. In time, he repudiated most of the radical and visionary aspects of his work. His weakening may not be justifiable but it was understandable. Although, at the end of his life, he lived in conventional fashion on a government sinecure, *Political Justice* was one of the books that inspired a generation of workers and laid the foundations of the labour movement in Britain.

Not everyone had turned against Godwin. Shelley read *Political Justice* during his last year at Eton, and it is easy to see why it made such an impression on him. Here was a book that seemed to explain, in a coherent way, the ideas that Shelley was struggling to comprehend. Tom Paine's *Rights of Man* was a polemic in defence of the revolution, written in the heat of the moment, and a clarion call to workers to fight for their rights. Godwin's was a more considered book, setting out to establish the permanent and fundamental principles on which a just society could be built. *Political Justice* is sometimes inconsistent, overlong and difficult to interpret. In contrast, William Blake saw instinctively what it took Godwin volumes to see – that human freedom was incompatible with any manifestation of state power, church or patriarchal family. Nevertheless, its discussion on the great issues of the day – government, law, religion, marriage, etc. – in a unified way, provided the template that the age demanded.

Godwin starts with an attack on the liberal tradition of the right of the individual to do as he pleases. He counterposes the concept of duties and the ideal of the common good:

> So much for the active rights of man…are all of them superseded and rendered null by the superior claims of justice… In the first place he is said to have a right to life and personal liberty… He has no right to his life when duty calls him to resign it. Other men are bound…to deprive him of life or liberty, if that should appear in any case to be indispensably necessary to prevent a greater evil.[7]

He repudiates the law, by which he means the codified laws of organised states. His examination of property rights, education and marriage led him to conclude that the majority of the faults of society arise from the oppression of the individual, and are inseparable from the coercive rule of the state: 'Government is nothing but regulated force'.[8] Above all, he demands the dissolution of political government. In its place he argues for smaller units – the parish, the village, which would end the tyranny of the state, and instill the values of community, cooperation and solidarity. Law and punishment are unnecessary in a devolved society. Instead there would be the spontaneous justice of the parish. Industrialisation had led to the immiseration and alienation of workers and he calls for a return to a simpler rural life. He desires 'a state of the most rigid simplicity'. In his parish society man would work only in essential manual manufacture and agriculture:

> There will be no rich man to recline in indolence, and fatten on the labour of his fellows. The mathematician, the poets and the philosopher will derive a new stock of cheerfulness and energy from the recurring labour that makes them feel they are men.[9]

Godwin was not a revolutionary. He believed people got the government they deserved, and change would only happen by a slow and gradual process. In time the omnipotence of truth and the perfectibility of humanity would give rise in an evolutionary way to a new and better society:

> It is only in a gradual way that the public can be instructed…
> Revolutions are the produce of passion, not of sober and tranquil reason.[10]

Reason, discussion and debate were the political tools of Godwin. He shared with the ruling class a fear of 'the mob', which led him to oppose associations, political parties or any form of agitation. His attack on associations was directed at the radicals, not the Whigs, fearing that their activities would stir up the passion of the masses. He was equally critical in his opposition to government repression, which left him politically isolated, effectively taking a position of 'a plague on both your houses'. Godwin shared with Edmund Burke a contempt for workers. His description of the masses as 'mere parrots', mouthing the slogans of their leaders,[11] is not any less insulting than Burke's 'swinish multitudes'. What alarmed him most about the radical societies was the absence of 'persons of eminence, distinction, and importance in the country' at their meetings, who could temper the enthusiasm of those not much in the habit of regular reading.

Edmund Burke, the founder of modern Toryism, played a surprising role in Godwin's intellectual development, which he acknowledged in later editions of *Political Justice.* In 1786 the *Political Herald and Review* published a long letter of support, addressed to Burke by Godwin, under the name of Mucius. This was before the ideas of liberty, equality and fraternity became common currency, and Burke was still identified with the liberal wing of the Whigs. In the same year they also published his letter *To the People of Ireland,* which shares some interesting similarities with Shelley's *Address to the Irish People,* though it is unlikely that Shelley was aware of its existence:

By a political union, everything you have gained and everything you looked for are to be given up together. From the independence you have earned you are to recede. The entire and unfictitious liberty, the conception of which you formed, you are to abjure forever. And what is it you are to gain by all this? The privilege of yielding a new sphere of patronage to the minister, of corrupting and poisoning the constitution of Britain, after you have barely yielded up your own.[12]

In a footnote Godwin cites Jonathan Swift's *Gulliver's Travels* as a source for his own views on legal and political matters:

Such is the idea of the author of *Gulliver's Travels* (Part IV), a man who appears to have had a more profound insight into the principles of political justice than any preceding or contemporary author. It was unfortunate that a work of such inestimable wisdom failed at the period of its publication from the mere playfulness of its form, in communicating adequate instruction to mankind. Posterity only will be able to estimate it as it deserves.[13]

Caleb Williams, Godwin's novel published in 1794, has sometimes been criticised as rendering 'the theme of *Political Justice* into fiction'. Godwin did intend to use *Caleb Williams* as a vehicle for his philosophical views. The novel grew out of the political milieu, of which the treason trials and the attempt to silence all opposition were the clearest expression. But it stands in its own right as a work of extraordinary power: 'It spoke in its own day as Hugo's *Les Misérables* and Tolstoy's *Resurrection* spoke to later generations'.[14] It is also a psychological thriller, in which the young Caleb discovers the terrible secret that his master Falkland is a murderer. Caleb, in the final volume, disguises himself by adopting an 'Irish brogue', and determines 'to bend my course to the nearest seaport on the west side of the island, and transport myself to Ireland'. At the same time, he understands the limitations of this course of action: 'Ireland had to me the disadvantage of being a dependency of the British government, and therefore a place of less security than most other countries which are divided from it by the ocean'.[15]

Godwin's novel *Mandeville*, published in 1817 and dedicated to John Philpot Curran, opens with an account of the narrator's birth in the north of Ireland, and his escape from the sectarian massacres during the 1641 rebellion in Ireland. Godwin had many radical Irish friends. Richard Brinsley Sheridan, John Philpot Curran and Henry Grattan were both political and personal acquaintances. In 1800 Godwin visited Curran in Ireland and wrote to Coleridge a long description of conditions there. His wife, Mary Wollstonecraft, was of Irish extraction – her mother was from Ballyshannon in County Donegal. In times of economic and personal trouble Ireland was a refuge for Mary and her sisters.[16] Through Mary, Godwin was in touch with many of the leaders of the United Irishmen. She had known Archibald Hamilton Rowan in Paris. His journals contain many references to meeting with Arthur O'Connor at a time when O'Connor was seeking French help for a rising in Ireland, and acting as the liaison between the United Irishmen and the London Corresponding Society.

Without question, in 1811 Shelley regarded Godwin as his political mentor. His letters express his reverence for Godwin's achievements and the intellectual rigour of *Political Justice*:

It opened to my mind fresh and more extensive views; it materially influenced my character, and I rose from its perusal a wiser and better man. I was no longer the votary of romance; till then I had existed in an ideal world – now I found that in this universe of ours was enough to excite the interest of the heart, enough to employ the discussions of reason; I beheld in short, that I had duties to perform.[17]

But, as we shall see, Shelley was never the mere disciple that supporters of Godwin claim. George Woodcock writes of the period after Shelley's return from Ireland:

From that day his mental activity came wholly under the influence of Godwin, and no other thinker of his own age ever rivalled Godwin as a mentor who shaped Shelley's aspirations and moulded the content of his poetry.[18]

Shelley was a far more complex thinker than Woodcock gives him credit for. Equally valid is Dawson's assertion that 'Paine's influence can be traced behind all of Shelley's political activities, and behind a good deal of his early political theory too'.[19] After his return from Ireland Godwin never changed Shelley's mind on any substantial political issue. By 1813, he was no longer a disciple of Godwin, but a thinker fully on his own. Shelley was constantly confronted by the events in the world around him. The revival of the movement in Ireland, the Pentridge uprising in 1817 and the Peterloo massacre in 1819, all of which provoked a furious response in Shelley, and his anger at the fireside reformers shine through:

This is the inspiration which drags Shelley again and again away from his liberal circle towards the masses. The prospect of mass action filled him with far more excitement – and his poetry with far greater resonance and power – than did the prospect of 'slow, gradual reform'.[20]

Before starting on his career as a political activist the 'votary of romance' had one more service to perform – his elopement and marriage to Harriet Westbrook. She was just 15 years old when his sister introduced them. According to the 'official history' she threw herself under his protection because of her unhappiness at school and at home. As both were under age with no hope of parental consent, they eloped and married in Edinburgh.

Harriet has always suffered by comparison with Mary, Shelley's second wife, and the daughter of Mary Wollstonecraft and William Godwin. Mary was reared in a household where books, philosophy and ideas were important. She was encouraged to think and speak for herself, and at 16 when Shelley met her, she was not overawed by the worldly 22 year old. They met and fell in love as equals.

Harriet Westbrook had none of these advantages. Her father was in trade, a vintner and coffee house owner. He amassed a considerable fortune and sufficient standing in society to educate Harriet alongside the daughter of Timothy Shelley, member of parliament and country gentleman. She was educated to be refined and genteel, and marry a man of substance.

But the Shelley worshippers demand perfection of their hero, and so Harriet was systematically denigrated to exonerate Shelley and Mary of any blame in the break-up of his first marriage. In time this became the accepted truth. Stephen Gwynn, writing in 1904, is typical in his description of their marriage and separation:

> Harriet Westbrook, [was] the pretty daughter of an intolerably vulgar family. Shelley, always a propagandist, successfully undertook to convert her to his views, and trouble arose with her parents, when the girl threw herself upon Shelley's protection and proposed that they should fly together.
>
> Here was a young man…who had hampered himself, on principle, by marriage to a woman neither socially nor intellectually his equal… From one reason or another, his home life grew distasteful to him; his wife and he were estranged.[21]

Worse still, as the Shelley legend gained momentum, were the lies of Harriet's descent into prostitution. Shelley's attempt to blame Harriet is indefensible, and one of the few times in his life that he failed to live up to his own ideals. In a letter to Harriet, trying to justify his actions, he rubs salt into the wound:

> Our connection was not one of passion and impulse. Friendship was its basis, and on this basis it has enlarged and strengthened. It is no reproach to me that you have never filled my hearth with an all-

suffiicing passion; perhaps you are even yourself a stranger to these impulses.[22]

The remorse he felt in later life over his treatment of Harriet was genuine, as Mary testified after his death. His subsequent letters to Harriet, though hurtful, show that their separation was not because of any fault in her character. It was simply that he had fallen hopelessly in love with Mary. Harriet shared his life for three years, crowded with incident and excitement, and at the time of their separation she was pregnant with their second child. Therefore, Shelley's alleged remark to Peacock reflects badly on him:

Everyone who knows me must know that the partner of my life should be one who can feel poetry and understand philosophy.
Harriet is a noble animal but she can do neither.[23]

Harriet would never match Mary in Shelley's eyes. But under his tutelage, she read history and philosophy and from the newspapers of Cobbett and Hunt she developed an interest in politics. Harriet shared his hopes for a free world, his efforts for the independence of Ireland, the fight for free speech, and campaigned with him to free imprisoned booksellers and publishers. Harriet was very young, just 16, when they arrived in Ireland, yet her letters show a maturity beyond her years. She understood and believed for herself the concepts of freedom that Shelley espoused. Her letters show an intuitive understanding of Irish politics – she saw through Curran very quickly:

I cannot bear Curran; what use is he to your country? No! If he had been, though his life had been the sacrifice, Ireland would have been saved. I have no patience with Curran. I shall convert Mr Lawless I hope from his idol.[24]

They differed radically on the question of marriage. Shelley, under the influence of Godwin, was an advocate of free love. Harriet understood the situation for a woman who dared to defy convention. In such a repressive society it was not practicable to live openly together. Even Godwin acknowledged this in the preface to his novel *Fleetwood* (1805). In an interesting intellectual reversal of roles, their discussion on marriage compared to the virtues of living together centred on two novels they exchanged in the period before their elopement. Shelley was reading a romantic love story, Sydney Owenson's *The Missionary*,[25] an exotic tale of the orient that gave the illusion of being instructive. In reality, all it offered was the titillation of the forbidden. Perhaps in Luxima, the heroine, Shelley imagined a perfection that was not the reality of their situation. Maybe his emotional turmoil accounts for the impact it made. He sent a copy to Harriet, expecting it would influence her views on living together. In reply she urged him to read Amelia Opie's *Adeline Mowbray*, a serious novel loosely based on the relationship between Mary Wollstonecraft (Adeline) and William Godwin (Glenmurray), and their views on marriage. The story is simple enough: Adeline becomes enamoured with Glenmurray, an advocate of a free union over marriage, through reading his book. They meet, fall in love and live together. Glenmurray, aware of the difficulties, is prepared to compromise and marry her, but Adeline refuses as a matter of principle. After Glenmurray's death, she is left a social outcast. Unable to earn a living, she is caught in a downward spiral that ends in her death. Adeline dies regretting that:

> I dared to act contrary to the experience of age, and became in the eyes of the world an example of vice, when I believed myself the champion of virtue.[26]

Perhaps the fate of Adeline left its mark. Two years after their separation Harriet, alone and in poor circumstances, threw herself into the lake in Hyde Park and drowned. Louise Schutz Boas, in her book, *Harriet Shelley*, has finally put the record straight, and best summarised her plight:

> She had been belittled and begrimed in an effort to lay her ghost, her story coloured by Victorian prejudice, by misguided hero-worship or hatred of her husband. Shelley's detractors shaped it into a stick to belabour him, his admirers into a whip to lash her.[27]

While Shelley accepted that marriage was the only practicable solution at the time, it did not mean that he intended living in conventional style. On their return from Edinburgh, Eliza, Harriet's elder sister, who was to become a permanent member of their household, joined them. For the rest of his life Shelley always lived with an extended circle of friends and relations.

In June 1811, a few months before his elopement, Shelley made the acquaintance of Elizabeth Hitchener, a Sussex schoolteacher, with whom he struck up an extraordinary intellectual friendship. She was 10 years older than Shelley, a self educated schoolteacher who was in contact with the radical circles in London. Their friendship and correspondence evolved into a forum for philosophical and political debate and an outlet for his attempts at emotional self analysis. Elizabeth Hitchener became in turn his pupil, confidante and soulmate. In the course of the following year the relationship changed to one of intense hatred on Shelley's part. However, in the letters to Elizabeth Hitchener we can trace the shift in Shelley's interests from religion and philosophy to politics. We now read of an increasing hostility to the establishment, and in particular to the army and big business.

By late 1811 Shelley was committed to a new career of political propagandist. He was aiming at two different classes of reader, the working class and liberal intellectuals. Influenced by Tom Paine, Shelley hoped to use popular political ballads distributed as broadsheets to arouse the working class to a realisation of their position. With intellectuals he was more influenced by Godwin, intending to use novels and essays to instruct them in their political duties and urge them to take up the leadership of the coming social upheavals, which he believed would be similar to the French Revolution. Shelley always hoped that revolution might be avoided, but if it happened he was clear that he would be on the side of the people:

> Popular insurrections and revolutions I look upon with
> discountenance. If such things must be, I will take the side of the
> People; but my reasoning shall endeavour to ward it from the hearts
> of the Rulers of the Earth, deeply as I detest them.[28]

This is the clearest summary of Shelley's views on revolution and throughout his life he remained constant to that position.

In October 1811 Shelley, Harriet and Eliza left for the Lake District. The poet Robert Southey lived in Keswick, Wordsworth and Coleridge nearby, which may have been the reason for moving there. Shelley never met Wordsworth or Coleridge, but his discussions with Southey appear to be the decisive catalyst that pushed him towards political activity. There is a common assumption that their relationship was wholly antagonistic – the young idealist set against the middle-aged Tory. However, Southey was better informed on political issues than anyone Shelley had met before. Southey had worked in Dublin as chief-secretary to the Irish chancellor of the exchequer in 1801-1802 and was therefore informed about Irish history and politics. It was Southey who suggested that he write to James Montgomery, the radical poet and editor of the *Sheffield Iris* about political pamphleteering. Southey was obviously taken by the young Shelley, who reminded him of his own radical past. Southey wrote to a friend: 'I tell him that all the difference between us is, that he is 19 and I am 37'.[29] It was not age or experience that led to the break between them, but politics. Southey, who in his youth was a supporter of the French Revolution and author of the revolutionary poem *Wat Tyler*, became an apologist for the establishment in later life. Shelley, writing to Godwin in January 1812, said:

> Southey the poet whose principles were pure and elevated once, is
> now the servile champion of every abuse and absurdity. – I have had
> much conversation with him. He says 'You will think as I do when
> you are old'. I do not feel the least disposition to be Mr S's proselyte.[30]

Robert Emmet's famous speech from the dock, before his execution in 1803 – 'When my country takes her place among the nations of the earth, then, and not till then, let my epitaph be written'[31] – had once inspired Southey to make an attempt at Emmet's epitaph:

> Here in free England shall an English hand
> Build thy *imperishable monument*[32]

Now the poet who had been so moved to raise an 'imperishable monument' to Emmet in 1803 took the opposite view, as Shelley explained: 'Southey hates the Irish, he speaks against Catholic emancipation, and parliamentary reform'.[33]

As one star set another arose. From Southey he learned that William Godwin was not dead, as he had assumed, but very much alive. The news filled him with delight and he wrote at once to Godwin in London:

> The name of Godwin has been used to excite in me feelings of reverence and admiration, I have been accustomed to consider him a luminary too dazzling for the darkness which surrounds him, and from the earliest period of my knowledge of his principles I have ardently desired to share on the footing of intimacy that intellect which I have delighted to contemplate in its emanations... I had enrolled your name on the list of the honourable dead. I had felt regret that the glory of your being had passed from this earth of ours: It is not so – you still live, and I firmly believe are still planning the welfare of humankind. I have but just entered on the scene of human operations, yet my feelings and my reasonings correspond with what yours were... I am ardent in the cause of philanthropy and truth, do not suppose that this is vanity… I am convinced I could represent myself to you in such terms as not to be thought wholly unworthy of your friendship.[34]

In fact, Godwin was far from 'planning the welfare of mankind'. Now in his mid-50s, he was no longer trying to convert the world to his views, and lived quietly with his second wife, publishing children's books. Godwin replied immediately, and thus began a correspondence that would transform both their lives. Shelley resplied on 10 January 1812 with a long biographical letter in which he asserted that, inspired by the ideas of *Political Justice*, he was:

> ...now earnestly pursuing studious habits. I am writing 'an enquiry into the causes of the failure of the French Revolution to benefit mankind'.[35] My plan is that of resolving to lose no opportunity to disseminate truth and happiness.[36]

In reply Godwin suggested that Shelley ought to repress any thoughts of publication, or even worse, from any involvement in political activity, until wisdom and knowledge had qualified him to become a teacher. He urged him to proceed with due calm and modesty, as it was one of the fundamental principles of *Political Justice* that change cannot take place by political associations or active campaigning, but by a process of reasoning and education carried on in private. Therefore, imagine the shock to the elderly philosopher when, a few days later, Shelley announced at the end of a long letter:

> In a few days we set off to Dublin. I do not know exactly where we shall be, but a letter addressed to Keswick will find me: Our journey has been settled some time. We go principally to forward as much as we can the Catholic Emancipation.[37]

This was not a whim or youthful enthusiasm on Shelley's part. His philosophy of social revolution was the central dynamic of his life, poetry and politics:

> Then we may hope the consummating hour
> Dreadfully, sweetly, swiftly is arriving.[38]

The 'consummating hour', which Shelley believed was approaching, arose from the general crisis affecting society in 1812, but its origins can be traced back to the French Revolution. Therefore, to make sense of Shelley's life and work we need to go back to the 1790s, to the events and people who ushered in 'a new era in the world's history'.

NOTES

1   R Holmes, *Shelley: The Pursuit*, op cit, p43.

2   W Godwin, *Selection from Political Justice* (London, 1943), p4.

3   R G Grylls, *William Godwin and his world* (London, 1953), p16.

4   W Hazlitt, *Spirit of the Age* (London, 1964), p202.

5   *Northern Star* (Belfast), October 1793 and 9 December 1796.

6   W Godwin, op cit, introduction, p13.

7   Ibid, p197.

8   Ibid, p242.

9   Ibid, p745.

10   Ibid, p252.

11   Ibid, pp260-61.

12   W Godwin, *Uncollected Writings,* (Florida, 1968), p58.

13   W Godwin, *Political Justice,* op cit, pp552-53.

14   G Woodcock, *William Godwin* (London, 1946), p120.

15   W Godwin, *Caleb Williams* (London, 1987), pp247-248.

16   Mary's brother Charles was involved in business with relatives in Cork, and her sisters eventually moved to Dublin where they opened a school. 'They lived in Hume Street and Everina had the drawing room upstairs where she taught the boys of the gentry. Mrs Bishop (Eliza) had the parlour downstairs where she taught the girls' (*Dowden Papers,* Trinity College Dublin, no 3,005).

17   F L Jones, op cit, 1, p227.

18   G Woodcock, op cit, p211.

19   P Dawson, *The Unacknowledged Legislator* (Oxford, 1980), p41.

20   P Foot, op cit, p168.

21   S Gwynn, *The Masters of English Literature* (London, 1938), pp358-59.

22   F L Jones, op cit, 1, p389.

23   T Peacock, *Memoirs of Shelley* (London, 1970), p57.

24   F L Jones, op cit, p321.

25   Sydney Owenson (1776-1859) was born in Dublin and lived in Kildare St. After her marriage in 1812 she was known as Lady Morgan. She is best known for her romantic melodramas, *The Missionary, The Wild Irish Girl,* etc. A republican, whose drawing room was known as 'a foyer of liberalism', she brought her interest in Irish history and politics together in *Patriotic Sketches of Ireland* (1807) and later in *The O'Briens and O'Flahertys* (1827), a serious novel about the political reality of Ireland leading up to the Act of Union. She had an undoubted influence on the Shelleys, as Harriet's letter shows: 'I have read Miss Owenson's *Missionary* and much do I admire the author. I am now reading her *Novice of St Dominick.* I regret not having known her when I was in Dublin. Her *Patriotic Sketches* have won my heart. She speaks so feelingly of your dear country that I love her for that'. (F L Jones, op cit, p234) See Appendix 1 for Miss Owenson's influence on Shelley's poetry. Mary Shelley met Lady Morgan in 1835 and they became lifelong friends.

26   A Opie, *Adeline Mowbray* (Oxford, 1999), p238.

27   Louise Schutz Boas, *Harriet Shelley* (London, 1962), preface, pv.

28   F L Jones, op cit, p221.

29   C C Southey, *Life and Correspondence of Robert Southey* (London, 1849), vol 3, p325.

30   F L Jones, op cit, p231.

31   R Emmet, *Speech from the dock* (Dublin, 1978), p8.

32   R Southey, 'Written immediately after reading the speech of Robert Emmet', *Poems of R Southey* (London, 1909), lines 14-15, p396.

33   F L Jones, op cit, p155.

34   Ibid, pp220-21.

35   This was his novel *Hubert Cauvin,* which was never finished – the manuscript was subsequently lost.

36   F L Jones, op cit, p229.

37   Ibid, p231.

38   P B Shelley, *Esdaile,* op cit, 'The Crisis', lines 13-14, p40.

CHAPTER THREE

The Morning Star of Liberty

The greatest event in human annals. Twenty six millions of our fellow
creatures…bursting their chains, and throwing off in an instant, the
degrading yoke of slavery.[1]

THE *Belfast Newsletter* did not exaggerate
when it described the French Revolution as 'the greatest event in human
annals'. Wolfe Tone described it more poetically as 'The Morning Star of
Liberty'.[2] France in 1789 was the catalyst for revolution across Europe.
Feudalism had outlived its usefulness and a rising capitalist class armed
with the ideas of the enlightenment was waiting to cast aside the old
order: 'It proclaimed the political order of a new European society… A
victory of enlightenment over superstition'.[3] For the United Irishmen,
the revolution showed that a Catholic country could be in the vanguard
of radical ideas, and this opened the possibility of a Protestant-Catholic
alliance against the British regime.

The industrial revolution and the invention of iron framed printing
presses democratised access to ideas. The cheap editions that flowed
from the presses, allied to the foundation of circulating libraries made it

possible for books, newspapers and especially pamphlets to be distributed and sold across the country in vast quantities. In Ulster in the 1790s, the United Irishmen encouraged popular education by forming plebeian book clubs and reading societies, which were in effect 'seminaries of sedition'. Arthur O'Connor wrote that the *Press* and the *Northern Star* illuminated intellectual life in Belfast and transformed it into 'the Athens of Ireland'.[4]

The French Revolution unleashed a debate that found expression not just in polemical terms, but also in organisational, cultural and political forms. The London Corresponding Society was formed in January 1792. This was the first mass party in the world with a substantial working class base. At its peak 20,000 members were organised (only the Republican Party in America predates it). They were shopkeepers, artisans and mechanics and their business was reform.[5] Like all great movements, the impetus of its own inspiration carried it beyond its immediate demands and inspired a movement for the reconstruction of all human institutions, even the amendment of human nature itself.

H N Brailsford, in his book *Shelley, Godwin, and Their Circle,* wrote, 'The history of the French Revolution in England begins with a sermon and ends with a poem'.[6] Dr Price was a well-known dissenting preacher who, on 4 November 1789, four months after the fall of the Bastille, delivered his famous sermon in London. His congregation was the Society for Commemorating the Revolution in Great Britain, a club that met annually to celebrate the glorious revolution of 1688. They were respectable members of society – lawyers, doctors of divinity, lords and nobles, not the shoemakers and the staymakers who were to form the London Corresponding Society and riot on the streets of England. Dr Price ended his sermon with this declaration:

> And now methinks I see the ardour for liberty catching and
> spreading, a general amendment beginning in human affairs; the
> dominion of the kings changed for the dominion of the laws, and
> the dominion of priests giving way to the dominion of reason and
> science.[7]

Price, an old man near death, made history that afternoon. His address opened the way for contact between the English radicals and French revolutionaries, which changed the face of English and Irish politics forever.

Great historical events sometimes find reflection in the art and literature that they inspire, and this was especially true of the French Revolution. In 1789 Cowper and Burns were the most innovative and popular poets in Britain. Cowper was an elderly religious man who pitied the poor, but thought reform was impossible. He was shaken out of his pious scepticism by the events in France and was transformed by this 'wonderful period in the history of mankind'.[8] Robert Burns, a Tory supporter, inspired by the events in France, became a Radical Whig and a champion of rights for women, a cause that gained ground during the French Revolution. In 1792 he wrote these lines for the actress Louisa Fontenelle when she appeared in Scotland:

While Quacks of state must each produce his plan,
And even children lisp the rights of man;
Amid this mighty fuss just let me mention,
The Rights of Women merit some attention.[9]

Burns, who was referring to Tom Paine's *The Rights of Man*, published a year earlier in defence of the French Revolution, did not have to wait long for his champion of women's rights to appear. In the same year Mary Wollstonecraft published *A Vindication of the Rights of Women*, a response both to her experience as a woman and to the prevailing tradition of ridicule and scorn for the reality of women's lives.

Though Cowper and Burns led the way, it was the Lake Poets – Wordsworth, Southey and Coleridge – who transformed poetry at the end of the 18th century. There have been few generations of writers more interested in the study of their society than the 'Romantic poets', from Wordsworth and Coleridge in the 1790s to Shelley and Byron 20 years later. Our very concept of the 'romantic artist' derives from our study of that period. But it is not a description of themselves that they would recognise or indeed have welcomed.

Any attempt at summarising or defining Romanticism implies a coherence that was not the reality of the situation and can end up oversimplifying the phenomenon. The Augustan or classic tradition considered poets and artists as interpreters. The Romantics regarded themselves as creators. What previously had been decorative, impersonal, bounded by convention, was now emotional, energetic, a celebration of freedom. To suggest that human emotions matter was another way of saying that all human beings have rights. The Romantics were firmly located in the material world, but one that was transcended by an ideal world of the imagination. This did not imply that they lived in a world abstracted from reality. They saw themselves in one sense as men of action – Wordsworth wished above all to be considered a teacher. The ideal world they constructed was often more real than the world they inhabited, but it also was a world full of imponderable forces, a site of change and transformation. They were rebels in their medium as in their social vision. The shock of the French Revolution cut them adrift from conventional literary moorings and started them on a search for a new conception of what poetry was and how it should be written. They explored different forms and structures. In Tom Paulin's view, 'Wordsworth's early poems take nature as their subject, but their treatment of nature as movement and process also makes them radical documents'.[10]

The new world of the poets was a place of turbulence and change, a process which was reflected in both the content and the form of their work. They shared a concept of imagination and a poetic style that was quite different from anything that went before it. On this all the Romantics are agreed. But their response to social change was more varied – sometimes welcoming change as constructive and progressive, at other times concerned, hostile and afraid. Coleridge was always uncertain and provisional in his attitude to these patterns of change and conflict. Wordsworth and Southey, initially enthusiastic for the radical philosophy of the enlightenment, moved to a position that was more 'inwardly focused, socially evasive and conservative'.

While Shelley understood their disillusionment at the outcome the revolution, he himself never wavered in his support for the ideals of the Enlightenment:

Gloom and misanthropy have become the characteristics of the age in which we live, the solace of a disappointment that unconsciously finds relief only in the wilful exaggeration of its own despair. This influence has tainted the literature of the age with the hopelessness of the minds from which it flows...But mankind appear to me to be emerging from their trance. I am aware, methinks, of a slow, gradual, silent change.[11]

No society disappears before it exhausts all the possibilities open to it, and England in 1790 was no exception. A description of the reaction in England against the French Revolution traditionally starts with the name of Edmund Burke. His *Reflections on the French Revolution*, published in the winter of 1790, stands as a permanent memorial to its effect on English society. Thomas McLoughlin, in his book *Contesting Ireland*, calls Burke 'a divided Irishman',[12] on the one hand he was a supporter of free trade for Ireland and Catholic emancipation and, on the other, one of the most eloquent advocates for the British Empire in the 18th century. Conor Cruise O'Brien speaks of 'the friction between the outer Whig and the inner Jacobite'.[13] The French Revolution forced Burke to resolve that contradiction:

Burke still proclaims the flower full-grown
The slow-maturing Constitution.
Mature himself and fixed in stone
He deprecates the Revolution.[14]

Tom Paine wrote a letter to Burke from Paris outlining the course of the revolution, predicting that it would spread beyond the borders of France. His account was to fuel one of the bitterest political controversies in British politics, and reshaped the political landscape to this day.

Reflections was written as a defence of monarchy, priesthood and privilege. Burke was alarmed at the similarities between Paine's sympathy for the French Revolution and Dr Price's sermon in support of the National Assembly. Burke saw that the bulk of Paine's letter and Price's sermon concerned the flaws in the English constitution, and would lead to demands for reform that could undermine the very basis of the existing order. Though addressed 'to a Gentleman in Paris', it was always the

English reader that Burke had in mind. In a famous passage he prophesied: 'Along with its natural protectors and guardians, learning will be cast into the mire, and trodden down under the hoofs of the swinish multitude'.[15] This reference to the masses as 'a swinish multitude' was received with indignation and amusement and was responsible for one of the few strands of humour in British radical literature. Shelley was one of the many who responded to Burke's jibe, when in 1819 he incorporated the phrase into a political satire, *Swellfoot the Tyrant,* directed against the Castlereagh administration. In Ireland, the United Irishmen replied with a popular ballad, 'The Swinish Multitude':

May you, By Bastille's ne'er appalled
See natures rights renewed
Nor longer unavenged be called
'The Swinish Multitude'[16]

Burke, isolated from the masses in the House of Commons, had misjudged the popular mood. The general public may not have shared the wholehearted enthusiasm of Wordsworth or Southey for the French Revolution, but they understood that it was a struggle for liberty and freedom. By characterising the mass of the population as 'brutish and inarticulate', Burke provoked a furious response. Within months Mary Wollstonecraft replied with *A Vindication of the Rights of Man.* In 1793 William Godwin published his *Enquiry Concerning Political Justice,* which was to be so influential in the young Shelley's political development. Though none would be as powerful or popular as Tom Paine's *The Rights of Man,* published in 1791.

Tom Paine was born in Norfolk in 1737, the son of a Quaker. He worked as an exciseman, only to be dismissed for writing a pamphlet in defence of an agitation for higher wages. Without hope of work he left for America. His arrival coincided with the events that led to the American War of Independence. Paine announced his arrival with a pamphlet entitled *Common Sense,* which had an immediate impact on American politics: 'It would be difficult to name any human composition which has had an effect at once so instant, so extended and so lasting'.[17] In 1775 he enlisted in Washington's army, and fought right through the campaign. In the intervals between forced marches, he wrote a series of pamphlets to rally the spirits of the disheartened American volunteers. In one of them Paine wrote:

> These are the times that try men's souls. The summer soldier and the sunshine patriot will, in this crisis, shrink from the service of his country; but he that stands it now, deserves the thanks of man and woman.[18]

These were sentiments that would find an echo during the United Irishmen's revolt in 1798.

At the end of the war Paine could have settled in America as an honoured citizen, but, tired of inaction, he returned to England to carry on the work of agitation and pamphleteering that he had started in America. What he had done for America with *Common Sense*, he sought to do for France with his *Rights of Man.*

Burke and Paine to this day are inextricably linked, but Paine was not primarily concerned with answering Burke. His description of the French Revolution was written before Burke's book appeared. Paine wrote *The Rights of Man* to prepare public opinion for revolutionary change. The moment threw up the man; for workers had grasped the simple fact that their position was not fixed by some immutable laws of nature, or incomprehensible economic laws, but was related to the way the country was governed. 'Paine spoke a language that the labouring man, the artisan, and the farmer could understand'.[19] For the most part, the workingmen's clubs were content to agitate for the reform of government, but many were prepared to go the whole way with Paine:

> His influence was perhaps on the whole greater than any other single revolutionary writer in 19th century England; and it is because of this continued influence that he came to be regarded, not without reason as the poor man's friend.[20]

Part two of *The Rights of Man* was published in February 1792 and Paine, in a letter to a friend, wrote that he hoped: 'It will produce something one way or the other. I see the tide is yet the wrong way, but there is a change of sentiment beginning'.[21] There were few places in Britain untouched by his book, which started an agitation at grassroots level unheard of since the Diggers and Levellers of the 1640s. We will never know the total sales of Paine's work, although John Keane estimates that in Britain alone it sold more than 200,000 copies.[22] Hannah More, a leading spokeswoman against revolution, observed that the supporters of Paine 'load asses with their pernicious pamphlets and...get them dropped, not only in cottages, and in highways, but into mines and coal-pits'.[23] In Scotland it was reported that his book 'is being circulated...at a very low price, and that 10,000 copies per week are being sold'.[24] Paine and the workingmen's clubs, which he inspired, were the cradle and the school, out of which the modern labour movement grew.

The Burke-Paine controversy was not just an issue at the grassroots of society. The Whig triumvirate of Fox, Sheridan and Burke, which intellectually dominated British politics at the end of the 18th century, split apart on the publication of Burke's *Reflections*. Sheridan supported Fox against Burke, which led to the split between the New Whigs of Fox and the Old Whigs of Burke. In time this split was to crystallise into the modern Liberal and Conservative parties.

This was a golden age, when everything seemed possible. Wordsworth, who was in France experiencing the revolution, felt that:

Bliss was it in that dawn to be alive

But to be young was very heaven.[25]

Burke was no longer alone in thinking that the constitution was under threat. In May 1792 the Pitt government issued a proclamation against seditious writings. A summons was issued against Paine, though no move was made to arrest him, for fear of mass unrest. The tide was turning against Paine and in September, fearing arrest, he fled to France, never to return. This was the beginning of the end for that generation, for whom 'bliss was it in that dawn to be alive'. England was at war with revolutionary France. It was 'the times that try men's souls'. Economic depression had blunted the workers movement, and the leaders were heading for jail or were about to start for Botany Bay.

In a letter written in November 1791, 'Paine said that 16,000 copies of his book had been sold in England, over 40,000 in Ireland'.[26] The impact in Ireland was immense. A committee was set up in Dublin to organise distribution of a cheap edition. In Belfast Republicans and Presbyterians were distributing 'six-penny pacquets of sedition' to a semi-literate population. Extracts were printed in the *Belfast Newsletter,* the *Morning Post* and the *Dublin Weekly Journal.* Wolfe Tone noted that 'it at once became the Koran of Belfast'.[27] The Society of United Irishmen, founded in 1791, inspired by the *Rights of Man* and the ideals of the French Revolution, made Paine an honorary member. But it was amongst the Irish Catholic peasants that Paine's book made the greatest impact. The Whiteboys, a peasant secret society, described by one contemporary as 'a vast trade union for the protection of the Irish peasantry',[28] had become more politicised under the impact of Paine's book and the economic unrest caused by the war with France:

> As early as 1793 Denis Browne of Westport was already attributing the changed political spirit of the ordinary people to the stream of paper emanating from Dublin, a spirit produced by the circulation of Paine's *Rights of Man,* of seditious newspapers, and by shopkeepers who, having been in Dublin to buy goods, have formed connections with some of the United Irishmen.[29]

They affirmed a militant republican catechism: 'I believe in a revolution founded on the rights of man'.[30] Despite Tone's friendship and admiration for Paine's republicanism, the United Irishmen had little inclination to accept Paine's social programme:

> Irish radicals were slow to suggest modifications to the economic structure. The middle-class businessmen who provided much of the driving and directing power in the radical reform movement accepted the existing relationships between capital and labour as axiomatic and in some instances they came into conflict with militant working groups.[31]

In the absence of a revolutionary social programme, separatism, republicanism and Catholic emancipation became the ideology driving the 'summer soldiers' towards the uprising of 1798: 'Not only did the United Irishmen perish on the fields of Ireland in 1798, so also in a sense did Paine and his ideology'.[32]

In France, the revolution was balanced between the Jacobins, under

Robespierre's leadership, and the forces of reaction. The masses were not yet defeated, and the outcome of the revolution was still to be decided. This was a difficult time for the supporters of the revolution. In England, after the first flush of excitement for 'a people risen up', some gave way to despondency. Southey and Coleridge, under the influence of Godwin, had been diverted to:

> A grander and simpler scheme. A plan to give nature and reason a new start on a new continent, free from the corruption which had poisoned reform in France and stifled reform in England.[33]

Their grand scheme was to build a new utopia in America, on the banks of the Susquehanna River in Pennsylvania. A few hundred pounds and the will to leave the Old World behind were all that was necessary. But like most utopias it was blown away by a blast of reality – no money was forthcoming. Southey departed for Portugal and Coleridge in his *Religious Musings* turned to a different millennium. Wordsworth was made of sterner stuff. His apostasy was still some years off. He went to France in May 1791 at the age of 19, because he 'felt himself so fascinated by the gorgeous festival era of the Revolution'.[34] He returned to England in 1793, a committed supporter of the revolution. He despised the England he found and, in the war with France, rejoiced at every English defeat. Despite government repression he planned a republican newspaper, the *Philanthropist.* In a letter he wrote of his hopes for the paper, 'I know that the multitude walk in darkness. I would put a lantern into each man's hand to guide him'.[35] Correspondents were to be appointed in all areas of Britain and Ireland. He believed that in England revolution was at hand. Wordsworth had an ambivalent attitude to revolution, supporting it in France, while hoping that reform was possible in England. He never resolved that ambivalence, which eventually led him into the camp of reaction.

There had never been a period for young writers and artists like that born out of the French Revolution. The *Lyrical Ballads* [36] were the work of men in their 20s An unmade reputation or unproduced masterpiece by the age of 30 was a rarity among the Romantics. Coleridge's great flowering of poetic genius took place in a period of five years, and in particular in the year 1797, at the age of 25. What the Russian revolutionary Leon Trotsky wrote in the late 1930s could just as easily serve as an epitaph for the 1790s: 'Life is beautiful, let the future generations cleanse it of all evil, oppression and violence, and enjoy it to the full'.[37] The poets and writers of the 1790s believed for a while they were that future generation.

Shelley was born into a world dominated by the struggle for the rights of man and political justice. But he came of age in an era of reaction and defeat, a grim period sometimes known as the 'Bleak Age', between the failure of the French Revolution and the Reform Bill of 1832. The first generation of Romantics, that of Wordsworth, Coleridge and Southey, had become disillusioned or conservative by the experience of defeat. However, a new generation of young writers grew up in the opening decades of the 19th century, for whom only the 'Liberating Flame of the Revolution' was visible across the years:

> The second generation of British romantics – that of Byron
> (1788-1824), the unpolitical but fellow-travelling Keats (1795-1821)
> and above all Shelley (1792-1822) – was the first thus to combine
> romanticism and active revolutionism: the disappointments of
> the French Revolution, unforgotten by their elders, paled beside
> the visible horrors of the capitalist transformation of their own
> country.[38]

Shelley saw no contradiction between art and revolution, and he elected from an early age to meet the challenge it presented. For Shelley, this was never easy, either in terms of the tragedies he suffered in his personal life or in terms of the political difficulties he encountered. Nevertheless, this was a challenge that he welcomed, and met with fortitude and courage. His experience in Ireland in the early months of 1812 was to shape and mould the 10 years of life that were left to him.

NOTES

1   J Bardon, *A History of Ulster* (Belfast, 1992), p218.

2   W Tone, *Memoirs* (Washington, 1826), vol 1, p356.

3   K Marx and F Engels, *Collected Works* (London, 1975), vol 8, p161.

4   Quoted in K Whelan, *The Tree of Liberty* (Cork, 1996), p62.

5   E P Thomson, *The Making of the English Working Class*, op cit, pp102-185.

6   H N Brailsford, *Shelley, Godwin, And Their Circle* (London, 1913), p7.

7   Quoted in E Trory, *Cradled into Poetry* (Hove, 1991), p30.

8   Quoted in P Brown, *The French Revolution in English History* (London, 1918), p32.

9   R Burns, *Poetical Works* (London, 1950), 'The Rights of Women', lines 3-6, p244. Some newly attributed poems by Burns are published in Noble & Scott Hogg, *The Cannongate Burns* (London, 2001). These radical poems from 1789 onwards were published anonymously for fear of arrest. The 'Ode (for Hibernia's Sons)' heaps praise on the Irish rebels living under the 'th' iron rod' of Britain.

10   T Paulin, *The Day-Star of Liberty* (London, 1998), p75.

11   *Poetical Works of Shelley,* 'The Revolt of Islam', preface, op cit, pp33-34.

12   T McLoughlin, *Contesting Ireland* (Dublin, 1999), p161.

13   Ibid, p171.

14   T S Faulks 'College Green', *Penguin Parade no7* (London, 1940), lines 7-10, p82.

15   E Burke, *Reflections on the French Revolution* (London, 1935), p76.

16   P O'Farrell, *The '98 Reader* (Dublin, 1998), p3.

17   G Trevelyan, quoted in, *Thomas Paine Reader* (Middlesex, 1987), p10.

18   Ibid, p116.

19   R R Fennessy, *Burke, Paine, And The Rights of Man* (La Haye, 1963), p244.

20   Ibid, p250.

21   Ibid, p239.

22   J Keane, *Tom Paine: A Political Life* (London, 1995), p333.

23   Ibid, p331.

24   Ibid, p331.

25   William Wordsworth, 'The Prelude', *The Poetical Works of Wordsworth* (London, 1946), book II, lines 108-9, p631.

26   R R Fennessy, *Burke, Paine, And The Rights of Man, op cit*, p3.

27   T A Jackson, *Ireland Her Own*,(London, 1947), p101.

28   E O'Connor, *A Labour History of Ireland* (Dublin, 1992), p4.

29   K Whelan, op cit, p65.

30   J Keane, op cit, p333.

31   R McDowell, *Ireland in the Age of Imperialism and Revolution*
(London, 1979), p365.

32   S Ensko, 'The Irish Readers of The Rights of Man', *Labour History News*
(Dublin, 1991), no 7, p18.

33   P Brown, op cit, p108.

34   F M Todd, *Politics and the Poet: A Study of Wordsworth* (London, 1957), p37.

35   Quoted in P Brown, 'Letter to W Matthew's, June 1794', op cit, p111.

36   *Lyrical Ballads* was published jointly by Wordsworth and Coleridge in 1798.
They were poems of nature and the imagination, the preface, added in 1800, has
been termed 'the manifesto of English Romanticism'.

37   T Cliff, *Trotsky,* vol 4 (London, 1993), p18.

38   E J Hobsbawm, *The Age of Revolution* (London, 1977), p323.

CHAPTER FOUR

Ireland in 1812

A crisis like this ought not to be permitted
to pass unoccupied or unimproved.[1]

THE Shelleys took rooms on the first floor
of a house belonging to Mr Dunne, a woollen-draper, at 7 Lower
Sackville Street (now O'Connell Street).[2] Standing on the balcony outside his window, Shelley could see an unbroken vista from the Rotunda
at its northern end to the former Houses of Parliament, over the river
Liffey to the south. In its time Sackville Street was one of the finest
streets in Europe, and home to the most wealthy and powerful people in
Irish society.[3] After the Act of Union in 1800, which abolished the Irish
parliament and created the union of Great Britain and Ireland, Dublin
slowly took on the appearance of a provincial slum, as silks and the bro-
cades turned to rags:

> The introduction of the Act of Union…has changed the appearance
> of Dublin; with the removal of its Parliament, the nobility of Ireland
> withdrew to England and left their places in Dublin either to fall
> into decay or to be converted into public offices, hotels or charitable
> institutions.[4]

As early as 1804 an English visitor remarked that 'in Dublin everything is pomp or poverty'. The same writer was also struck by 'how political the city was, how political pamphlets featured markedly in the wares of the booksellers'.[5] The Act of Union was a disaster for the city. Within a few years Dublin Castle was run down, the paths of St Stephens Green were choked with weeds, and there were more beggars on the streets of Dublin than ever before. The clauses in the act that produced the most immediate effect were those that related to Ireland's financial obligations. The war with France had increased the British national debt, and a disproportionate amount was imposed on the Irish exchequer.[6] The servicing of this debt was a serious drain on Irish capital at a time when it could least afford it. The deteriorating relations with America, which led to the declaration of war in 1812, had severe economic repercussions in Ireland because of the dependence of the linen industry on the US market. The magnificent Linen Hall, deprived of its function by the collapse of the linen trade, was by now staggering towards its demise.[7] Unemployed weavers were forced to emigrate to the already depressed textile towns in the north of England. Dissent was on the rise. Economic depression and the sudden rise in prices had inflamed popular passions.

This was the background to the national campaign for Catholic emancipation, which reached a climax in 1811. The campaign grew dramatically from small beginnings in 1804-05 to pose one of the greatest threats to the Protestant Ascendancy and the legitimacy of the state since the rebellion of 1798. The agitation around the elections for a more representative Catholic Committee produced a revival of disaffection in the old Defender and United Irish areas and brought many former militants into activity again. The secret societies were once again growing in size and influence. The origins of the Ribbonmen – Defenderism's direct offspring – are to be found in this period, and in similar conditions that had fostered the union of the United Irishmen and the Defenders almost 20 years earlier. The importance and extent of the secret societies in Irish history has been emphasised recently in the work of Marianne Elliott, Kevin Whelan and others. Tom Garvin writes of them:

The submerged peasantry and labourers of 18th-century Ireland had evolved a localist political culture that emphasised collective solidarity, the enforcement of folk custom in matters of land-tenancy, marriage, inheritance, support for the clergy and relations with landlords. A crude village democracy existed; Whiteboy captains were commonly elected, as were the leaders of factions and hurling teams. In classic Hobbesean fashion, the political state which was denied to them by the Ascendancy tried to create itself at village level in the form of a sort of underworld polity, complete with the functions of judgement and execution.[8]

This almost fits the description of Godwin's village democracy in his *Political Justice.* But the conditions of state repression under which they had to operate made it quite different from that envisaged by Godwin. The secret societies have a long history in Irish political and social life, and they adopted many forms and titles – Defenders, Whiteboys, Hearts of Steele, Shanavests, Ribbonmen and many others. They were not just a rural phenomenon, they also drew support in the towns from the expanding artisan and working classes. As well as the nascent trade union organisations, Dublin in the 1790s had political clubs and reading societies based on the city's journeymen and artisans, which was fertile ground for Defenderism and its successors.[9] They were mainly Catholic defensive organisations:

The 'midnight legislators' could always call, as they pointed out 'we will know you the darkest night when you will not know us the brightest day'.[10]

Sometimes they assumed a sectarian form, as in the clashes between the Protestant Orange Order and the Defenders in Ulster at the end of the 18th century. The role played by the two main societies leading up to the rebellion of 1798 showed that such organisations could be mobilised and politicised in the interests of a wider cause, and used to promote or suppress an emerging ideology that threatened the very existence of the state. The defeat of the United Irishmen in 1798 dealt a blow to political organisation, but, because of their nature the secret societies survived, battered but intact, to resurface during the agitation for Catholic emancipation. By now they called themselves Ribbonmen, with the most political elements still harbouring thoughts of a national uprising with French help.

The Act of Union had two main purposes: to secure Protestant Ascendancy in Ireland, and protect Britain from the danger of a French invasion through 'the back door'. In the opening decade of the 19th century, this also gave rise to unforeseen political and social developments. There was the rapid decline of Presbyterian radicalism, and a shift from opposition to support for the Union. This was hastened by the sectarian polemics, which opened divisions in the old Presbyterian/Catholic alliance, and by the growing dependence of industry in the north east on the British market. The area, which had been noted for its radicalism and opposition to British influence in Ireland, became in time famous for its unbending support for the Union. Republican ideology survived the defeat of 1798 and the Act of Union, but its base in the 19th century was largely confined to the Catholics. Emmet's speech from the dock during his trial in 1803, which had so impressed Shelley, was a powerful propaganda tool in the republican revival. But this revival must be seen against the backdrop of rising rural and urban agitation and the economic crisis that Britain was now seen to be responsible for. The campaign for Catholic emancipation, around which the different strands of resistance were to coalesce, was destined to become the most powerful movement in the history of 19th century Ireland.

The Catholic Relief Act of 1793 and the establishment of Maynooth[11] in 1795 were part of a process by which the government attempted to reconcile Catholics to the Crown. The Protestant Ascendancy and the hierarchy of the Catholic Church had a common interest in cooperating against the anti-religious ideas of the republicans, while the British army, in the war with France, offered the only hope of salvation for the Catholic church on the continent. A consensus existed between the Catholic hierarchy, the old Catholic aristocracy, the Protestant reformers and the English Whigs that an arrangement could be reached on the Catholic question. As a result the Catholic bishops meeting in Maynooth in January 1799 agreed that the British government should be given the right of veto over the appointment of bishops by the pope. These arrangements remained secret until 1808, but were understood to be part of an agreement for emancipation after the union:

> Help us carry the Union and there will be no insuperable difficulty, with such aid as may be had from Cornwallis and Pitt in admitting a Catholic minority into the imperial parliament.[12]

After the union the Catholic question was dismissed and the Catholic leadership were left to brood over their wrongs and their credulity in sullen indignation. When Henry Grattan in 1808, believing the time was now right, announced in parliament that the Catholics of Ireland had authorised him to accept the veto as part of the solution to the Catholic question, he was quickly repudiated in a spontaneous rejection of his proposals. Catholic opinion was changing. In the eight years since the union Catholics had become more assertive. They were more self confident and believed that emancipation was a right rather than a concession in the gift of the British government. In Daniel O'Connell they found a leader who could represent their impatience and their determination to fight for emancipation on their own terms. Their vehicle was the Catholic Committee, established in 1806 on the basis of an older Catholic organisation, which expressed the interests of the Catholic aristocracy. A struggle for power took place, as the Irish merchant and professional classes led by O'Connell challenged the old leadership:

> The question has now become acute, whether the influence of the Catholic peers, who deplored any policy that might embarrass the English Whigs, or the more adventurous policy of the young Catholic barristers was to prevail.[13]

The veto controversy led to the marginalisation of the aristocracy and their conservative allies in Catholic politics and also their strategy of reliance on the British establishment to honour their commitment to emancipation.

The Irish hierarchy at a synod of bishops in February 1810, sensing the shift in opinion, rejected the veto and, in doing so, explicitly endorsed the position of O'Connell and his faction in the Catholic Committee. By rejecting qualified emancipation O'Connell and the more radical elements in the Catholic Committee were forced to shift the emphasis towards political demands as the only means of achieving their aims. O'Connell, recognising the need for a broad alliance, now argued for repeal of the union as the main objective, even at the cost of Catholic demands. His speech at a meeting of Dublin Corporation in September 1810 emphasised the separateness of Ireland from Britain. It encouraged a sense of Irish identity that excluded the British and he argued for the necessity for unity among all sections of Irish society, if anything was to be achieved:

> The Protestants alone could not expect to liberate his country – the Roman Catholic alone could not do it – neither could the Presbyterian – but amalgamate the three in the Irishman, and the Union is repealed. Learn discretion from your enemies – they have crushed your country by fomenting religious discord – serve her by abandoning it forever… I trample under foot the Catholic claims, if they interfere with the repeal.[14]

O'Connell was formulating a view of Irish nationalism that was inclusive and non-sectarian. This was O'Connell at his most principled, but it was a high-risk strategy that cut against the political grain:

> There is a prima facie case to be made that even by 1810 a majority of Irish Protestants and a significant proportion of Irish Catholics continued to support the Union, or if the latter did not actively support it they did not see an alternative to it, certainly not the one which O'Connell was advocating.[15]

O'Connell's political views were formed during his time in London between 1794 and 1796. He read all the radical journals and books of the period, and was particularly impressed by Godwin's *Political Justice*: 'I admire this work more, beyond comparison more, than any I ever met with'.[16] His hatred of violence and revolution and his belief that political reform could best be achieved by moral force came from Godwin and it was on these two propositions that his lifelong political philosophy was built. He came out of the liberal tradition of the Enlightenment, but he was not a republican or radical in the tradition of Wolfe Tone or the United Irishmen. He declared his ideal to be 'an

Irish King, an Irish House of Lords and an Irish House of Commons'.[17] In effect a capitalist-aristocratic Ireland, with the right to justice and religious and civil freedom.

The nature of O'Connell's influence on Irish political life is an argument that is still unfolding, but in the period we are concerned with, 1811-12, when Shelley decided to go to Ireland, O'Connell's star was in the ascendant and the whole country was astir. No wonder Shelley considered 'the state of Ireland as constituting a part of a great crisis in opinions', which 'ought not to pass unoccupied or unimproved'.

Shelley set out on his mission the morning after their arrival in Dublin. His first stop was at the house of John Philpot Curran, on St Stephens Green.[18] As Curran was not at home, he left a note with the letter of introduction that Godwin had provided. Now his most urgent task was to find a printer for the manuscripts he had brought from England.[19] Shelley had a long list of publishing projects, his book of poems, the two Irish pamphlets, an essay and two broadsheets. We know that he engaged John Stockdale and Sons of 71 Abbey Street[20] to print his book of poems, probably because of Stockdale's former connections with the United Irishmen. Stockdale had been the printer of their paper, the *Press*, for which he was imprisoned for six months in 1797 and condemned to pay a fine of £500 for seditious libel. In addition the militia had destroyed 'not only the papers ready for publication, but the types and other printing materials, amounting in value to about £500'.[21] After his release from jail he resumed his political activities, and during Emmet's insurrection in 1803 he printed the address of the 'Provisional Government', which was issued on the day of the rising. He was imprisoned for two years for his part in the rebellion and, according to the historian R R Madden: 'Came out of jail a ruined man…and died in 1813 poor and abandoned by associates and survivors'.[22]

Madden is mistaken in this. Stockdale survived financially and went on to print prestigious volumes of '*The Speeches of the Right Honourable John Philpot Curran*' in 1808 and 1811. But he was broken by the experience. Under pressure from the authorities he reluctantly became an informer. Stockdale is named in a report dated 1 January 1805 as a government informer.[23] Possibly it was with government money that he reestablished his business.

Shelley printed two pamphlets and two broadsheets in Dublin, but only the *Proposals for an Association of Philanthropists* lists the printer on the title-page: I Eton of Winetavern Street. However, no printer of this name can be traced in Dublin. Most likely this was a cover-name to protect Stockdale from possible prosecution. There was no reason for Shelley to engage another printer. He would have been aware of Stockdale's political reputation and his printing works were convenient, less than 100 yards from where Shelley was staying in Sackville Street. This also explains why Stockdale refused to complete the printing, or return the manuscripts of Shelley's poems, *Songs of Liberty* and his collection of *Essay's, Moral and Religious* until 1813, when Shelley paid the bills for the pamphlets and broadsheets.

That afternoon in a Dublin newspaper Shelley read with great excitement the latest news of the Mexican Revolution.[24] Perhaps this was the harbinger of the worldwide revolt that he had hoped for in his *Address to the Irish People*:

> I desire Catholic Emancipation…all steps however good and salutary, which may be taken…can only be subordinate and preparatory to the great and lasting one which shall bring about the peace, the harmony and the happiness of Ireland, England, Europe, the World.[25]

But the newspaper report was six months out of date; by the time Shelley read the news the revolution was already lost. The movement in Mexico developed in conditions not terribly different from those that threw up the United Irishmen. Literary and reading societies were formed to circumvent the ban on the works of Paine, Voltaire and Rousseau, which quickly became centres of political dissent. In spring 1811 the revolutionary army moved on Mexico City, but at a crucial moment they hesitated and the moment was lost. Within months they were defeated and the leadership executed.

That evening in a long letter to Elizabeth Hitchener he included a copy of the poem, *To the Republicans of North America*, written to celebrate the revolution in Mexico. He commands the Ecuadorian volcano Cotopaxi to 'bid the sound' of revolution across the mountains of the American continent:

Cotopaxi! Bid the sound
Through thy sister mountains ring,
Till each valley smile around
At the blissful welcoming![26]

This is the first time Shelley used what was to become one of his favourite metaphors for revolution – the erupting volcano – and to explore the question that his intervention in Irish politics raised, his attitude to violent revolution! Can bloodshed ever be justified in the cause of liberty? Using the imagery of The Liberty Tree with its long tradition in revolutionary movements and popularised in the 1790s by the United Irishmen's Catechism:

What is that in your hand?	*It is a branch.*
Of what?	*Of the Tree of Liberty.*
Where did it first grow?	*In America.*
Where does it bloom?	*In France.*
Where did the seeds fall?	*In Ireland.*[27]

Shelley writes clearly and confidently of his commitment to revolution, as he did in periods of optimism throughout his life. But, when he copied the poem into the letter to Elizabeth Hitchener he omitted the following verse, perhaps because he had promised her that his writings in Ireland would 'breathe the spirit of peace, toleration and patience':

Blood may fertilise the tree
Of new bursting Liberty.
Let the guiltiness then be
On the slaves that ruin wreak,
On the unnatural tyrant-brood
Slow to Peace and swift to blood.[28]

Near the end of this letter he added a number of lines, whose title, *To Ireland,* was given by Rossetti in his 1870 edition of Shelley's poems:

Bear witness, Erin! When thine injured isle

Sees summer on its verdant pastures smile,
Its cornfields waving in the winds that sweep
The billowy surface of thy circling deep![29]

And so ended the Shelleys' first day in Dublin. They settled down to wait for the first copies of the *Address to the Irish People* to arrive from the printer. They were full of ideas for publishing schemes. Eliza Westbrook agreed to edit a selection of Tom Paine's works, which they intended to print in Dublin, as a way of introducing radical ideas to the Dublin working class. For the next few days they lived in comparative seclusion, educating themselves in Irish affairs and preparing their various manuscripts. Shelley quickly realised the political limitations of the *Address* – that his arguments lacked focus and were not specific enough on the issues of repeal and emancipation and what was now clear to him was the need for an organisation, if anything was to be achieved. He set about writing his second Irish pamphlet, whose complete title shows the direction of Shelley's thought, *Proposals for an Association of Philanthropists who convinced of the inadequacy of the Moral and Political State of Ireland to Produce Benefits which are nevertheless Attainable are Willing to Unite to Accomplish its Regeneration.*

Four days later, on 18 February, the first sheets of the *Address* arrived from the printer. The plan to print in broadsheet form and paste them on the walls of Dublin had to be abandoned, due to its length – in total it came to 22 pages. Within a week 1,500 copies were ready, and on 25 February Shelley's *An Address to the Irish People* was offered to the public by way of an advertisement in the *Dublin Evening Post*, which also appeared in the issues of 29 February and 3 March:

> *This day is published, price Fivepence, to be*
> *had of all the Booksellers,*
> AN ADDRESS TO THE IRISH PEOPLE
> *By Percy B. Shelley*

Advertisement. – The lowest possible price is set on this publication, because it is the intention of the Author to awaken in the minds of the Irish poor a knowledge of their real state, summarily pointing out the evils of that state, and suggesting rational means of remedy. Catholic Emancipation, and a Repeal of the Union Act (the latter the most successful engine that England ever wielded over the misery of fallen Ireland) being treated in the following Address, as grievances which unanimity and resolution may remove, and associations conducted with peaceable firmness, being earnestly recommended as means for embodying that unanimity and firmness which must finally be successful.

The advert was obviously intended to publicise the *Address*, but also, to act as a bridge between the broad analysis of the 'real state' of affairs in Ireland, as outlined in the *Address*, and the proposals that he intended to put forward in his second pamphlet – the need for an organisation to fight for the specific demands of Catholic emancipation and repeal of the union.

Within three days, 400 copies of the *Address* were distributed. Copies were mailed to Irish radicals such as Curran, Hamilton Rowan and Roger O'Connor. Shelley engaged a local man, Dan Healy, to distribute copies around the city. Following the example of Tom Paine, Shelley sent him out with instructions to pin them up in public houses and coffee shops. In a letter to Elizabeth Hitchener he described his progress:

I have already sent 400 copies of my little pamphlets into the world, and they have excited a sensation of wonder in Dublin. The persons with whom I have got acquainted, approve of my principles, and think the truths of the equality of man, the necessity of a reform and the probability of a revolution undeniable. But they differ from the mode of my enforcing these principles and hold expediency to be necessary in politics… I hope to convince them of the contrary of this… I send a man out every day to distribute copies, with instructions how and where to give them. – His accounts correspond with the multitude of people who posses them.[30]

The *Weekly Messenger* reported that 'the publications which he has circulated with such uncommon industry…has set curiosity on the wing to ascertain who he is'.[31] By 18 March only a few copies remained. Despite the amusement of future biographers at Shelley's methods,[32] he did all that was possible to secure an effective distribution. Even by today's standards this was a remarkable achievement.

He renewed his efforts to make contact with various Irish leaders. 'I have not seen Mr Curran', wrote Shelley in a letter to Godwin on 8 March. 'I have called repeatedly, left my address and my pamphlet. I will see him before I leave Dublin.' Curran was clearly avoiding Shelley. The Curran of 1812 was not the fiery advocate who had passionately defended Wolfe Tone, Hamilton Rowan and Peter Finnerty, and whose speeches Shelley had read with such admiration the year before. Though his daughter Sarah, Curran's family was implicated in Emmet's rising of 1803. Sarah was in love with Emmet and attempted to help him escape after the collapse of the rising. To distance himself from the affair, Curran refused the brief to defend Emmet and subsequently disowned Sarah. He sent a letter full of self abasement to the Castle authorities, referring to Emmet as 'that miscreant' and to his daughter as 'that poor deluded creature'.[33] He also refused to defend Thomas Russell, charged for his part in the rebellion and for breaching the terms of the amnesty of 1798. Commenting on this and the anger in Dublin over the execution of Emmet and Russell, the chief secretary in a letter to London wrote, 'It is fortunate that Mr Curran is completely in our power'.[34] Curran had long put his reforming sympathies behind him and made his peace with the establishment. He expected to be offered the position of attorney-general from the Grenville government in 1806, but the Irish Whigs were betrayed by their English allies, and he was forced to settle for the position of Master of the Irish Rolls.

Shelley had sent Curran a copy of his pamphlet along with Godwin's letter of introduction, and the prospect of meeting with Shelley probably terrified him. According to Godwin, Curran would not want to be associated with a young hothead like Shelley:

> It was like making an acquaintance with Robert Emmet, who, I believe, like yourself, was a man of very pure mind, but respecting whom I could not have told, from day to day, what calamities he might bring upon his country.[35]

If this was intended as a warning to Shelley as to the dangers of his actions, he was badly mistaken. To be compared to Emmet was in Shelley's eyes, high praise indeed. In late March Godwin wrote a letter to Curran, which misrepresented Shelley's intentions, but did facilitate a meeting between the two:

> I supposed he had kept himself aloof from you on account of your pamphlet, and [stating] that at my importunity you had given up your project, and that being the case, I trusted he would oblige me by seeking out the man, whom, under different circumstances, he had thought himself bound to shun.[36]

They dined together on two occasions. Much to Shelley's disgust, Curran refused to discuss politics and contented himself with witty turns of speech. Shelley, writing to Godwin, could not hide his disappointment, for he had expected more from the former defender of the United Irishmen: 'I should not have beheld him with the feelings of admiration which his first visit excited had he not been your intimate friend'.[37]

There was further disappointment, as Hamilton Rowan did not reply to the letter that Shelley had enclosed with a copy of the *Address to the Irish People*.[38] Rowan, like Curran, had grown conservative, and left the heady days of the 1790s behind him, when the radicals of London, Paris and Dublin formed an intimate personal and political circle:

> A venerable tradition of co-operation between Irish freedom fighters, English Whig aristocrats of the liberal wing and radical and revolutionary intellectuals of the nineties with backgrounds as diverse as Godwin, Condorcet, Paine and Mary Wollstonecraft. Shelley was to keep coming across this influential network in later life, in locations as far apart as London, Paris, Pisa and Rome.[39]

His attempt to make contact with other Irish radicals and the old leaders of the United Irishmen, whom Shelley 'worshiped and revered', is evident from a letter to Elizabeth Hitchener:

> O'Connor, brother to the Rebel Arthur is here, I have written to him. Do not fear what you say in your letters. I am resolved. Good principles are scarce here. The public papers are either oppositionalist or ministerial; one is as contemptible and narrow as

the other. I wish I could change this. I of course am hated by both of these parties. The remnant of the United Irishmen whose wrongs make them hate England I have more hopes of. I have met with no determined Republicans, but I have found some who are democratifiable.[40]

Roger O'Connor and his brother Arthur were prominent members of the United Irishmen, and despite many terms of imprisonment, remained committed to Irish independence. Arthur O'Connor had been the proprietor of the *Press*, the paper of the United Irishmen. After the 1798 rebellion he went to France where he acted as their spokesman and attempted to raise support for a new French expeditionary force to Ireland. Roger was a personal friend of the English reformer Sir Francis Burdett, and in the 1830s his son, Feargus, edited in England, the *Northern Star,* the Chartist paper named after the Belfast paper of the United Irishmen. There is no record of any reply or whether Shelley ever met Roger O'Connor. But, what is clear from this letter, and was implied in the *Address*, is that Shelley had no interest in the Irish Whigs, who were largely controlled by the Irish Catholic aristocracy.

What he understood instinctively was confirmed when he was invited to speak on 28 February at the Catholic Committee's aggregate meeting in the Fishamble Street Theatre. In order to understand the significance of this meeting we need to look back a few years. The following extracts are taken from a 26-page paper entitled 'Précis of the Formation and Proceedings of the Catholic Committee in Ireland, 1809, 1810, 1811'[41] in the Public Record Office in London:

> At an aggregate meeting held at the Repository in St. Stephen's Green, Mr Finnerty recommended a Petition to Parliament for Catholic Emancipation, one for the repeal of the Union…and it was resolved, that the Catholic Committee should have sole management of Catholic affairs (November, 1810).

> The aggregate meeting assembled at the Private Theatre, Fishamble Street, Among other resolutions it was resolved, 'That the Committee be appointed; that the Catholic Peers, Baronets, and the survivors of 1793 have the management of Catholic affairs' (July, 1811).

These records show the tensions inside the Catholic Committee. Peter Finnerty was in favour of linking the issue of emancipation with that of repeal in support of O'Connell's attempt to build a broader political base for the campaign. But the older, more conservative elements were still in control at the leadership level as late as 1811. A subsequent report notified the secretary of state that a subscription had been opened in Dublin for Peter Finnerty. This was, of course, the fund to which Shelley had subscribed while at Oxford:

> Young Mr Curran, son of the Master of the Rolls, has been very active in soliciting from the Catholics subscriptions for Mr Finnerty, and letters from persons associated in London for promoting that object have been addressed to the Catholics here.

The same report noted:

> Many Protestants were present and the theatre was full in every part… Great pains [were] taken, particularly by the Catholic clergy to keep the lower orders from attending in the streets.[42]

Finnerty's speech[43] and the attempt by O'Connell to politicise the campaign prompted the British government to use the Convention Act against the Catholic Committee. The act was introduced in 1793 to curb the activities of the United Irishmen, and declared unlawful all committees or assemblies, that were appointed to represent the people, 'under pretence of petitioning' for any alteration in matters established by law in church or state. From that year until 1812, when Shelley arrived in Ireland, the act, though latterly little used, was a cause of resentment. In a direct challenge to the law and the leadership of the aristocrats, O'Connell proposed that permanent local committees should be set up throughout the country similar to the one in Dublin. A general committee of 36 delegates from the parishes of Dublin and 10 from each county was elected. Fearing the consequences for his supporters when the secretary of state for Ireland issued instructions for the arrest of all persons implicated in the elections, O'Connell dissolved the committee. Curran, to his credit, was one of the privy councillors who refused to sign the order. O'Connell was now intent on forcing the pace and, in defiance of a proclamation by the lord lieutenant, a delegate meeting was arranged for July 1811, where elections for a new committee on the same basis were organised. They met in October, with 150 delegates from all parts of Ireland and managed to finish their business before the police arrived. Following the meeting six delegates were arrested. The future of O'Connell and his faction on the committee was on the line. At the trial the courts set out to show what Catholics must expect if they dared to raise their voice in public in this manner. In the first case to come before the courts, the jury found in favour of the defendant, Dr Sheridan. The *Dublin Evening Post*, a Protestant opposition paper, hailed the acquittal as significant:

> A jury composed of Protestants and Presbyterians has found a verdict in favour of the aggrieved Catholic – in favour of Public Right – in favour of Ireland – in favour of the Empire.[44]

The O'Connellites had won the first round. In December, the committee called another meeting with O'Connell as the main speaker to protest against the government attack on their rights, and this protest grew into a nationwide agitation. Meetings were summoned all over the country. And what had been a conservative movement, led by the most respectable elements in Irish Catholic society, grew into a mass movement that linked the demand for emancipation with that for repeal of the union, and propelled O'Connell on to the pages of Irish history.

Though Sheridan was acquitted, the government pursued the other defendants. Thomas Kirwin was found guilty, even though it was the same charge and he put forward the same defence. This was a setback for O'Connell, and in order to circumvent the Convention Act the Catholic Committee now organised what they termed 'aggregate meetings', which were open to all. Speakers were invited without ever stating whether they were guests or officials of the committee. Despite the ascendancy of O'Connell, the main tactic of the Catholic Committee was still to put their faith in the Prince Regent, whom they regarded as the 'enlightened friend of Ireland'. The Prince of Wales was appointed regent because of the insanity of George III in February 1811. He had spoken in favour of Catholic emancipation, and the Catholic Committee presumed he would support their claims when certain restrictions on his powers expired in February 1812. With this expectation the meeting in November 1811 voted to present an *Address* to the regent, and a petition to both Houses of Parliament, in favour of emancipation. The meeting adjourned after deciding to reassemble on 28 February 1812 in the Fishamble Street Theatre. It was this meeting that Shelley was invited to address.

NOTES

1   F L Jones, op cit, p258.

2   The balcony was removed in 1884. The building was substantially damaged during the Easter rising in 1916. It was rebuilt in the 1920s as a cafe and it is now a bank.

3   E Walsh, 'Sackville Mall', in D Dickson (ed), *The Gorgeous Mask: Dublin 1700-1800* (Dublin, 1987), p41.

4   G N Wright, *An Historical Guide to Ancient and Modern Dublin* (London, 1829), p8.

5   A Cosgrave (ed), *Dublin Through the Ages* (Dublin, 1988), p95.

6   In 1791 the debt amounted to £2.4 million. By 1800 it was £24 million and in 1810 £95 million. E Dowden, *The Life of Percy Bysshe Shelley* (London, 1886), vol 1, p236.

7   For details see, P Somerville-Large, *Dublin* (London, 1981), p220.

8   T Garvin, 'O'Connell and the making of Irish political culture', in M O'Connell, (ed), *Daniel O'Connell: Political Pioneer* (Dublin, 1991), p9.

9   For details see D Lindsay, 'The Defenders', in M Cullen, (ed), *1798: 200 Years of Resonance* (Dublin, 1998), pp15-25.

10   *Drogheda Papers*, National Library of Ireland, ms 9749.

11   St Patrick's College, Maynooth, was established in 1795 as a seminary for Irish priests. Since the time of the penal laws Irish priests were forced to train abroad, usually in France or Spain. Fearing that priests trained in France would be influenced by republican ideas, the British government agreed to the establishment and financial support of Irish seminaries.

12   Quoted in E Dowden, op cit, p238.

13   D Gwynn, *Daniel O'Connell the Irish Liberator* (London, nd), p97.

14   J O'Connell, (ed), *The Life and Speeches of Daniel O'Connell, MP* (Dublin, 1846), vol 1, pp34-52.

15   B Girvin, 'Making Nations: O'Connell, Religion and the Creation of Political Identity', in M O'Connell, (ed), *Daniel O'Connell Political Pioneer*, p17.

16   A Houston, *Daniel O'Connell: His Early Life, and Journal, 1795 to 1802* (London, 1906), p107.

17   D Gwynn, op cit, p101.

18   Number 80 St Stephens Green was owned by Earl Mountcashell from 1767 to 1809, (see Chapter 7, p144 for connection with Mary Wollstonecraft). It was purchased by John P Curran who lived there from 1809 to 1817. The house came into the possession of the Guinness family and was eventually donated to the Irish Government by Lord Iveagh. It is now the Department of Foreign Affairs.

19   According to R Holmes (*Shelley: The Pursuit*, op cit, p117), after calling on Curran: 'On his way back, at Winetavern Street he found a printer, Isaac Eton, who was prepared to set up the manuscript of his first Irish pamphlet, *An Address to the Irish People*'. Holmes is mistaken in this. The *Address* has no printer listed on the title-page. His transformation of I Eton, who is listed as the printer on the title-page of the *Proposals for an Association of Philanthropists*, into Isaac Eton, appears to be a confusion with a printer in London named Daniel Isaac Eaton, who was brought to trial for publishing Paine's *The Age of Reason*. Shelley defended Eaton and the freedom of the press in a pamphlet, *Letter to Lord Ellenborough*, which he published in London in July 1812. There is no I Eton listed in Winetavern Street, (see *Wilson's Dublin Directory* of 1812). In fact there are no printers of that name listed in Dublin in that whole period (see M Pollard, *A Directory of the Dublin*

Book Trade: 1550-1800 (London, 2000) and Charles Benson, *A Directory of the Dublin Book Trade: 1800-1850* (forthcoming)). The political climate was such that it was common for pamphlets not to have a printer's name, as in the case of the *Address,* or to use a fictitious name for fear of prosecution. See *Annual Register, 1812,* p124, for details of the prosecution of Fitzgerald, the Dublin printer of a pamphlet on Catholic emancipation. The Oxford edition of *The Prose Works of Percy Bysshe Shelley,* edited by E Murray (Oxford, 1993) believes that the typographical evidence makes it probable that the *Address, Proposals* and *A Declaration of Rights* were 'printed by the same Dublin printer' (p338), whom they presume to be I Eton. All the evidence points to John Stockdale as the printer of all of Shelley's Irish works. The typefaces used in the Shelley pamphlets are comparable with those used by Stockdale in books and pamphlets printed by him around 1812 (I am grateful to Bob Sharpe of the Print Museum in Dublin for his opinion on this). While it is true that these typefaces would have been common to a number of printers of that period, taken with other evidence it establishes Stockdale as almost certainly the printer of Shelley's manuscripts in Dublin.

20   Sometime between 1810 and 1812 the numbering system on Abbey Street was changed, number 62 became number 71.

21   D F MacCarthy, *Shelley's Early Life,* (London, 1872), p81.

22   R R Madden, *The United Irishmen* (London, 1860), vol 7, p246 and vol 8, p334.

23   *State of Country Reports* 1805, nos 1031/35/36.

24   The *London Morning Chronicle* carried a report of the Mexican Revolution on 7 December 1811, which Shelley may have seen.

25   Appendix 3, p272.

26   *Poetical Works of Shelley,* op cit, lines 21-24, p872.

27   K Whelan, op cit, p57. The United Irishmen took the tradition of planting Liberty Trees from France as a symbol of liberty. They were usually adorned with ribbons and sometimes mounted with a red cap. According to a report in the *Irish Times* (16 December 2000) it is possible that at least one is still extant in Ireland. Tom Paine wrote a poem in its honour in 1775, the *Liberty Tree* (*The Thomas Paine Reader,* op cit, p63).

28   P B Shelley, *The Esdaile Notebook,* op cit, lines 35-40, p72.

29   *Poetical Works of Shelley,* op cit, lines 1-4, p873. See note in Appendix 1, p194 for discussion of Rossetti's interpretation.

30   F L Jones, op cit, p263.

31   *Dublin Weekly Messenger,* 7 March 1812.

32   See D King-Hele, *Shelley, His Thought and Work* (London, 1971), p20.

33   L Hale, op cit, p230.

34   L Hale, Ibid, p233.

35   F L Jones, op cit, p278.

36   F L Jones, op cit, p278.

37   F L Jones, op cit, p278.

38   F L Jones, op cit, p262.

39   R Holmes, *The Pursuit*, op cit, p124.

40   F L Jones, op cit, p264.

41   See D F MacCarthy, op cit, p228.

42   Ireland, 1811, January to June, no 652, Public Record Office, London.

43   *Dublin Weekly Messenger,* 10 November 1810. Report of Finnerty's speech.

44   *Dublin Evening Post*, 23 November 1811.

CHAPTER FIVE

The Fane of Liberty

FISHAMBLE Street rises up from the river
Liffey at a spot where fishing boats tied up at the river's bank. The name
is derived from the old market, the Fish-Shamble, which was a thriving
commercial area in the old city famous for its clubs and music venues.
This was the site of a famous theatre built in 1741, where in the following
year Frederick Handel conducted the premiere of the *Messiah*. But by 1812
both the street and the theatre had succumbed to the gradual decay common to Dublin at that time.

On 28 February three days after the publication of Shelley's *Address to
the Irish People*, the Catholic Committee reconvened in the Fishamble
Street Theatre to consider the draft of an address to the Prince Regent
and a petition to both Houses of Parliament. Daniel O'Connell was the
principal speaker and star attraction. It was a day of great social and
political excitement. The theatre was brilliantly lit, the elite of Catholic
society were present and the ladies dressed as if it was the first night of
the opera. Harriet and Eliza accompanied Shelley, who was already
known to some in the audience by his pamphlet:

Harriet and Eliza on either arm,
He walked the foulest lanes,
Beggars, drunkards everywhere,
Up a rickety verandah
To the Fishamble theatre, once a church
Where God had stayed to laugh
In a music-hall with stalls and boxes.[1]

O'Connell started by thanking the previous speakers, 'and first let me offer the tribute of my warmest gratitude to two of the Protestant gentlemen who have already addressed you'. He went on to say that Catholics and Protestants had a common cause – 'the right of Petition is at stake, and the Protestants risk as much as we do'. He continued with a review of the Kirwin case and the fake plot that the authorities had used as 'a scheme to dupe the poor, in order to continue the vassalage of the rich'. He concluded that emancipation 'is certain and will be immediate'. After some discussion a special resolution was moved thanking the 'distinguished Protestants who have this day honoured us with their presence'.

Shelley rose to speak to this resolution. This was his first public speech, but he had prepared well using material from the *Address to the Irish People*, and his forthcoming pamphlet, *Proposals for an Association*. He claims to have spoken for over an hour.[2] But, this must be an exaggeration. The resolution was the sixth of the afternoon and little to do with the main business, which explains why O'Connell had probably left the meeting by the time Shelley spoke. The newspaper reports point to a speech of much shorter duration, perhaps 15 minutes, but the fact that six newspapers[3] saw fit to report his remarks indicates its impact. The most comprehensive report is taken from the *Patriot*, Dublin, 2 March 1812:

Mr Shelley then addressed the Chair. He hoped he should not be accounted a transgressor on the time of the meeting. He felt inadequate to the task he had undertaken, but he hoped the feelings which urged him forward would plead his pardon. He was an Englishman; when he reflected on the outrages that his countrymen had committed here for the last 20 years he confessed that he blushed for them. He had come to Ireland for the sole purpose of interesting himself in the misfortunes of this country, and impressed with a full conviction of the necessity of Catholic Emancipation, and of the baneful effects which the union with Great Britain had entailed upon Ireland. He had walked through the fields of the country and the streets of the city, and he had in both seen the miserable effects of that fatal step. He had seen that edifice which ought to have been the fane of their liberties converted to a temple of Mammon. Many of the crimes which are daily committed he could not avoid attributing to the effect of that measure, which had thrown numbers of people out of the employment they had in manufacture, and induced them to commit acts of the greatest desperation for the support of their existence.

He could not imagine that the religious opinion of a man should exclude him from the rights of society. The original founder of our religion taught no such doctrine. Equality in this respect was general in the American States, and why not here? Did a change of place change the nature of man? He would beg those in power to recollect the French Revolution: the suddenness, the violence with which it burst forth, and the causes which gave rise to it.

Both the measures of Emancipation and a Repeal of the Union should meet his decided support, but he hoped many years would not pass over his head when he would make himself conspicuous at least by his zeal for them.

The 'fane of their liberties converted into a temple of Mammon' refers to the old parliament building in College Green sold after the Act of Union to a bank company, on condition that the interior was altered so that it could never be used as a debating chamber in the future. All the reports refer to the suffering and distress he encountered.[4] Shelley had never experienced human misery on this scale before, though, as he explained to Elizabeth Hitchener, the reasons seemed so obvious: 'The rich grind the poor into abjectness, and then complain that they are abject. They goad them into famine, and hang them if they steal a loaf'.[5] His compassion existed at a personal level as well as a political one:

But not forever at my needy door
Let Misery linger speechless, pale and lean;
I am the friend of the unfriended poor.[6]

What little money he possessed he willingly shared with the poor and the destitute. Late one evening, he encountered a widow with three children arrested for stealing a penny loaf. He pleaded with the constable for her release: 'I asked him if he had a heart, he said – to be sure he had, as well as any other man, but, that he was called out to business of this nature sometimes 20 times a night'.[7] He saved her from arrest that night, though he knew that nothing could save her from 'ultimate ruin and starvation'. He tried to help a young boy he found starving with his mother. Before he could do anything, the boy was seized by the constables and brought before a magistrate who gave him the choice of 'the tender or military service, he preferred neither, but was compelled to be a soldier'. The misery and suffering he encountered almost overwhelmed him. He wrote that he was 'sick of this city', and longed to be at peace. But the experience hardened his resolve – 'my views on this subject changed; yet how deeply has this very change rooted the conviction on which I came hither'.[8]

Also in attendance at the meeting were two government spies, one a chief constable, Michael Farrell, well known in the history of the period. His report mentions Shelley very slightly: 'Lord Glentworth said a few words – a Mr Bennett spoke, also Mr Shelley, who stated himself to be a native of England'.[9] This report, along with a copy of the *Dublin Evening Post*, containing an account of the meeting, was forwarded to the home secretary in London. This was the first entry in what was to be an extensive file on Shelley's political activities.

A week later, shortly after the publication of Shelley's second pamphlet, *Proposals for an Association*, a highly flattering article appeared in the *Dublin Weekly Messenger*. Shelley sent copies to his father and to Godwin with the following note: 'You will see an account of me in the newspaper. I am vain, but not so foolish as not to be rather piqued than gratified at the eulogia of a journal'.[10] He also instructed Elizabeth Hitchener to insert it in the Sussex newspapers. Despite the odd spelling of his name this is the first account of Shelley in the press and therefore worth reproducing in full:

The Weekly Messenger, Dublin, Saturday, March 7th, 1812

PIERCE BYSHE SHELLY, ESQ.

The highly interesting appearance of this young gentleman at the late Aggregate Meeting of the Catholics of Ireland, has naturally excited a spirit of enquiry, as to his objects and views, in coming forward at such a meeting; and the publications which he has circulated with such uncommon industry, through the Metropolis, has set curiosity on the wing to ascertain who he is, from whence he comes, and what his pretensions are to the confidence he solicits, and the character he assumes. To those who have read the productions we have alluded to, we need bring forward no evidence of the cultivation of his mind – the benignity of his principles – or the peculiar fascination with which he seems able to recommend them.

Of this gentleman's family we can say but little, but we can set down what we have heard from respectable authority. That his father is a member of the Imperial Parliament, and that this young gentleman, whom we have seen, is the immediate heir of one of the first fortunes in England. Of his principles and his manners we can say more, because we can collect from conversation, as well as from reading, that he seems devoted to the propagation of those divine and Christian feelings which purify the human heart, give shelter to the poor, and consolation to the unfortunate. That he is the bold and intrepid advocate of those principles which are calculated to give energy to truth, and to depose from their guilty eminence the bad and vicious passions of a corrupt community; that a universality of charity is his object, and a perfectibility of human society his end, which cannot be attained by the conflicting dogmas of religious sects, each priding itself on the extinction of the other, and all existing by the mutual misfortunes which flow from polemical warfare. The principles of this young gentleman embrace all sects and all persuasions. His doctrines, political and religious, may be accommodated to all; every friend to true Christianity will be his religious friend, and every enemy to the liberties of Ireland will be his political enemy. The weapons he wields are those of reason, and the most social benevolence. He deprecates violence in the accomplishment of his views, and relies upon the mild and merciful spirit of toleration for the completion of all his designs, and the consummation of all his wishes. To the religious bigot such a missionary of truth is a formidable opponent, by the political monopolist he will be considered the child of Chimera, the creature of fancy, an imaginary legislator who presumes to make laws without reflecting upon his materials, and despises those considerations which have baffled the hopes of the most philanthropic and the efforts of the most wise. It is true, human nature may be too depraved for such a hand as Mr Shelly's to form to anything that is good, or liberal, or beneficent. Let him but take down one of the rotten pillars by which society is now propped, and substitute the purity of his own principles, and Mr Shelly shall have done a great and lasting service to human nature. To this gentleman Ireland is much indebted, for selecting her as the theatre of his first attempts in this holy work of human regeneration; the Catholics of Ireland should listen to him with respect, because they will find that an enlightened Englishman has interposed between the treason of their own countrymen and the almost conquered spirit of their country; that Mr Shelly has come to Ireland to demonstrate in his person that there are hearts in his own country not rendered callous by six hundred years of injustice; and that the genius of freedom, which has communicated comfort and content to the cottage of the Englishman, has found its way to the humble roof of the Irish peasant, and promises by its presence to dissipate the sorrows of past ages, to obliterate the remembrance of persecution, and close the long and wearisome scene of centuries of human depression. We extract from Mr Shelly's last production which he calls *Proposals for an Association*, &c. [A long quotation from this pamphlet followed, which, as it is printed entire in this book, need not be given.] We have but one word more to add. Mr Shelly, commiserating the sufferings of our distinguished countryman Mr Finerty, whose exertions in the cause of political freedom he much admired, wrote a very beautiful poem, the profits of which we understand, from undoubted authority, Mr Shelly remitted to Mr Finerty; we have heard they amounted to nearly a hundred pounds. This fact speaks a volume in favour of our new friend.

Shelley was pleased with the article in the *Weekly Messenger*, which gave him some hope for the success of his mission. But he was not deceived into believing that it would be easy. Shelley hated political expediency. None of the newspapers report the hisses that greeted him when he spoke on religion. The Catholic gentry applauded the sentiments that pleased them, but ignored the solutions that Shelley advanced as a remedy. Their focus was still on the Prince Regent and the English Whigs. Therefore, they wished to avoid any agitation that linked Catholic emancipation with repeal of the union. Though flattered by the reports, he was by no means elated by the response:

I do not like Lord Fingal or any of the Catholic aristocracy. Their intolerance can be equalled by nothing but the hardy wickedness and intolerance of the Prince. My speech was misinterpreted. I spoke for more than an hour. The hisses with which they greeted me when I spoke of religion, though in terms of respect, were mixed with applause when I avowed my mission. The newspapers have only noted that which did not excite disapprobation.[11]

But it was not all praise. A renegade Englishman would not be allowed to escape unscathed by the Anglo-Irish supporters of the establishment. Two letters appeared in the *Dublin Journal,* a government-subsidised paper, one signed 'An Englishman', on 7 March, the other 'A Dissenter' on 21 March. Neither mentions Shelley by name, but it would have been obvious to most astute readers that he was the target of their attack:

To the Editor of the *Dublin Journa*l. Saturday, 7 March 1812.
Curiosity and the expected gratification of hearing a display of oratory by some of the leading members of the Catholic body led

me on Friday, for the first time, to the Aggregate Meeting in Fishamble Street. Being rather late I missed the orations of Mr O'Connell and the leading orators, and only heard a dry monotonous effusion from Counsellor _ , and, to me, a most disgusting harangue from a stripling, with whom I am unacquainted, but who, I am sorry to say, styled himself my countryman – an Englishman. This young gentleman, after stating that he had been only a fortnight in Ireland, expatiated on the miseries which this country endured in consequence of its connexion with his own, and asserted (from the knowledge, I presume, which his peculiar sagacity enabled him to acquire in so short a period) that its cities were depopulated, its fields laid waste, and its inhabitants degraded and enslaved; and all this by its union with England. If it revolted against my principles, Mr Editor, to hear such language from one of my own countrymen, you will readily conceive that my disgust was infinitely heightened to observe with what transport the invectives of this renegade Englishman against his native country were hailed by the assembly he addressed. Joy beamed in every countenance and rapture glistened in every eye at the aggravated detail: the delirium of ecstasy got the better of prudential control; the veil was for a moment withdrawn. I thought I saw the purpose, in spite of the pretence, written in legible characters in each of their faces, and though emancipation alone flowed from the tongue, separation and ascendancy were rooted in the heart.

As for the young gentleman alluded to, I congratulate the Catholics of Ireland on the acquisition of so patriotic and enlightened an advocate; and England, I dare say, will spare him without regret…
'AN ENGLISHMAN'.

The second letter is clearly a reply to the article on Shelley in the *Weekly Messenger,* and his pamphlet *Proposals for an Association.*

To the Editor of *The Dublin Journal.* Saturday, 21 March 1812.
Through the medium of your paper, however, the attention of the public has been called to another of the Catholic performers, and a

late worthy correspondent has obliged you with some deserved and judicious animadversions upon his debut. In a weekly paper, the appearance of this 'very interesting' personage is announced with as much parade as if Dogberry, Verges,[12] and the Watch graced the scene… His panegyrist has described him with the minuteness of an interested biographer; the prospects and the talents of the 'stranger' and his generosity, his amazing generosity to an incarcerated individual [Mr Peter Finnerty], whose crime was not loyalty, are made the subjects of commendation; and in illustration of the excellence of this modern Apollonius, who travels but for the improvement of the human race, a specimen of his composition is printed and circulated… He proposes to 'exterminate the eyeless monster Bigotry', and 'make the teeth of the palsied beldame Superstition chatter'. This, which is doubtless designed as an allegorical allusion to the Romish Church, must, if actually accomplished, be its death…

In a style less elevated and Heliconian this modern annihilator of moral and political evil roundly proposes an association throughout Ireland for the attainment of 'Catholic Emancipation and the repeal of the Union Act'. That the abolition of the aristocracy of the country is a feature in his picture of Utopian amelioration, though, for reasons obvious, but lightly touched, and as yet kept in the shade, is evident from the manner and connexion in which he disapproves 'of other distinctions than those of virtue and talent' – disapproval specious indeed, worthy the head of him who expects a new Jerusalem on earth, or seeks divine perfection among created beings. But ignorant, shamefully ignorant, must they be of human nature, and of the awful events which have taken place in Europe of late years, who can be gulled by such a pretext now…

Leaving this 'interesting stranger' to amuse the admirers of the Catholic Drama by puffing at 'the meteors' of his own creation, 'which play over the loathsome pool' of his own pantomimic invention, I will ask you, sir, what has the Protestant cause, and what has that consummation of political wisdom the British constitution, to fear from a party which has to shelter in the shade of such paltry and unmeaning bombast?

A DISSENTER.

On 2 March, three days after the Fishamble Street meeting, Shelley's second pamphlet, *Proposals for an Association of Philanthropists,* was published. Shelley wrote the *Proposals* during his first few weeks in Dublin and the benefits of his actual contact with the political situation in Ireland are obvious. Shortly after his arrival in Dublin he recognised the shortcomings in the *Address to the Irish People* and added a postscript at the last moment: 'For information respecting the principles which I possess, and the nature and spirit of the association which I propose, I refer the reader to a small pamphlet which I shall publish in the course of a few days'.[13] His plan now, was for 'proselytising the young men at Dublin College'. *Proposals* was aimed at educated liberals, with the intention of founding an association to advance the cause of repeal and emancipation. This was to be the first of many associations that Shelley hoped would be formed across the country. Letting his thoughts run ahead of him he wrote to Elizabeth Hitchener: 'Whilst you are with us in Wales, I shall attempt to organise one there, which shall correspond with the Dublin one. Might I not extend them all over England, and quietly revolutionise the country'.[14] Shelley believed that the struggle in Ireland was the key that could ignite a movement that would revive the ideals of the French Revolution for all of humanity:

I desire that the means should be taken with energy and expedition, in this important yet fleeting crisis, to feed the unpolluted flame at which nations and ages may light the torch of Liberty and Virtue![15]

The pamphlet opens with the statement that 'man cannot make occasions, but he may seize those that offer',[16] and with all the enthusiasm of a 19 year old, Shelley set out to seize the moment. His first pamphlet and the publicity surrounding his speech at the Catholic Convention had brought him to public attention. But he recognised that, unless a movement was built that would bridge the gap between theory and practice, the opportunity would be lost – 'Individuals acting singly, with whatever energy can never effect so much as a society'.[17] His plan for an association was an attempt to reach back to the best traditions of the French Revolution and the United Irishmen and apply them to the specific conditions of Ireland in 1812. But there were risks in Shelley's proposals, association was a dangerous word – it reeked of the Jacobin club – and such organisations were illegal under the Corresponding Societies Act of 1799. Shelley was aware of the aims and methods of the United Irishmen from a 50-page essay on the secret societies of Ireland and Great Britain appended to Abbe Barruel's book on the Illuminati by his translator, Robert Clifford:[18]

> Its members are to be chosen from among men in the prime of life, without distinction of religion; true philanthropists… It will make the light of philanthropy converge.[19]

The 19th century meaning of philanthropist is hard to recover at this remove, but it includes, solidarity, benevolence and the promotion of the social and political wellbeing of one's fellow man. Shelley outlined a number of 'suggestions' or rules for his proposed association in a letter to Godwin[20] on 8 March. They were never published, but Shelley had intended to circulate them to interested parties as the organisational basis for his association.

In the *Proposals* Shelley spelt out what he considered to be the essence of the problem. Emancipation meant that upper class Catholics would gain some legal rights, but it would do little to ease the misery of the masses. Nevertheless, it should be supported as a progressive measure. Repeal of the union was different, this was a measure that would directly benefit the mass of the people: 'The latter affects few, the former thousands. The one disqualifies the rich from power, the other impoverishes the peasant, adds beggary to the city, famine to the country'.[21] Writing in 1846, O'Connell's son John commented on Shelley's pamphlet:

> The allusion to the effect on the 'higher orders' of Catholics was so far as those of them who have benefited by the Emancipation Act, truly prophetic. 'Power and wealth' have sadly injured, with them, 'the cause of freedom and virtue'… In the remarks upon Repeal there is the same singular oppositeness to the present day.[22]

Shelley had every right to feel that his 'proposal' was important. Therefore, it was with a certain confidence that he ended his pamphlet with an appeal:

Such as are favourably inclined towards the institution would highly gratify the proposer if they would personally communicate with him on this important subject, by which means the plan might be matured, errors in the proposer's original system be detected, and a meeting for the purpose convened with that resolute expedition which the nature of the present crisis demands.[23]

Shelley had not given up on the idea of a popular broadsheet to be pasted up on the walls of Dublin. He began work on a *Declaration of Rights*,[24] one of the most radical documents ever produced, which summarises his republican ideals in 31 short paragraphs. While it reiterates many of the points made in the *Address to the Irish People*, its inspiration was the French *Declaration of Rights* adopted by the Constituent Assembly in 1789. This was a popular form of political agitation. The *Morning Chronicle* in London reported that a 'Bill of Rights' had been distributed in Dublin in December 1811.[25] Shelley was indebted to Paine and Godwin for many of the formulations of general rights. But Paine's influence is much more persuasive. Shelley follows Paine in arguing for the equality of man, not with relation to their property but to their rights. Shelley insisted on absolute freedom of speech and press. The quotations from Paine's works, which Eliza Westbrook collected, probably formed the basis for Shelley's broadsheet. *Curran's Speeches*[26] provided Shelley with much background information. Article 19 of the declaration, states: 'Man has no right to kill his brother, it is no excuse that he does so in uniform'.[27] Curran defended Hamilton Rowan in 1794 for publishing the manifesto of the United Irishmen. In the course of the trial Curran said: 'If they continue to make us fight and kill one another in uniform, we will continue to write and speak, until nations are cured of this folly'.[28] We do not know if the *Declaration of Rights* was ever pasted on the walls of Dublin, but Walter Peck suggests that it may have been distributed with the other pamphlets as a supplementary document.[29] While this is possible, it must have been in small numbers, for the first mention of the broadsheet[30] was on 18 March, when Shelley was aware that his project held out little prospect of success.

Shelley certainly made mistakes in his enthusiasm for action, but, given his circumstances, he did remarkably well to publicise his programme to the extent that he did. Shelley has been unfairly criticised for his lack of understanding of the situation in Ireland. Richard Holmes believes that 'Shelley had arrived in Dublin with little more knowledge of the true state of Irish politics than that which could be gleaned from the Duke of Norfolk's drawing-room and the library of Robert Southey'.[31] This misses the importance of Irish affairs in British politics in the early 19th century. With a population of 6 million to Briton's 12 million, its relative importance was far greater than today, as can be seen from the reports in the British press of the period. The *Morning Chronicle,* the *Times*, the *Edinburgh Review,* the *Annual Register* and especially Cobbett's *Political Register* all carried extensive reports of Irish political affairs.[32] William Cobbett's change of heart from champion of the British government to one of its harshest critics had many reasons, and by no means the least was its policy on Ireland.[33] Over the years scarcely a month went by without some article on Ireland appearing in the pages of the *Political Register*. Cobbett spelt out for his readers, the effect of British policy in Ireland. Typical, was an article on the repressive measures contained in the Irish Insurrection Act of 1807, illustrated by the story of Roger O'Connor, who was falsely held on suspicion of aiding the rebels in 1798:

Reader, if you be an Englishman, Say how should you like to be treated as Mr O'Connor was? How should you like to have your house, your gardens, your fields, your plantations laid waste and destroyed? How should you like to be hurried from prison to prison, to be thrown into dungeon after dungeon, and when you demanded trial, refused that trial? But surely I need not ask these questions. Well, then, is there to be no feeling for him because he is an Irishman?[34]

Shelley was an avid reader of newspapers, and would have been aware of the debates on Irish Catholic rights, which dominated the news in

1811. He grew up in a political household and was widely read among the most advanced thinkers of his time. Thomas Hogg believed that Shelley's interest in Ireland may have been fired by some 'Hibernian Hampden brimful of sympathy for his persecuted country' in the coffee house in Mount Street which was 'infested by Irish patriots'.[35] Mrs Beauclerc, a neighbour and acquaintance of Shelley's in Sussex, was the stepsister of Lord Edward Fitzgerald, who was killed during the 1798 rising in Dublin, and may have sparked an early interest in the United Irishmen. Walter Peck in his 1927 biography was amongst the first to unearth the sources for Shelley's Irish pamphlets, principally cited as *Curran's Speeches*, *The Prospectus of the United Irishmen,* Abbe Barruel's *Memoirs of Jacobinism,* and the works of Godwin and Paine. This ignores the hundreds of pamphlets that were published and eagerly read in the circles that Shelley moved in. The 'no-popery' election of 1807 gave rise to a flurry of publications,[36] both legal and illegal, and the controversy over Catholic emancipation unleashed a pamphlet war that resembled Jonathan Swift's *Battle of the Books* in 1698.[37]

In the 1790s the British policy of winning Irish loyalty to the crown and of reconciling English opinion to Irish self government broke down as a result of the fears instilled by the French Revolution and the rebellion of 1798. The Act of Union was intended to achieve by coercion what could not be obtained by persuasion. Lord Cornwallis's remark to William Pitt that: 'While Ireland could not be saved without the union, you must not take it for granted that it will be saved by it,'[38] proved all too true. While the Union removed the symbols of Irish independence, Pitt intended that Ireland would be compensated by gaining religious emancipation and agrarian reform. Pitt, to his credit, resigned when these promises were not fulfilled, and, as a result, a movement that had its origins in the demand for Catholic emancipation developed over time into a physical force campaign for the total separation of the two countries. Shelley came to Ireland in 1812 because he believed that the general crisis affecting British society found its most militant expression in Ireland and in particular in the struggle for Catholic emancipation. Shelley was not alone in believing in the explosive potential of the Irish situation. Charles Grey in late 1810 refused to support Richard Brinsley Sheridan's ambition to be appointed chief secretary of Ireland on the grounds that it would be like 'sending a man with a lighted torch into a magazine of gunpowder'.[39]

This is the background against which we must judge Shelley's Irish pamphlets. *The Address to the Irish People*, at its best, is a stirring and powerful document that transcends the issues of the day into a universal application. His emphasis on rights left him politically isolated on the left of the democratic movement. Shelley insisted on perspectives: behind Catholic emancipation lies the issue of all political oppression; behind the Act of Union lies economic exploitation. Shelley argued that all the issues of the day must be joined together as part of a greater struggle to end all oppression, not just in Ireland, but the world over. This sense of historical perspective in Shelley's pamphlet is almost unique in the Irish political literature of the day, which were more concerned with current tactical questions. But this is also its weakness, Shelley was so absorbed in presenting the bigger picture that he failed to adequately address the immediate issues. The *Address* lacked focus – he stated the problem but the solution is lost in a haze of platitudes. He wrote about concepts of freedom without putting forward actual proposals for the specific circumstances that existed. It appeared as if Catholic emancipation and repeal of the Union were merely stepping stones that allow him to move on to the bigger issues that affect mankind. We know from his letters[40] that his *Address* was intended to be the first in a series of pamphlets whose ultimate aim was the undermining of Catholicism itself. The pamphlet opens with an attack on religion – Catholics once persecuted Protestants, just as now Protestants persecute Catholics – therefore neither can claim the high moral ground. His attack on the Catholic religion misses the point that, in the historical circumstances of Ireland in 1812, Catholics were denied their rights. His anti-Catholic remarks therefore alienated him from the very audience that he hoped to influence. Yet in spite of these mistakes the pamphlet contains the core of a programme that could have cut across the conservatism of the Catholic Committee and offered a way forward to the more radical elements within the movement: he called for unity between Catholic and Protestant, for an open rather than secret organisation using legal means, for Irish radicals to have confidence in their own strength and organisation, rather than depend on the Prince Regent or the British government, and he argued that friendly relations should be developed with the people of England because they suffer under the same government.

The Address to the Irish People was a direct appeal aimed at the masses. It suffers from being written in a style that Shelley believed was accessible 'to the lowest comprehension that can read'. In reality, it is overlong, repetitive and at times patronised the audience he was trying to reach: 'Do not drink, do not play, do not spend any idle time…give no offence'.[41] In Shelley's defence it must be said that this emphasis on moral restraint was part of the political culture of the time and no different in tone from similar appeals issued by the United Irishmen:

> Let not drink and idleness dishonour United Irishmen… Be
> discreet and avoid drunkenness. Be firm but be patient and avoid
> riots.[42]

However, the more direct style of a leaflet circulating in Dublin in January 1812 managed to say in half a page what Shelley said in 10.

> Roman Catholics of Ireland
> For Christ's sake, and for the tender mercy of God, do not take up
> arms in your own defence, or any one else's, on any account
> whatsoever, in that respect act exactly like the Quakers, (hear and
> forbear) suffer wrongs patiently and for Christ's sake, and the Lord
> in time will relieve you, do not be foolishly led away by any show of
> false promises, to leave your poor parents, wife and families
> breaking their hearts after you; forfeiting your religion or duty to
> god, the church and your neighbours.
> Remember 'He that lives by the sword must die by the sword' –
> Therefore for the Lord's sake, enter not into combination or private
> meetings of any sort that may give the least offence to the
> Government. – Be thoroughly resigned to the will of the Lord, and
> god will bless you and yours.[43]

Shelley tried to draw a fine line between reform and revolution, which Godwin recognised immediately. Godwin was certain that if the masses were encouraged to take action it would inevitably lead to revolution. This was a risk Shelley was prepared to take, because for him repression was even more intolerable. That is why he spends so many pages in the *Address* urging restraint on the Irish – he knows it may lead to revolution but he is prepared to accept such an outcome.

The French Revolution opened Shelley's mind to the potential of the masses. But he could never fully break from the old Whig fear of 'the mob' and therefore he clung to the idea that educated leaders were necessary to tell them what to do. Nevertheless, the *Address* is significant as a manifesto of Shelley's new faith that would later find expression in a more complete and lyrical style.

Shelley's second pamphlet, *Proposals for an Association,* was aimed at a different audience, the educated professional class who could provide the leadership of his proposed associations. His treatment of Catholic emancipation and repeal of the union is more thought out and presented in greater detail than in the *Address.* The class emphasis he puts on these issues has been refined by his experience in Ireland and the debates at the Catholic Committee meeting of 28 February. His genuine internationalism is evident in the opening paragraph of the *Proposals*:

Man cannot make occasions, but he may seize those that offer. None are more interesting to Philanthropy than those which excite the benevolent, passions that generalise and expand private into public feelings and make the hearts of individuals vibrate not merely for themselves, their families, and their friends, but for posterity, for a people; till their country becomes the world and their family the sensitive creation.[44]

In the second half of the pamphlet he shifts from the specific conditions in Ireland to the general application of his theories. Influenced by Paine and Godwin, he develops his ideas both on the nature of government and on the issue of individual rights versus collective rights. In his unfinished novel *Hubert Cauvin* Shelley explored the tragedy of the French Revolution and in the *Proposals* he offers his thoughts, most likely drawn from his novel, on what he considers to be the essence of the problem. He examines the role of writers and intellectuals, the degeneration of the revolution, and the role of 'the mob'. To avoid such a tragedy in the future educated leaders will be needed to guide the masses, hence the need for political associations. 'To the dream of the world republic of the *Address* is now added that of a world organisation to accomplish it'.[45]

Proposals was written in his own natural style, and is a marked advance over his earlier prose, and infinitely superior to his poems and letters of the same period. But, it reflected a duality both in his thinking and in his language. In the postscript to the *Address* Shelley writes that, 'I have but translated my thoughts into another language' – the language of the masses. Shelley only partially solved the problem of writing for different audiences; the style and language he used almost defined the audience he was writing for. Shelley could assume many voices. His major poems are interwoven with innumerable threads from earlier literature and philosophy, which sometimes adds to the complexity. *Prometheus Unbound*, a difficult and challenging poem, assumed an educated audience. By contrast, his best poems and prose from around 1819 make no assumptions about his readers. They were written in his own natural style and accessible to all, as in *Ode to the West Wind, The Mask of Anarchy* and *A Philosophical View of Reform.*

By the end of the 18th century language itself had become a class issue. Books such as Johnson's *Dictionary*, Blair's *Rhetoric* and Murray's *Grammar* codified the English language, which had a number of consequences. They laid down the rules for language, which made it easier to learn, but Johnson's model was the classics and hence his correct form of language was even less accessible to ordinary people. The concept of vernacular and refined language was used to dismiss any writings addressed to or originating from the uneducated that did not conform to these rules. Only refined language was considered adequate for political or public debate. To write in vernacular or vulgar language (the language of the masses) was by definition to place oneself outside of society:

Anger, vehemence, a non-abstract vocabulary, and an abundance of metaphor could be dismissed according to Blair and others as primitive both morally and intellectually.[46]

The effect of this was to make the language of debate more difficult to learn, which in turn served to exclude the mass of the population from the political arena. Petitions to parliament were dismissed because of the form in which they were written. But, as the Catholic Committee found out, the ideas behind the petitions were the real reason they were denied rather than the roughness of the language.

The French Revolution transformed political debate. Up to that time different realities were being expressed by the different forms of language. Burke's *Reflection on the French Revolution* and Paine's *The Rights of Man* demonstrated that it was possible to write in a language that was neither refined nor vulgar. This broke the link between a classical education and political life and opened up public debate to the masses. *The Rights of Man* has commitment, anger, metaphor, impassioned speech, arguments based on experience – all the faults that Blair had warned against. Paine imposed syntax and structure on the language of the people that heightened the rhythm of the prose. The words and structure flow from the ideas rather than conforming to an arbitrary or artificial set of rules. Building on Paine's achievement the United Irishmen cultivated a style of writing based on the spoken language that was meant to be 'read by the many rather than admired by the few'. They emphasised cheap newspapers, pamphlets and broadsheets to be read out to the illiterate artisans and farm labourers rather than expensive books, and in the process they democratised political debate itself.[47] In England, William Cobbett gave expression to those without a voice. His *Political Register* first published in 1802, championed a style that was accessible to all. Cobbett's *English Grammar* (1818) was written for the labouring classes and sold an amazing 100,000 copies, which indicates the thirst for education.

In the last decade of the 18th century language was freed from the shackles of the past. Wordsworth and Coleridge in the *Lyrical Ballads* challenged the prevailing view of how poetry should be written. They explored how far the language of the lower and middle classes could be adapted 'to the purposes of poetic pleasure'. In the preface to the *Lyrical Ballads* in 1800 they set out their manifesto:

> The principal object, then, proposed in these poems was to choose incidents and situations from common life, and to relate or describe them, throughout, as far as was possible in a selection of language really used by men, and at the same time, to throw over them a certain colouring of imagination.[48]

The Irish language scholar George Thomson, writing about the oral tradition of the Blasket Islanders off the west coast of Kerry over 100 years later, almost perfectly described the ambition of Wordsworth and Coleridge and the literary possibilities of vernacular language:

> The conversation of those ragged peasants, as soon as I learned to follow it, electrified me. It was as though Homer had come alive. Its vitality was inexhaustible, yet it was rhythmical, alliterative, formal, artificial, always on the point of bursting into poetry.[49]

That Shelley in 1812, given his class background and education, still had to learn the possibilities of the 'conversation of the ragged peasants' or the voice of the English labourers is to some extent understandable. By then the alliance between radicalism and literature no longer existed. Coleridge and Wordsworth now denounced any attempt at literary inclusion with all the vehemence of those who once denounced the *Lyrical Ballads*. Shelley's Irish writings display all the problems of a writer trying to come to terms with his audience and how to use words in a way that could reach out to a broader layer of readers. The writer who departed from Ireland in April 1812 was not the same man who had arrived two months earlier. He learnt more in that time than many do in a lifetime. He learnt of the reality of people's lives and also, I suspect, how to use language more effectively. Shelley's poetry is sometimes complex and can present stylistic difficulties. There are a number of 'styles within Shelley's style', but there is one strain that runs consistently throughout much of his work that is natural, accessible and with a simple imaginative process. George Thomson's characterisation of Homer's poetry is perhaps the most apt description of the transformation that took place in this strand of Shelley's work after his return to England:

> He was a people's poet – aristocratic no doubt...his language was artificial, yet strange to say, this artificiality was natural. It was the language of the people raised to a higher power'.[50]

NOTES

1   B Kennelly, *Shelley in Dublin* (Dun Laoire, 1974), verse 5, lines 3-9, p13.

2   F L Jones, op cit, p273.

3   *The Freeman's Journal*, 29 February 1812. Reprinted in the *Hibernian Journal*, 2 March 1812; Walker's *Hibernian Magazine*, March 1812; *Dublin Evening Post*, 29 February 1812; *Saunders Newsletter*, 29 February 1812; *The Patriot*, 2 March 1812.

4   We know very little about the Shelleys time in Ireland. The newspaper reports and their letters indicate that they travelled widely about Dublin and the surrounding countryside. The terrible poverty and suffering they encounted that winter almost overwhelmed them. The experience left a lasting mark on Shelley and his hatred of poverty and oppression is obvious in almost everything he wrote.

5   F L Jones, op cit, p270.

6   *Poetical Works of Shelley,* 'On Leaving London for Wales', op cit, lines 33-35, p880.

7   F L Jones, op cit, p270.

8   Ibid, p266.

9   See D F MacCarthy, op cit, p239.

10   F L Jones, op cit, p266.

11   Ibid, p273.

12   Two police constables from Shakespeare's *Much Ado about Nothing*. The 'Watch' performed the duties of police before the introduction of the modern force.

13   Appendix 3, p281.

14   F L Jones, op cit, p264.

15   Appendix 4, p286.

16   Appendix 4, p285

17   Appendix 4, p289

18   The Abbé Barruel, *Memoirs Illustrating the History of Jacobinism,* (London, 1798) 4vols. The translator Robert Clifford appended his history of Abbe Barruel's influence in Ireland and Great Britain at the end of volume four: *Application of Barruel's Memoirs of Jacobinism to the secret Societies of Ireland and Great Britain.*

19   Abbé Barruel, op cit, appendix 1, pp2-3. A philanthropic society existed in Dublin in the 1790s which was a forum for deist discussion and a centre for the United Irishmen. Perhaps Shelley took the name from this society?

20   F L Jones, op cit, p267.

21   Appendix 4, p287.

22   J O'Connell, op cit, p138.

23   Appendix 4, p301.

24   Appendix 5, p303.

25   *Morning Chronicle,* London, 23 December 1811.

26   See W Peck, *Shelley: His Life and Work* (Boston, 1927), vol 2, appendix E, p341, for Shelley's indebtedness to John Philpot Curran in *The Address to the Irish People.*

27   Appendix 5, p305.

28   J Curran, *Speeches of the Rt Hon. John Philpot Curran* (Dublin, 1808), p161.

29   W Peck, op cit, p239.

30   Letter from Harriet Shelley to Elizabeth Hitchener, in F L Jones, op cit, p279.

31   R Holmes, op cit, p123.

32   See *Annual Register* for 1811, pp12-18 and pp51-58. The *Times* of London carried over 40 articles on Irish politics in the six months to 31 January 1812. The *London Morning Chronicle* covered the trial of Dr Sheridan, the activities of the Catholic Association and the campaign for Catholic Emancipation. In November and December 1811 only the Peninsular War received more coverage.

33   See M Townsend, *Not by Bullets and Bayonets* (London, 1983). See also 'W Cobbett and Ireland,' in J Osborne, *Studies,* (Dublin, 1981), no 278/279, p187.

34   *Political Register,* XVII, 12 May 1810. This Roger O'Connor was a supporter of the British government and should not be confused with one of the O'Connor brothers of the same name, who was a member of the United Irishmen.

35   T J Hogg, The *Life of Percy Bysshe Shelley,* vol 1, op cit, p318. The 'Hibernian Hampden' refers to the number of Irish radicals who joined the Hampden Clubs,

which were formed in 1812. The Mount Street coffee house in London was owned by John Westbrook, Harriet's father, and frequented by Shelley. Coffee houses were the traditional meeting place for political clubs and organisations. Hogg is voicing his opinion here rather than making a statement of fact.

36   Catholic emancipation was one of the key issues in the 1807 election. See W J McCormack, *From Burke to Beckett* (Cork, 1994) also *The Veto Controversy* (Belfast, 1985) and *The Scully Papers* (Dublin, 1988) for details.

37   This pro-government pamphlet, one of many, which was widely distributed in London, outlined the activities of the Catholic Committee, petitions for emancipation, and legal affairs in Ireland in 1810-11, and is typical of the period. *Substance of a speech of the Rt. Hon. Will. Wellesley Pole in the House of Commons on the 11th of June 1811* (London, 1811).

38   Quoted in N Mansergh, *Britain and Ireland* (London, 1942), p28.

39   Quoted in F O'Toole, *A Traitor's Kiss* (London, 1998), p428. Richard Brinsley Sheridan, Irish playwright and MP, was a member of the Duke of Norfolk's circle in the Whig party. He was an advocate of Catholic emancipation and Irish independence.

40   F L Jones, op cit, p241.

41   Appendix 3, p264 – 'Play' in this context means gambling.

42   *Rebellion Papers,* National Archives of Ireland, 620/54/37,40 United Irishmen leaflets issued in Meath and Dublin in 1797.

43   *Evening Herald,* 8 January 1812, p2.

44   Appendix 4, p285.

45   K Cameron, op cit, p151.

46   O Smith, *The Politics of Language 1791-1819* (Oxford, 1984), p29.

47   See M H Thuente, *The Harp Re-strung* (New York, 1994). One issue that is still unclear is how far the United Irishmen's propaganda penetrated into the majority Irish speaking areas of the country. K Whelan in 'The United Irishmen, The Enlightenment and Popular Culture', in D Dickson, D Keogh and K Whelan eds, *The United Irishmen,* (Dublin, 1993) quotes Lord Dillon as being convinced that the United Irishmen had 'paid interpreters in remote parts of the country to translate for the ignorant'. (p278).

48   W Wordsworth, 'Preface to the Lyrical Ballads', *Poetical Works,* p935.

49   G Thomson, *Island Home: The Blasket Heritage* (Dingle, Co Kerry, 1998),

p137. George Thomson (1903-1987) was born in England and learned Irish at the Gaelic League classes in London. His first visit to the Blasket Islands in 1923 transformed his life and he devoted his time to learning and writing about their culture. The island's oral culture even changed his method of writing so that he would never commit anything to paper without first reciting it out loud. A Greek scholar, he was appointed lecturer in Greek at Galway University, where he taught through the medium of Irish. An active Marxist, among his many publications was *Marxism and Poetry* published in 1946. He translated and edited Muiris O'Sullivan's classic book on the Blasket Islands, *Twenty Years A-Growing* (London, 1933).

50   G Thompson, *Island Home,* op cit, p138.

Chapter Six

Optimism of the Will

For a nation to love liberty it is sufficient that she knows it,
to be free it is sufficient that she wills it.

SHELLEY concluded his *Address to the Irish People*
with the words of Lafayette quoted above. He understood the nature of
the crisis in Ireland and the political opportunities this presented. But
he overestimated the extent and the ability of the forces available to him.
The legacy of the defeat in 1798 and the failure of Emmet's rising in 1803
meant that there was no enthusiasm for instant solutions. When Shelley
wrote his first pamphlet, he had no perception of the circumstances in
which the majority of the Dublin poor lived. Their conditions were such
that they were incapable of responding to his call:

Are you slaves, or are you men? If slaves then crouch to the rod, and
lick the feet of your oppressors, glory in your shame; it will become
you, if brutes, to act according to your nature. But you are men; a
real man is free, so far as circumstances will permit him. Then
firmly, yet quietly resist.[1]

They were neither slaves nor free men, but a class trying to emerge from the poverty and chaos of an emergent capitalism. To his credit, Shelley quickly realised the difficulties he faced. In a letter to Godwin on 8 March, he confessed, 'I had no conception of the depth of human misery until now. The poor of Dublin are assuredly the meanest and most miserable of all... These were the persons to whom, in my fancy, I had addressed myself: how quickly were my views on this subject changed'.[2] Having experienced the wretchedness of the poor at first hand, Shelley quickly abandoned any idea that he could inspire them to take action on their own behalf. He was profoundly depressed by the experience, but equally, determined to press ahead: 'With what eagerness do such scenes as these inspire me'.[3] His anger is evident in a letter he sent to the *Weekly Messenger*, which was not published, but it indicated a more realistic understanding of the political situation: 'You will see my letter next week to the editor of the panegyrising paper. Some will call it violent. I have at least made a stir here, and set some men's minds afloat'.[4]

Shelley had no illusions in the Catholic Committee, which was in the hands of business and professional people whose only interest was to obtain advancement for their own class. Shelley wanted to emphasise the bigger issues that would affect the welfare of the masses – the class nature of the British government, economic exploitation and the fight for the vote – with the ultimate aim of an egalitarian society.

His hopes for success were now pinned on the scattered remnants of the United Irishmen and the liberal intelligentsia coming together to form an association on a platform of Catholic emancipation and repeal of the union. Influenced by Godwin and the failure of the United Irishmen, Shelley was adamant that the association should renounce violence and secrecy. Its function was to educate its members through debate and discussion, and agitate among the masses for its programme. This was the embodiment of a proposal that Shelley had made to Leigh Hunt a year earlier. There was room for an organisation that placed itself to the left of the O'Connell group, yet was prepared to work within the movement to achieve its aims.

Shelley awaited developments with great anticipation at 7 Sackville Street during the first week of March. But his inexperience was soon exposed. John Philpot Curran, Hamilton Rowan and their circle had long traded in their green coats and made their peace with the British establishment. Given the level of oppression, an immediate response from Roger O'Connor and other elements of the United Irishmen still active was unlikely. The enthusiasm of youth is seldom tempered with patience. Therefore, it was almost inevitable that the initial response to his proposals would fail to live up to Shelley's expectations. His frustration is evident, 'I have daily had numbers of people calling on me; none will do. The spirit of bigotry is high'.[5] Doubtless many callers were just curious, or worse, opportunists attracted by the information in the *Dublin Weekly Messenger* that Shelley was 'heir of one of the first fortunes in England'. But despair was coupled with hope. In a letter to Elizabeth Hitchener, Shelley mentions that Harriet and Eliza 'are walking with a Mr Lawless (a valuable man).' In a postscript Harriet added, 'Has Percy mentioned to you a very amiable man of the name Lawless, he is much attached to the cause yet dare not act'.

John Lawless was born in Dublin in 1773, the son of a respectable brewer. He trained for the legal profession, but was refused entry to the bar on account of his association with the United Irishmen. He moved to Belfast as editor of the *Belfast Magazine*, and published the *Belfast Politics*,[6] a collection of debates and resolutions in 1792-93 relating to the United Irishmen. This caused so much offence to the government that they ordered all copies to be burnt. After the Act of Union he returned to Dublin and became active in the campaign for emancipation. He was identified with the O'Connell wing of the Catholic Committee, but politically was well to the left of O'Connell, opposing any compromise with the British establishment. In time this led to a rupture with O'Connell, who spoke of him as 'Mad Lawless' and in 1831 opposed his candidature for the House of Commons.

Lawless was a colourful, if controversial figure in Irish politics. He was a contributor to the *Dublin Weekly Messenger* and most likely the author of the complementary article on Shelley that appeared on 7 March. Despite their differences regarding the prospects for the success of Shelley's proposals, they agreed to work together on a number of projects: 'Mr L tho he regards my ultimate hopes as visionary, is willing to acquiesce in my means. He is a republican'.[7]

As expectations for the association grew fainter, hope came from a new quarter. John Lawless offered him a share in a newspaper.[8] Shelley was excited by this proposal, for it offered the prospect of a platform for his politics and a powerful voice in the debate on reform. None of the surviving records mention the paper referred to, but, according to a report in the Dublin *Evening Herald* of 26 February 1812, plans were afoot to launch a literary and political paper on the lines of the *Edinburgh Review,* the pro-Whig paper founded in 1802 in Scotland:

> Notice of *Dublin Quarterly Review* to be launched by a number of Literary and Professional Gentlemen resident in this city and in London, of whose Talents the public has had some specimens, and in whose Principles Irishmen have had cause to confide.

The *Dublin Quarterly Review* never went into production. But, from the details in the prospectus, it is likely that this was the paper Shelley referred to. Shelley was in Dublin at the time the notice appeared and given the description of those behind the *Review,* Lawless was always likely to be involved. Against this, Shelley is specific in saying it was a 'newspaper' rather than a 'review': 'I shall soon however have command of a newspaper, with Mr Lawless'.[9] Whatever the proposal was, it lifted Shelley's spirits as the difficulties in forming his association became apparent.

Lawless was in charge of a project to prepare and publish *A Compendium of the History of Ireland.* Shelley enthusiastically agreed to assist with the manuscript. Whatever literary contribution Shelley made to the book, if any, it is clear from a letter to his uncle on 20 March that his role was to raise funds for the completion of the project and use his position to obtain distribution for the book:

> I am now engaged with a literary friend in the publication of a voluminous History of Ireland, of which two hundred and fifty pages are already printed, and for the completion of which, I wish to raise two hundred and fifty pounds. I could obtain undeniable security for its payment at the end of eighteen months. Can you tell

me how I ought to proceed? The work will produce great profits.[10]

We do not know if Shelley ever managed to raise any money for Lawless, or whether he had any further involvement with the book, which was finally published in 1814.[11] If Lawless was the 'undeniable security' referred to by Shelley, then the hints in Harriet's letters in November 1813 that they were let down by Lawless in financial matters make sense. And, as we shall see, this may have been one of the issues that led to a breach in their friendship.

Traditionally the victors get to write the history of their age. The vanquished seldom have the means or the opportunity to record their version of events. In either case the masses are generally hidden from history and we know little of their lives and aspirations. Thankfully this has changed, due to the work of historians such as Christopher Hill and Edward Thompson. An immense body of work now exists that chronicles the attempts of the common people to impose their own solutions on the problems of their time. If we carefully sift the records, it is sometimes possible to uncover the lives of working class people who existed in the slipstream of others deemed worthier in history. Such a woman was Catherine Nugent. What we know of her is almost entirely a consequence of her relationship with Shelley. Alfred Webb, whose father was acquainted with Catherine, published the letters of Harriet Shelley to Catherine Nugent[12] in 1889 and added some notes about her life. Limited as it is, Catherine emerges as a woman of principle, vitality and integrity, worthy of a place in history in her own right.

Catherine Nugent was born in Dublin in 1771. She was an active and valued member of the United Irishmen and corresponded extensively with her fellow revolutionaries in the movement. Relatively little has been published dealing specifically with women and 1798. Nancy Curtin describes the role of the United Irishwomen as 'a kind of female auxiliary which attended to fund raising and providing amenities for imprisoned United Irishmen'.[13] A contemporary, Mary McCracken, who was familiar with the writings of Mary Wollstonecraft, was sceptical of the United Irishwomen as she believed they did nothing to emancipate women and were merely 'teapot clubs' where politics was not discussed. Catherine Nugent's activities went beyond discussion. She was active in the rebellion to such an extent that, if she were a man, she certainly would have been executed. Harriet Shelley describes Catherine's activities in the aftermath of the rebellion: 'She visited all the prisons…to exhort the people to have courage and hope. She said it was a most dreadful task; but that it was her duty, and she would not shrink from the performance of it'.[14] A friend described her in 1826 as 'a wonderful woman – altho' very plain, little and republican looking', and a letter of 1827 reveals her to be an educated and intelligent woman.[15] Catherine Nugent was 40 years old in 1812. She was not married, declaring that 'her country was her only love', but she styled herself Mrs Nugent, as was the fashion of the time. Though born a Catholic, she did not hold strictly by the creed or practice of her religion, an attribute that would not have gone unnoticed by Shelley.

She obtained a copy of Shelley's *Address to the Irish People*, probably from Dan Healy, and immediately sought out Shelley at his rooms in Sackville Street. He was not at home, but he returned the visit and thus began a friendship based on mutual respect and admiration. Catherine Nugent was a great practical help to the Shelleys during the difficult month of March, and on her account they moved to rooms at 17 Grafton Street, opposite the house where she lived. Unlike any of Shelley's other acquaintances she was working class. She sewed furs for the rich in the shop of John Newman at 101 Grafton Street.

Shelley had immense compassion for the sick, the undernourished, and the downtrodden. But in Catherine Nugent he encountered for the first time a working class woman not as a victim of society, but as an individual who was fighting for what she believed to be her right. She met Shelley as an equal, as he acknowledged in a letter to her in May 1812:

Had you the millions which the Prince will possess how would England not be benefited! Were he compelled to sit in Mr Newman's shop and sew fur on to satin in what would she be injured? – that this remark is not meant for flattery you will believe.[16]

His respect for her personally and politically was such that in August

1812, he sent her a copy of his pamphlet *A Letter to Lord Ellenborough* to obtain her opinion of it. From her Shelley must have derived a more detailed and intimate appraisal of the political climate in Ireland and the prospects for his proposals, and also a sense that change from below was possible. After her day's work she would visit with the Shelleys to discuss the issues of the day. The Shelleys were recent converts to vegetarianism but on her account departed from their regime. Harriet's invitation to dinner stated that 'a murdered chicken has been prepared for her repast'.

Their friendship was such that in April they tried to persuade her to go with them to Wales, but she replied that she had never been out of her country and had no wish to leave it. After their departure from Ireland the Shelleys remained in contact, and Harriet's letters to Catherine are one of the main sources of information concerning the Shelleys affairs during 1812-14. Harriet's last letter, written a year before her death, shows both the closeness of their friendship and her despair after the separation from Shelley:

What will you do my dear Catherine? Now those Newmans retire you will not like to go to another house of business. The few years you have to live may surely be passed more pleasantly. Do make up your mind at once to come and stay with me. I will do everything to make you happy. For myself happiness is fled. I have lived for others. At nineteen I could descend a willing victim to the tomb… Your letters make me more happy. Tell me about Ireland. You know I love the green Isle and all its natives.[17]

Catherine Nugent never forgave Shelley for his treatment of Harriet and in later life 'could scarcely bear to think, much less speak of him'. She continued her political activity and in the 1820s set up a small discussion group that met in her rooms in Grafton Street. She lived with the Newmans after their retirement and when she died in December 1847 she was buried alongside them in St Anne's churchyard in Dublin.[18]

In early March a letter sent to a Mr Reynolds,[19] a friend of Catherine Nugent's, came to Shelley's attention. Redfern, an Irishman living in

Lisbon as an exile, was press-ganged into the Portuguese army with the connivance of the British authorities. He appealed to Reynolds for help. Shelley had an abiding hatred of the military. In January 1812 Shelley sent a number of verses from *The Voyage* to Elizabeth Hitchener.[20] They describe how the activities of the press gang reduced the parents of a young soldier to poverty. We do not know when Shelley completed the poem, but it could just as easily describe Redfern's case.

> Her son, compelled, the tyrants foes had fought,
> Had bled in battle, and the stern control
> That ruled his sinews and coerced his soul
> Utterly poisoned life's unmingled bowl
> And unsubduable evils on him wrought.
>
> And now cold charity's unwelcome dole
> Was insufficient to support the pair,
> And they would perish rather than would bear
> The law's stern slavery and the insolent stare.[21]

Shelley set about the campaign to free Redfern. He printed up copies of Redfern's letter and mailed it to prominant individuals including Sir Francis Burdett in London: 'You will soon see a copy of his letter, and soon hear of my or Burdett's exertions in his favour. He shall be free; this nation shall awaken'.[22] In May he reminded Catherine Nugent to 'remember me to Reynolds, tell him I shall not be idle about Redfern and that as soon as I have done anything I will write to him'.[23] Elizabeth Hitchener sent a copy of the letter to the *Sussex Weekly Advertiser*, which refused to print it, on the grounds that any publicity might irritate the government and lead to further oppression against the unfortunate Redfern.[24] We do not know whether Shelley, Burdett or Reynolds made any impact in publicising the case, and Redfern's fate is still unknown.

Shelley achieved little of political consequence in Ireland. His impatience worked against him. The conditions existed for a movement to the left of the O'Connell faction in the Catholic Association. In Cork, William Thompson,[25] who was branded a 'Red Republican' because of his support for the French Revolution, campaigned on terms similar to Shelley in the 1812 election. Catherine Nugent represented the best of what Shelley was trying to achieve. With people like her, Reynolds and John Lawless, given time and hard work, a small but significant movement could have been built to influence the political agenda in a more radical direction.

Shelley was a great admirer of Robert Emmet. His interest may have been stimulated by Southey's poem on Emmet or the story of Sarah Curran's love affair with Emmet. Many of the Romantic poets were drawn in guilty fascination to Emmet's tragic life. Coleridge's description of Emmet bears an almost uncanny similarity to the 'dirty protest'[26] undertaken in the 1980s by Republican prisoners in the H-Block prison camp in Northern Ireland in support of their campaign for political status: 'A mad Raphael, painting ideals of beauty on the walls of a cell with human excrement'.[27] Shelley made a political pilgrimage to St Michan's Church, where tradition has it that Emmet was buried in an unmarked grave covered by a large grey stone on the west side of the church.[28] There he may have met with the rector, the Reverend Thomas Gamble, who attended Emmet on the scaffold and arranged for his interment in a temporary grave after his execution in 1803. Gamble was radical, a social reformer and an intimate friend of the leaders of the United Irishmen. Shelley, no less than Southey and Coleridge, was inspired by Emmet's sacrifice and his admiration shines through in his poem *On Robert Emmet's Tomb*:

May the tempests of Winter that sweep o'er thy tomb
Disturb not a slumber so sacred as thine;
May the breezes of summer that breathe of perfume
Waft their balmiest dews to so hallowed a shrine.

May the foot of the tyrant, the coward, the slave,
Be palsied with dread where thine ashes repose,
Where that undying shamrock still blooms on thy grave
Which sprung when the dawnlight of Erin arose.[29]

The length of time that Shelley intended to spend in Ireland was to some extent open-ended, depending on the impact of his campaign. Shortly after his arrival, full of enthusiasm, he wrote to Elizabeth Hitchener: 'Everything proceeds well. I could not expect more rapid success'. He planned to publish his pamphlets, make contact with the leaders of the movement and set up an organisation which he hoped might spread to England and beyond. However, by mid-March Shelley realised the problems he faced. The prospects for the association were minimal: 'As to an Association my hopes daily grow fainter on the subject, as my perceptions of its necessity gain strength'.[30] The misery and poverty that surrounded him intensified his growing sense of failure to make his proposals effective. Out of his own experience he realised the need to retrench and rethink his strategy.

This was the background to a political debate, in a revealing exchange of letters, between Godwin and Shelley on the issues raised in the latter's pamphlets. Shelley had sent a copy of the *Address to the Irish People* to Godwin on 24 February, with an outline of his *Proposals for an Association*. Godwin replied on 4 March:

> In the pamphlet you have just sent me, your views and mine as to the improvement of mankind are decisively at issue. You profess the immediate object of your efforts to be 'the organisation of a society, whose institution shall serve as a bond to its members'. If I may be allowed to understand my book on *Political Justice*, its pervading principle is, that association is a most ill-chosen and ill-qualified mode of endeavouring to promote the political happiness of mankind. And I think of your pamphlet, however commendable and lovely are many of the sentiments it contains, that it will be either ineffective to its immediate object, or that it has no very remote tendency to light again the flames of rebellion and war. It is painful to me to differ so much from your views on the subject, but it is my duty to tell you that such is the case.[31]

Shelley replied by return of post defending his position:

> I am not forgetful or unheeding of what you said of Associations. But *Political Justice* was first published in 1793; nearly twenty years

have elapsed since the general diffusion of its doctrines. What has followed? Have men ceased to fight, has vice and misery vanished from the earth. – Have the fireside communications which it recommends taken place? – Out of the many who have read that inestimable book how many have been blinded by prejudice, how many in short have taken it up to gratify an ephemeral vanity and when the hour of its novelty had passed threw it aside and yielded with fashion to the arguments of Mr Malthus! I have at length proposed a Philanthropic Association, which I conceive not to be contradictory but strictly compatible with the principles of *Political Justice.*[32]

Godwin responded in what only can be described as a state of panic, accusing Shelley of inciting violence by his actions:

Shelley, you are preparing a scene of blood! If your associations take effect to any extensive degree, tremendous consequences will follow, and hundreds, by their calamities and premature fate, will expiate your error. And then what will it avail you to say, 'I warned them against this; when I put the seed into the ground, I laid my solemn injunctions upon it, that it should not germinate'?

If you wish to consider the sentiments which in the earnestness of my soul I have presented to you, you should consider my two letters as parts of the same discourse, and read them together. Do not be restrained by a false shame from retracting your steps; you cannot say, like Macbeth, 'I am in blood stepp'd in so far that should I wade no more, returning were as tedious as go o'er'.[33]

There is a common assumption that Godwin convinced Shelley to abandon his political activity in Ireland in the course of this debate. This was not the case. Shelley deferred to Godwin's destructive criticism out of respect; he accepted that he was young, over-confident and inexperienced, but he never accepted that he was wrong. Godwin was out of touch with the issues of the day. His arguments that associations would lead to violence were being disproved by the activities of Cobbett, Burdett and Cartwright at the very time he was writing. In Ireland the Catholic Association showed on a large scale what Shelley's more modest proposals could have achieved.

From this time on Shelley was never absolutely frank with Godwin about his political views. He said nothing of his publishing schemes with Lawless or his hopes for the future. The difference between them was not age or experience, but that Godwin wrote for the middle classes who would not take action, while Shelley tried to write for the masses, who would. He continued on his own course until convinced by events that he could do no more in Dublin. In his final letter to Godwin he would only accept that his scheme for an association was 'ill-timed' not wrong:

> I have withdrawn from circulation the publications wherein I erred & am preparing to quit Dublin: It is not because I think that such associations as I conceived would be deleterious, that I have withdrawn them… My schemes of organising the ignorant I confess to be ill-timed: I cannot conceive that they were dangerous.[34]

By 18 March all thoughts of an association in Ireland were given up as impractical. His attention now turned to how the movement might be advanced in England and Wales. Their departure was fixed for 7 April, unless the suspension of the Habeas Corpus Act forced them to leave earlier for fear of arrest. A box containing the pamphlets, the broadsheets and the printed version of Redfern's letter was sent ahead to Elizabeth Hitchener as material for the development of the Lewes Association. Despite the failure in Ireland he still hoped for success: 'Dublin is the most difficult of all. In Wales I fear not. In Lewes fear is ridiculous. I am certain your book club is a beautiful idea'.[35] Elizabeth Hitchener had set up a radical book club, as the basis for their association. Shelley had written to the chairman outlining his plans, and Elizabeth Hitchener sent reports of Shelley's activities to the Sussex newspapers.[36] He urged her to prepare the ground by distributing the *Declaration of Rights* among the Sussex farmers, as Benjamin Franklin had done during the American Revolution.

Shelley could only afford the freight for his box of pamphlets as far as Holyhead in Wales. After some days customs officials opened the box to see if the contents were dutiable. What they found was sufficiently alarming to warrant sending a report directly to Lord Sidmouth, the home secretary. In a bureaucratic panic the local officials outlined the action they had taken:

> It contained, besides a great quantity of pamphlets and printed papers, an open letter, of a tendency so dangerous to government, that I urged him to write without further loss of time, a confidential letter, either to the Secretary of State, or to Mr Percival, and enclose the letter, and one each of the pamphlets and printed Declarations.[37]

Sidmouth appears to have taken no action beyond informing Wellesley-Pole, the secretary of state for Ireland, who returned the letter without comment.[38] In due course the box and its contents was forwarded to Elizabeth Hitchener. Even as they landed at Holyhead the Shelleys were under suspicion as dangerous radicals, whose activities would have to be monitored by the government. But, as the son of a member of parliament with influential friends, he was safe from prosecution, and he was never aware that another incident concerning him was entered on his file at the Home Office.

They departed from Dublin on Saturday 4 April 1812. Dan Healy, who was by now a valued member of the household, left with them.

NOTES

1   Appendix 3, p273. A similar formulation was published in the *Political Register* and *Impartial Review of New Books* (London, 1768), August, p94.
An Address to the Freeholders of the Kingdom of Ireland.
If you choose to be slaves, 'tis in vain to talk to you; and you will remain, what you ought to remain, the dependants of swoln up bashaws, and petty tyrants. – Habit, perhaps may have reconciled your minds to the thraldom – if that be the case, you are not fit members of a free community – Turkey or Morocco should be your abode.

2   F L Jones, op cit, p266.

3   Ibid, p266.

4   Ibid, p270.

5   Ibid, p270.

6   H Joy and W Bruce, (eds), *Belfast Politics* (Belfast, 1794). William Bruce (1757-1841) was an active member of the United Irishmen, but he opposed the rising in 1798 and served in the yeomanry against the rebels. He was a founder member of the Unitarian Society in Ireland, which may be the reason Shelley sent him a copy of his pamphlet *A Proposal for Putting Reform to the Vote* in 1817.

7   F L Jones, op cit, p273.

8   Ibid, p270, p273.

9   Ibid, p273. Another possibility is the *Dublin Political Review*, which was published by F W Conway. The first of 13 weekly issues was published on 6 February 1813.

10   F L Jones, op cit, p280.

11   J Lawless, *A Compendium of the History of Ireland* (Dublin, 1814). An examination of the text does not reveal any evidence of a contribution by Shelley.

12   A Webb, 'Harriet Shelley and Catherine Nugent', *Nation* (New York, 1889), issue 48, 6 June 1889. Harriet Shelley wrote 22 letters to Catherine Nugent. Unfortunately Catherine's letters to Harriet have not been preserved. Alfred Webb (1834-1908) was a radical Quaker, a supporter of Home Rule for Ireland and a campaigner against slavery and colonialism. See M L Legg, (ed), *Alfred Webb* (Cork, 1999).

13   N Curtin, 'Women and Eighteenth-Century Irish Republicanism', in M MacCurtin and M O'Dowd (eds), *The Women of 1798* (Dublin, 1991), p134.

14   F L Jones, op cit, p279.

15   *Nation*, p486.

16   F L Jones, op cit, p296.

17   Ibid, p424.

18   The headstone reads 'Also of Catherine Nugent friend of the above who died 14 December 1847 aged 76 years'. The headstones were removed in the 1970s to make way for a playground and are now stored in the crypt. According to the *Nation* (p464) a silhouette exists, also a mask and daguerreotype taken after her death.

19   I cannot identify for certain the Reynolds referred to by Shelley. But he was obviously a friend of Catherine Nugent's, a supporter of Catholic emancipation and possibly a former member of the United Irishmen.

20   F L Jones, op cit, p221.

21   P B Shelley, *The Esdaile Notebook*, 'A Tale of Society as it is from facts', lines 60-63, 72-75, p62. (Originally titled 'Mother and Son').

22   F L Jones, op cit, p270.

23   Ibid, p296.

24   K Cameron, op cit, p167.

25   William Thompson (1785-1833) Irish socialist, feminist and pioneer of the co-operative movement. His labour theory of value influenced Karl Marx and James Connolly. He co-authored with Anna Wheeler the *Appeal*, the first socialist statement on feminism in 1824. See D Dooley, *Equality in Community* (Cork, 1996). Anna Wheeler was influenced by Mary Wollstonecraft. She loved Shelley's poetry, particularly his views on women's liberation. She ended a letter to Robert Owen: '"Shall man be free and woman a slave" – and idiot? says Shelley. "Never, say I."'

26   In the early 1980s IRA prisoners in Northern Ireland refused to cooperate with the prison authorities unless they were granted political status. They refused to slop out their cells and as a result were forced to smear their excrement on the prison walls to dispose of it.

27   K Coburn and M Christensen, (eds), *The Notebooks of S T Coleridge* (London, 1957-73), entry no 1522.

28   The final resting-place of Emmet is still shrouded in mystery. The best account is by Joseph Hammond 'The Rev Thomas Gamble and Robert Emmet' (*Dublin Historical Review*, 1953), vol 14, no 4, 1953. Hammond says that Emmet was buried in a shallow grave in St Michan's and later his body was removed to an unknown grave. In 1903 an unsuccessful attempt was made to locate Emmet's remains. The search concentrated on the unmarked grave in St Michan's, the Emmet family vault in St Peters in Aungier Street and an unmarked grave in Old Glasnevin Church. The following year further investigations in St Paul's Church in King Street North revealed the remains of a headless man of Emmet's build. Both St Peters and St Paul's was demolished in the 1980s. It would be interesting to know where the remains were removed. We are approaching the 200th anniversary of Emmet's execution and modern methods of DNA testing could clear up the mystery.

29   P B Shelley, *The Esdaile Notebook*, op cit, lines 1-8, p60.

30   F L Jones, op cit, p273.

31   Ibid, p260.

32   Ibid, p266.

33   Ibid, p269.

34   Ibid, p276.

35   Ibid, p270.

36   Elizabeth Hitchener sent copies of Shelley's *Address*, Redfern's *Letter* and the report in the *Dublin Weekly Messenger* to the Sussex papers. The *Sussex Weekly Advertiser* assured her it was under consideration, but nothing more was heard of it.

37   See D F MacCarthy, *Shelley's Early Life,* op cit, p310.

38   For details of this incident see Public Record Office London, *State Papers, Ireland. January to April 1812.*

CHAPTER SEVEN

The Sensitive Plant

ENGLAND in 1812 was in a state of near rebellion. Disaffection swelled for a hundred reasons, which gave rise to an army of redressers legislating by night. Reports of a possible revolution reached the Home Office, which overstated the situation, but indicated the depth of the crisis:

> There was talk of a general rising, the disaffected of Manchester and district rising in concert with their fellows in the Midlands, in London, in Scotland, and in Ireland… It was widely believed that the first few days of May would see a general, national outbreak verging upon revolution.[1]

The economic struggles gave birth to a new kind of radicalism, which had its origins in the secret societies, such as the United Englishmen, that were formed at the end of the 1790s. This was a working class radicalism, concerned primarily with economic and social issues, organised from below, without as yet any kind of parliamentary orientation:

> No account of Luddism is satisfactory which is confined to a limited

industrial interpretation, or which dismisses its insurrectionary undertones with talk of a few 'hotheads'. Even in Nottingham where Luddism showed greatest discipline in pursuing industrial objectives, the connection between frame-breaking and political sedition was assumed on all sides.[2]

In Britain as a whole and especially in those parts where Shelley was travelling as an outcast from his family, class identities were forming as the new industrial workers came into conflict with the owners of property, the law and the establishment:

By the end of December [1811] the Nottingham correspondent of the *Leeds Mercury* declared: 'The insurrectional state to which this country has been reduced for the last month has no parallel in history, since the troubled days of Charles the First'.[3]

On 11 May 1812 a deranged man assassinated the prime minister, Spencer Percival. This was an act of personal desperation, yet symptomatic of the political atmosphere that spring. Harriet's report of the affair to Catherine Nugent conveyed the mood in the Shelley household:

It had been better if they had killed Lord Castlereagh. He really deserved it… Do you not think it nonsense for all the little towns and villages to send petitions to the Prince on the occasion. I suppose Ireland has not done anything half as silly.[4]

Even the radicals were terrified at the prospect of revolution; Cobbett campaigned in the *Political Register* to shift the emphasis of working class activity from rioting and machine breaking to mainstream political action. On 20 April the first Hampden Club was formed by middle and upper class reformers, who wished to divert insurrectionary discontent into constitutional forms. The young Lord Byron was an enthusiastic recruit, though his speech in the House of Lords in a debate on Catholic emancipation marked him out as someone who was prepared to go beyond the reforms proposed by the radical Whigs. As Shelley had done, he linked the campaign for emancipation with repeal of the union: 'If it must be called a union, it is the union of the shark with his prey'.[5] Like Shelley, he was fascinated by talk of more active times, such as the treason trials of 1794 and the United Irish rebellion of 1798, and imagined himself as an 'English Lord Edward Fitzgerald'.[6]

 By mid-April the Shelleys were settled in Rhayader, in Mid Wales. Their departure from Ireland was more of a shift of base than an acknowledgement of defeat: 'We left Dublin because I had done all that I could do, if its effects were beneficial they were not greatly so, I am dissatisfied with my success, but not with the attempt'.[7] His departure from Dublin is generally viewed as a defeat. Richard Holmes makes the point that when Shelley returned to England 'it was not to carry the fight into any of the disturbed urban centres… He sought rural seclusion to recoup his energies and meditate on what he had experienced'.[8] But, defeat was not in Shelley's mind. He ordered books for a library to be used for the benefit of humanity, and urged Catherine Nugent and Elizabeth Hitchener to join him in Wales to plan their next course of action. The large industrial cities were now the centre of agitation, and the political opportunities that Shelley had recognised in Dublin were being openly fought for in England. The experience he gained from his Irish venture would be invaluable in such circumstances. He was aware of the opportunities the situation presented and the problem of isolation from living outside the centres of agitation: 'Manchester, Carlisle, Bristol and other great towns are in a state of disturbance… In Wales they are all very apathetical on the subject of politics'.[9] Shelley spent some time reflecting on the lessons of his intervention in Ireland. The failure of his association was a sobering experience, which led him to conclude that his political future lay in propaganda rather than in agitation:

> When Shelley's associations do not become a reality, the idea of
> world revolution does not pass away, but enters the realm of poetry,
> aesthetics and the imagination.[10]

Shelley now looked for ways that he might be useful to the movement, rather than centrally involved in its activities. This did not lead to quietism or defeatism. Instead he developed a unique synthesis of the romantic and the radical tradition in the realm of his poetry that leads to a revolutionary demand for the destruction of the old world allied to a vision of the new. He searched for points of intersection between his politics, his imagination and his vision of the future.

Traditional political activities were not entirely abandoned and he set about distributing his broadsheets, the *Devils Walk*, and the *Declaration of Rights.* He employed the most imaginative methods; launching bottles filled with broadsheets into the Bristol Channel and balloons sent skywards trailing copies of the *Declaration*, which he recorded in one of his better early poems; *To a Balloon laden with Knowledge.* The imagery he uses is common to many poems from that period – the ideals of past revolutionaries, and in particular those of Robert Emmet and the United Irishmen will light a spark that will roar 'through the tyrant's gilded domes' and liberate the world:

A watch-light by the patriots lonely tomb;
A ray of courage to the oppressed and poor;
A spark, though gleaming on the hovels hearth,
Which through the tyrant's gilded domes shall roar;[11]

Dan Healy was dispatched to paste the *Declaration of Rights* on the walls of the outlying areas. On 19 August he was arrested in Barnstaple. When the authorities realised the contents of the broadsheets, he was brought before the mayor and interrogated about his activities. The matter was viewed with such seriousness that Lord Sidmouth at the Home Office was informed, and it is from this letter that we know what happened. Healy did not inform on Shelley, and kept to the cover story that had been agreed:

On being apprehended and brought before the Mayor, stated his name to be Dan Hill, and that he is the servant to P B Shelley, Esq.… On being asked how he became possessed of these papers, he said, on his road from Linton to Barnstable yesterday he met a Gentleman dressed in black, who he had never seen before, who asked him to take the papers to Barnstaple and post and distribute them, and on Hill's consenting, the gentleman gave him five shillings for his trouble.[12]

Dan Healy gave an assumed name, and made no mention of Ireland, perhaps for fear of arousing suspicion of a connection with Irish revolutionaries. He was fined £200, but had to serve six months in prison as Shelley was in no position to pay a fine of that size. However, Shelley arranged to pay a sum of 15 shillings per week, to obtain extra food and better conditions for Healy. This was the third occasion that the Home Office received reports on Shelley's subversive activities. Prosecution was considered, but without Healy's evidence, a conviction would be difficult to obtain, and Healy would never betray Shelley to English officials. Instead Shelley was placed under careful observation and his correspondence noted.

The exact nature of the relationship between Healy and the Shelleys is difficult to ascertain at this distance. Our information is limited to the letters that have survived, where he is always referred to as their servant. Shelley on one occasion referred to him as 'their Irish servant, simple blundering Dan Healy'.[13] Possibly Healy saw himself as more than a servant, perhaps as part of the household, and certainly as part of Shelley's political project. This may have led to the eventual rupture between Healy and the Shelleys. Healy had distributed Shelley's pamphlets in Dublin, moved with them to Wales, and tramped the lanes of Devon flyposting the broadsheets. His belief in Shelley was such that he served six months in jail on his behalf. He went without wages, as the Shelleys had not the wherewithal to pay him. Surely this entitled him to better treatment than Harriet's dismissive comment in a letter to Catherine Nugent, 'For the whole time he stayed with us he never did anything. Afterwards he turned out to be very ungrateful and behaved so insolently that we were obliged to turn him away'.[14] In order to sustain the myth of Shelley as a man without blemish, whose actions must always be shown in the best light, Edward Dowden tried to destroy Healy's reputation. This was despite the fact that Dowden's papers in Trinity College Dublin contain a letter testifying that Dan Healy 'would go through fire and water'[15] for Shelley:

At length the faithful Dan, like other friends too quickly won, was discovered to be a traitor in disguise; he grew insolent and ungrateful, and arrived in Dublin to put in circulation there the pathetic story of his wrongs.[16]

Whatever the reason for his dismissal and return to Dublin, John Lawless believed that Healy was badly treated and wrote an angry letter of complaint to Shelley, which amongst other reasons effectively ended their friendship. Catherine Nugent also met with Healy, and from the tone of Harriet's letters in reply, it is clear that she had expressed some sympathy for his position. If Dan Healy was just a servant, it is unlikely that a person of Lawless's standing would get involved to the extent that he did. Healy may have been an uneducated working class man employed as a servant by the Shelleys, but from the little we know of him he was respected for his political beliefs. Shelley's friend Thomas Hogg, who knew Healy, described him as 'an emancipator and philan-thropist',[17] hardly the description of a mere servant by a man who had an abiding hatred of working class people and the Irish in particular. This was also the opinion of the Shelleys up to the time of their last few months together, whatever his shortcomings as a servant.

Stockdale, the Dublin printer, refused to return Shelley's manuscripts until he was paid, and for most of 1812 the Shelleys were engaged in various subterfuges to obtain them. Lawless was asked to intercede on their behalf, but to no avail. In October, Shelley asked Catherine Nugent to go to Stockdale's and use her ingenuity to obtain the manuscripts: 'I am afraid you will be obliged to use a little manoeuvre to get them. In the first place you can say that you wish to look at them, and then you may be able to stout them away from him'.[18] Catherine was no more success-ful than Lawless. Shelley's desperation implies that the only copies of some or all of the poems were those in Dublin. Shelley retrieved the manuscripts during his second visit to Dublin in March 1813. He had arranged to borrow £120 before leaving Wales, which may explain how he overcame Stockdale's reluctance to part with them. The fortunes of these poems became entangled with that of Shelley's first great poem, *Queen Mab*. Shelley asked Thomas Hookham in London to print his early poems together with *Queen Mab* as one volume. But Hookham refused, fearing prosecution for blasphemy, and Shelley was obliged to publish *Queen Mab* in a limited private edition. After his death the guardians of the Shelley legend tried to hide the reality of his politics from the world. We had to wait 150 years for those early poems,[19] which Shelley intended to be a celebration of liberty, to be published in their entirety in the order he arranged them.

In August 1812 Irish life and affairs were still an important part of the Shelley household. Catherine Nugent sent them Irish patriotic songs and airs for their entertainment. Shelley was reading William MacNevin's book, *Pieces of Irish History, Illustrative of the conditions of the Catholics of Ireland, of the origins and progress of the political system of the United Irishmen and of their transactions with The Anglo-Irish Government,*[20] which he obtained from America. Its very title indicates why Shelley was so anxious to have it published in England, and on 18 August he sent a copy to Thomas Hookham:

> I send you a copy of a work which I have procured from America and which I am exceedingly anxious should be published. It develops as you will perceive by the most superficial reading, the actual state of republicanised Ireland, and appears to me above all things calculated to remove prejudices which have too long been cherished of that oppressed country, to strike the oppressors with dismay.[21]

Pieces of Irish History, consists of seven essays outlining the history of Ireland up to and including a summary of the penal laws and the events surrounding the revolution of 1798. Thomas Addis Emmet, brother of Robert, wrote the first and longest essay, which was probably enough to inspire the outburst of Irish patriotism that is evident in Harriet's letter to Catherine Nugent:

> Good God, were I an Irishman or woman how I should hate the English. It is wonderful how the poor Irish people can tolerate them. But I am writing to one who from her example shows them how they ought to tolerate this barbarous nation of ours. Thank God we are not all alike, for I too can hate Lord Castlereagh as much as any Irishwoman. How does my heart's blood run cold at the idea of what he did in your unfortunate country. How is it that man is suffered to walk the streets in open daylight![22]

The impact of MacNevin's book on Shelley's circle was immense; Elizabeth Hitchener, outraged by its contents, demanded that Shelley should publish it immediately:

> Bessy [Elizabeth Hitchener] has been reading [*Pieces of Irish History*] and is much enraged with the characters there mentioned, that nothing will satisfy her desire for revenge but the printing and publishing of them.[23]

Shelley was well aware of the difficulties that any bookseller would face in publishing or selling such a book given the political climate, and alternate plans were made. He intended to sell *Pieces of Irish History* only by subscription: 'Five hundred subscribers at seven shillings each will amply repay the printing and publishing'.[24] They were depending on Catherine Nugent for subscribers in Ireland: 'As being on the spot where so many of your exalted and brave countrymen suffered martyrdom. I should think there were very many [who] would be glad to put their names to it'.[25] But like so many of Shelley's publishing projects, it failed to come to fruition.

Shelley continued to distribute his Irish pamphlets while in England, but his stocks were low and he set about reprinting the two Irish publications with the 'suggestions' as one pamphlet. He intended writing an introductory preface that would explain his intentions. He wrote to Thomas Hookham requesting his 'opinion as to the probable result of publishing them'.[26] By printing in London he would overcome the problem with Stockdale, and by distributing through suitable friends, such as Catherine Nugent and John Lawless, he hoped they might find their way to Dublin and make an impression in Ireland. If Hookham was doubtful about the prospects for *Pieces of Irish History*, then we can be sure that he advised Shelley of the dangers of prosecution if he reprinted the Irish pamphlets. They were never reprinted in his lifetime and were not seen again until 1872 when MacCarthy published them as part of his book, *Shelley's Early Life*.

Thomas Hogg recalls visiting the Shelleys in London in November 1812. Their hotel room was strewn with ill printed books and newspapers dealing with Irish history and 'the affairs of that country'. Shelley did not say a word about Ireland, but Harriet handed him a broadsheet, 'as if it was something sacred and full of edification'. This was a report of the trial of Robert Emmet, filled for the most part with Emmet's speech from the dock with an engraving of Emmet as its centrepiece. When asked his opinion, Hogg replied that 'the sooner all such rascals are hanged the better'. Therefore it was no surprise that the Shelleys looked at him 'with calm contempt, and mute languid disgust'.[27] Shelley and Hogg were close personal friends, but Hogg knew nothing of Shelley's politics. His *Life of Shelley* cannot be relied upon on almost any issue of substance and his version of Shelley's interest in Irish politics is a travesty of the truth.

Dan Healy was released from jail on 26 February 1813, and made his way to Shelley's house in Wales. That night an incident occurred that resulted in the Shelley household taking flight for Ireland. An armed intruder broke into the house and, when confronted by Shelley, fired a shot that narrowly missed him. Harriet believed Robert Leeson, a local employer, to be the instigator of the attack. Leeson was a member of a prominent Irish Protestant family, hostile to the movement for Catholic emancipation, and his father, the Earl of Milltown, a landowner in County Wicklow, had supported the Act of Union in 1800. Leeson had been given a copy of one of Shelley's Irish pamphlets and was heard to say that he would drive them out of the country. John Williams, a friend of the Shelleys in the locality, had told Leeson that the pamphlet contained matter dangerous to the state and that Shelley was 'in the practise of haranguing 500 people at a time when in Ireland'.[28] The attack on Shelley remains one of the most controversial incidents in his life. Many are of the opinion that the attack was the product of Shelley's imagination, others that it was a ploy to leave the country without paying his bills. Harriet's account of the incident[29] supports the explanation put forward by H Dowling[30] that the attack was 'a contemptible trick…played upon him to get him out of the country on account of his liberal principles'. The Shelleys quit Wales the next day and on 6 March boarded the Bangor ferry for Ireland.

Shelley was desperate to escape from Wales. He was worried that government agents might have followed Dan Healy after his release from prison and feared that they were under surveillance. Ireland held many attractions as a place of refuge, despite the expense and discomfort of the journey. After a long and stormy boat journey the Shelleys arrived in Dublin and found lodgings near the home of John Lawless in Cuffe Street. Shelley was working on the final version of *Queen Mab* and intended to complete the notes while in Ireland. The notes explain and develop the ideas in the poem. They include his pamphlet *The Necessity of Atheism*, his views on love and marriage and practically his entire philosophical outlook. Shelley wanted those without a traditional education to read and understand his poem – which explains why *Queen Mab* became such a favourite with working class readers, and was known in later years as 'the Chartists' bible'. The idea of appending notes to democratise access to poetry was relatively new. Thomas Moore in 1808 had published *Corruption and Intolerance, two poems with notes addressed to an Englishman by an Irishman.* In the introduction he wrote:

> The practice, which has lately been introduced into literature, of writing very long notes upon very indifferent verses, appears to me to be a rather happy invention.[31]

The Shelleys remained in Dublin for two weeks waiting for their loan to come through. Shelley used the time to reacquaint himself with old friends, such as Catherine Nugent, and to negotiate the return of his manuscripts from Stockdale. Most likely he helped Lawless with the *Compendium of Irish History*, which was published a year later. In due course his money arrived, and, having completed his business in Dublin, they set off on the 21 March for the south of Ireland. They were accompanied by Dan Healy, Eliza Westbrook and the books that went everywhere with them. They rented a cottage on one of the islands that dot the Lakes of Killarney,[32] hoping to escape the attentions of the world and complete the notes for *Queen Mab*. We know nothing about their visit to Kerry, only Shelley's opinion of its natural beauty has survived. In 1818 he wrote that 'only the arbutus lakes in Killarney could compare with the beauty of Lake Como'.[33]

Thomas Hogg, having planned to visit his friends in Wales during March, accepted their altered invitation to meet them in Dublin. To his annoyance, he found the Shelleys had departed for Killarney. His account of the time he spent sightseeing in Dublin tells us a lot about the state of the country since the Act of Union. Hogg's description of Dublin is unreservedly depressing: 'The fashionable world had a mean and poverty stricken aspect. A conspicuous, glaring poverty pervaded the whole city'.[34]

Shelley's retreat in Killarney was interrupted by a note from Hogg announcing his arrival in Dublin. City life in the company of Hogg seemed infinitely more attractive than the wet and windy Killarney. The notes for *Queen Mab* were put aside and Shelley and Harriet set off for Dublin, leaving Healy and Eliza Westbrook to follow with his books at a more leisurely pace. Without pausing for sleep they travelled through the night, only to find that Hogg had departed for London the previous day. Shelley borrowed a small sum of money, and two days later on 2 April 1813, they embarked for Holyhead, never to set foot in Ireland again.

Shelley came of age in more ways than one in 1813, and after the hectic activity of the previous year it was time to take stock of his life. He felt that he had 'sunk into a premature old age of exhaustion'. Harriet was pregnant with their first child. Shelley was tired of the constant travel and wanted to settle down. He needed time and space to prepare *Queen Mab* for publication. While his radicalism was deepened by his experience in Ireland, his commitment to political action lost its force and attraction. He found the life of a political agitator to be hard and, at times, unrewarding. For the rest of his life his dedication to the radical cause was never in doubt, but his trust and confidence in the mass movement came to depend on the ups and downs of the struggle itself. It was this struggle that time and again heralded the upturn in Shelley's political confidence and, with it, his faith in the common people.

Queen Mab was published at the end of May 1813. Shelley prefaced it with Archimedes' statement: 'Give me one firm spot on which to stand, and I will move the earth'.[35] Shelley spent the rest of his life looking for that 'one firm spot'. His search took him across half of Europe, and perhaps it was that quest that he wrote about in *Queen Mab*:

Therefore, O Spirit! Fearlessly bear on:
Though storms may break the primrose on its stalk,
Though frosts may blight the freshness of its bloom,
Yet Springs awaking breath will woo the earth,
To feed with kindliest dews its favourite flower,
That blooms in mossy banks and darksome glens,
Lighting the greenwood with its sunny smile.[36]

Shelley had few expectations for *Queen Mab* – 'Let only 250 Copies be printed. A small neat Quarto, on fine paper so as to catch the aristocrats: They will not read it, but their sons and daughters may'.[37] No bookseller would dare stock it for fear of prosecution, and only 70 copies were distributed between England, Ireland and America. Their trusted friend, Catherine Nugent, was asked to supply a list of likely candidates in Ireland:

> His poem *Queen Mab* is begun, tho' it must not be published under
> pain of death, because it is too much against every existing
> establishment. It is to be privately distributed to his friends, and
> some copies sent over to America. Do you [know] any one that
> would wish for so dangerous a gift? If you do, tell me of them, and
> they shall not be forgotten.[38]

After its publication *Queen Mab* took on a life that was quite independent of Shelley. Over the next 25 years thousands of copies appeared and it became the most widely read, the most notorious and the most influential of all of Shelley's works. *Queen Mab* was never read by the sons and daughters of aristocrats, or even for its lyrical qualities. It was published in cheap pirate editions, and quickly established itself as a basic text in the self taught workers' culture of the early trade union and Chartist movement. *Queen Mab* was reviled by the establishment, but in 1815 it was championed by a most curious and short lived publication, the *Theological Inquirer*,[39] which printed almost one third of the poem over a number of issues, together with favourable letters and comment, and was in effect the first public edition. The editor was George Cannon, an Irish radical who wrote under the unlikely name of Erasmus Perkins.[40] Despite the fact that Shelley took an instant dislike to Cannon, he was pleased with its appearance, and connived with him in its publication.

Over the summer of 1813 the Shelleys lost touch with their Irish friends to the extent that John Lawless wrote to Thomas Hogg asking if they had some cause for not writing. Shortly afterwards, in May 1813, Lawless was confined to the debtors' prison in Dublin, which led many to believe that money was the reason for the rift in their friendship later that year. In March 1812 Shelley had asked Thomas Medwin for advice on how to raise £250 to complete the publication of *The Compendium of Irish History*, on which security could be raised 'for its payment at the expiration of 18 months'.[41] We do not know if Shelley managed to raise the money, but it is unlikely that money would ever have been an issue with Shelley when friendship was involved. In 1842, five years after the death of Lawless, F W Conway indirectly accused Lawless of swindling Shelley in an article in the *Dublin Evening Post*: 'And we know that he [Shelley] was made a pecuniary dupe of a person not less sincere in his politics, but in money matters less honest'.[42] Conway and Lawless had lifelong political and personal differences and, in MacCarthy's opinion, Conway cannot be relied upon in this matter. MacCarthy also exposed the fact that Conway was a government spy[43] and therefore had an interest in blackening Lawless's reputation and by association the repeal of the union movement in the 1840s. The Shelleys were well aware of Lawless's financial problems. It was not for nothing that he was called, in that peculiar Irish way, 'Honest Jack Lawless'. In June 1813 Harriet wrote sympathetically on the matter to Catherine Nugent: 'I am sorry to hear that poor Lawless is confined. If he had taken his friends' advice all his debts would have been settled long ago'.[44] By October their attitude had changed:

> Is Lawless out of prison yet? Had he not taken us in as he did, Bysshe would have done something for him; but his conduct was altogether so dishonest that Mr Shelley will not do anything for him at present. If he wished it he could not, for he is obliged to pay 3 for 1, which is so ruinous that he will raise only a sufficient [sum] to pay his [Shelley's] debts.[45]

If Shelley had managed to find the money for Lawless in 1812, the security referred to would have been due for payment by October or November 1813. Lawless's inability to pay his debts may have been the reason for the change in attitude that is evident in Harriet's letters to Catherine. But the Shelleys had known for some time that Lawless was bankrupt. A closer reading of Harriet's letters indicate that their friendship ended for reasons other than money – most likely the Shelleys' treatment of Dan Healy.

Domestic matters dominated Shelley's life for the next few years, in particular his separation from Harriet and his elopement with Mary Godwin Wollstonecraft. Social or political life became impossible, as there was no place even in the radical Whig section of English society for an avowed atheist, separated from his wife and living openly with another woman. Despondent and in poor health after Harriet's death and the subsequent legal battles for the custody of his children, Shelley had little time for writing or politics, and his only major work during this time was *Alastor*. In October 1814 Shelley, Mary, Claire, his two sisters and Thomas Peacock even contemplated running away to the west of Ireland to set up an idealised society, most likely inspired by Godwin's utopian ideals. By 1817 the Shelleys were living in Marlow, Buckinghamshire. The post-war economic depression had devastated the livelihoods of the lace workers in the area. Shelley was shocked by what he saw and it had the effect of galvanising him into action. There was an outpouring of poetry and prose, with two political pamphlets; *Proposals to put Reform to the Vote*[46] and the *Address to the People on the death of Princess Charlotte*, followed by his long revolutionary poem, *The Revolt of Islam*. This was the Shelley of 1812, once more writing for a mass audience, but with the experience of real struggle and personal involvement. Unfortunately, his enthusiasm was short lived, his pamphlets met with little response and the working class revival petered out. He felt hopeless and, given the difficulties in his personal life, Shelley, Mary and her sister Claire decided to leave England.

When early youth had passed, he left

His cold fireside and alienated home
To seek strange truths in undiscovered lands.[47]

The lines are from *Alastor,* which Shelley wrote in 1816, and they seem to foretell what in 1818 was to be the third and final retreat of his life, and according to Paul Foot, the most tragic:

For although he was to write his best-known work in Italy during his last four years, he was completely cut off there from the experience of the English working people, for whom so many of his works were written. His confidence in them, upon which so much of his political writing depended, rose and fell according to what he could glean from newspapers or from unsympathetic accounts from friends or tourists…he had no Dublin masses, no Welsh dam workers, no unemployed lace workers to talk to. He was politically isolated and his isolation ran through his writing like an open wound.[48]

Shelley took little interest in Italian politics. He never identified with the Italian poor, as he had with the impoverished workers in England and Ireland. Like so many exiles, his interest in politics was rooted in his own country. He became an exile in a 'paradise of exiles'. His letters are full of the beauty of Italy and his appreciation for its art and culture. Perhaps this was an attempt to escape from his loneliness and isolation, which was reflected in a pathetic letter to Peacock, where he described himself as 'an exile and a pariah', – there were only five people in England who did not regard him 'as a rare prodigy of crime and pollution'.[49] The old network of radicals and revolutionaries, which had sustained him politically and socially in Ireland and England, now acted to cut him off from the reality of Italian life.

Italy was a favourite haunt for Irish revolutionaries and radical socialites who could not adapt to conditions in Ireland in the dull and depressing years after the Act of Union. In April 1819, while sightseeing in Rome, Claire spotted Amelia Curran, the eldest daughter of John Philpot Curran, whom they knew through Curran's friendship with Godwin. Shelley had met her during his stay in Dublin in 1812. She was a cultural and sexually emancipated woman, a radical in politics and her personal life and a friend of Robert Emmet's at the time of the rebellion in 1803.

Her house in Rome was a stopping-off point for artists, mainly Irish, and she supported herself in Italy by painting society portraits. Amelia was a welcome addition to the Shelley circle. During those early summer months she painted portraits of Claire, Mary and Shelley, and their son William. She is best known for her portrait of Shelley, the only one painted from real life, which now hangs in the National Portrait Gallery in London.[50] Amelia never completed the painting and she considered it such a poor likeness that she threw it aside. It was a mere accident that she did not burn it along with other discarded works and in 1822, at Mary's request, she finished it to satisfy Mary's desire for a painting of her dead husband.

In January 1820 the Shelleys established themselves in Pisa, where they lived on and off for the next two years. It was the nearest thing that Shelley ever had to a home during all his adult life. His friendship with the Masons dates from this time:

> We see no one but an Irish lady and her husband, who are settled here… You will think it my fate either to find or to imagine some lady of 45, very unprejudiced and philosophical…in every town that I inhabit.[51]

Margaret King was born in Tipperary in 1772, the eldest daughter of Viscount Kingsborough and later wife of Stephen Moore, Earl of Mount Cashell. She was born into the Irish aristocracy, but by temperament was destined to walk with radicals and republicans. Her young world was transformed in 1786 by the arrival of Mary Wollstonecraft as her governess. Mary was 27 at the time and the Kingsboroughs were not to know that they were engaging a woman who in the next decade was to achieve notoriety throughout Europe greater than any other woman writer of her time. In her lifetime she was made an object of calumny and abuse. After her death she was branded a 'whore' whose vices and follies had brought about her providential end. She suffered because for the first time, in *A Vindication of the Rights of Women,* a woman had dared to write a book that was not an echo of men's thinking, nor an attempt to do well what a man had done better. Mary Wollstonecraft exerted a profound and lasting influence on the 14 year old who, in that one year acquired the liberal and republican principles that were to dominate her life. But, despite her attachment to the children, Mary could never hide her dislike of the Kingsboroughs, and the inevitable rupture came in August 1787, when she was dismissed. The following year she published her educational book, *Original Stories*, based on her experience as a governess with the Kingsborough family. After Mary's dismissal, though they corresponded, they were never to meet again.

Margaret's marriage was a failure, and from the beginning she led a separate life. In London in 1794 Lady Mount Cashell, as she was now known, attended the trial of the 12 men charged with conspiracy to overthrow the government. She went to the shop of the shoemaker Thomas Hardy and ordered a pair of shoes to show her support for the man who was a founding member of the London Corresponding Society and a defendant in the recent treason trials. Thomas Hardy made her a pair of shoes fit for an aristocrat, but she returned them requesting shoes fit for a democrat, which impressed Hardy to the point that he refused payment for either pair. She was a republican and a United Irishwoman, and was certainly under suspicion by the government. While her husband dined with his aristocratic friends, she entertained Wolfe Tone and the leaders of the United Irishmen.[52] She was a friend and correspondent of William Godwin, who later published her books and stories. Godwin met her in Dublin in 1800 and was struck by how plainly she dressed in order to break free of sexual and class stereotypes. In France in 1801 she associated with the likes of Tom Paine, Charles Fox and Robert Emmet, which would have endeared her to Shelley.

She left her husband in 1805 to live with George Tighe, an Irish absentee landlord with scientific and literary aspirations. She could no longer be known as Lady Mount Cashell, though this caused her no regret, nor could she be known as Mrs Tighe. They took the name Mr and Mrs Mason from a character in Mary Wollstonecraft's *Original Stories from*

Real Life, in which her counterpart, the little girl, had said, that when she grew up she wished to 'be like Mrs Mason'. Freed from the world she was born into, she could dedicate herself to a life that would have had the approval of her former governess, and live with a man who was both her lover and companion. Her intellectual energies were devoted to writing books for children and a book for mothers on education, a project that Mary Wollstonecraft had planned, but did not live to realise.

The Masons were part of what became known as the Pisan circle, which in time also included Lord Byron, Edward Trelawny, Leigh Hunt and John Taaffe, an Irish writer who eventually achieved fame for his *History of the Knights of the Order of St John of Jerusalem.*[53] The discussions between the Catholic Taaffe and the atheistic Shelley and Byron must have been intriguing, but they admired him enough to assist him in finding a London publisher for his *Comment on Dante.*[54] Another acquaintance in that exile community was Mrs Beauclerc, a former neighbour in Sussex and the stepsister of Lord Edward Fitzgerald of the United Irishmen. Everyone in Shelley's circle admired Mr Mason, but it was Mrs Mason, despite acquiring, in Shelley's eyes, an annoying perverseness, who influenced them most. Her house was the centre for long discussions about the Irish rebellion, and the horror of Castlereagh's administration.[55] The Act of Union broke her heart, as she recorded in a letter to Mary Shelley:

Since my country sank never to rise again, I have been a cool politician; but I cannot forget how I once felt, and can still sympathise with those capable of similar feelings. By the by, it may perhaps cause you to see what struck me as a prophecy, in looking over an old Anti-Union pamphlet which I found amongst a parcel of rubbish last summer. In reply to some honours and advantages pointed out by the writer it wishes to confute, the author says: 'I cannot perceive what advantage it could be to Ireland to have a servile, artful, and ambitious; native of that country pursuing his own interest in the British Cabinet, nor how it would benefit our island to have him reproached with being an Irishman. Would this produce any commercial advantages to our cities? Would this occasion any civilisation in our provinces? Would the prostituted talents of a selfish and crafty schemer rebound to our honour, or add to our prosperity?' The date of this pamphlet is June 1799, a time at which no one guessed what Lord Castlereagh would arrive at.[56]

Claire spent many days reorganising her library, which was frequently raided by the Shelley household for books and pamphlets on Ireland. Mrs Masons stories of the United Irishmen and the rebellion of 1798 enrich the diaries of Claire and Mary,[57] and her influence on the household can be seen in a letter from Mary to Marianne Hunt in which she complains that England had been turned into 'Castlereagh land or New Land Castlereagh – heaven defend me from being a Castlereaghish woman'.[58] The Mason's were a source of stability and refuge in Shelley's life. Mrs Mason's affection for Claire Clairmont was evident, particularly at the time of the troubled relations between Claire and the Shelleys, and she came to look on Claire as something of a grown-up daughter. She introduced them to the Irish language, the poetry of Gaelic Ireland[59] and provided them with books and information on Ireland's history and topography.[60] Shelley's poem *The Sensitive Plant* is traditionally associated with Mrs Mason:

A Lady, The wonder of her kind,
Whose form was upborne by a lovely mind.[61]

NOTES

1   F Darvall, *Popular Disturbances and Public Order in Regency England,* (London, 1934), p5.

2   E P Thompson, *The Making of the English Working Class,* op cit, p587.

3   Ibid, p554.

4   F L Jones, op cit, p304.

5   *Hansard,* (London, 1812), no. XXII, p651.

6   See K Cameron and D Reiman, (eds), *Shelley and his Circle, 1773-1822* (Massachusetts, 1961), vol 3, p309.

7   F L Jones, op cit, p281.

8   R Holmes, *The Pursuit,* op cit, p131.

9   F L Jones, op cit, p281.

10   M Scrivener, *Radical Shelley* (New Jersey, 1982), p51.

11   *Poetical Works of Shelley*, op cit, lines 8-11, p877.

12   W Rossetti, 'Shelley in 1812-13', *Fortnightly Review* (London, 1871), no IX, January 1871, p68.

13   R Holmes, op cit, p149.

14   F L Jones, op cit, p379.

15   *Dowden Papers*, Trinity College Dublin, no 3,014.

16   E Dowden, op cit, p392.

17   T J Hogg, op cit, p392.

18   F L Jones, op cit, p326.

19   P B Shelley, *The Esdaile Notebook*, op cit.

20   W MacNevin, *Pieces of Irish History* (New York, 1807). This is an expanded version of a *Memoir* presented to the government in 1798 in return for immunity from execution for its authors. They represented the most conservative elements within the United Irishmen who were keen to distance themselves from the military wing of the movement.

21   F L Jones, op cit, p324.

22   Ibid, p321.

23   Ibid, p321.

24   Ibid, p321.

25   Ibid, p321.

26   Ibid, p324.

27   T J Hogg, op cit, pp368-69.

28   F L Jones, op cit, p357.

29   Ibid, p355.

30   H Dowling, 'The Attack at Tanyrallt', *Shelley Memorial Association Bulletin*, no XII, 1961, pp28-36.

31   T Moore, *Corruption and Intolerance* (London, 1808), pv.

32   Probably Ross Island, which is joined to the mainland by a causeway. The most likely house according to the 1842 survey was either Ross Cottage or the Gate Lodge of Ross Castle.

33   F L Jones, op cit, 2, p6.

34   T J Hogg, op cit, p410.

35   *Poetical Works of Shelley,* 'Queen Mab', op cit, p762.

36   Ibid, verse IX, lines 164-70, op cit, p762.

37   F L Jones, op cit, p360.

38   Ibid, p367.

39   The *Theological Inquirer* – seven numbers were issued in London between March and September 1815. The first and second issues printed Shelley's *A Refutation of Deism* and an extended review of *Queen Mab.*

40   E S Boas, 'Erasmus Perkins and Shelley', *Modern Language Notes,* LXXX, 1955.

41   F L Jones, op cit, p280.

42   The *Dublin Evening Post,* 17 November 1842.

43   *State Papers,* 'Ireland 1812, August - December', Public Records Office, London. See also D F MacCarthy, *Shelley's Early Life,* op cit, pp306-7.

44   F L Jones, op cit, p372.

45   Ibid, p378.

46   Shelley drew up a mailing list of 42 people, of these, three were Irishmen: (1) *John Philpot Curran* (2) *George Ensor* (1769-1843), well known Anglo-lrish radical, whose writings Shelley was familiar with, and which were aimed at reforming British rule in Ireland, (3) *William Bruce* (1757-1841), a supporter of the Irish Volunteers in the 1780s, he opposed the rising in 1798 to the extent of enlisting in the government militia against the United Irishmen. Bruce was a leading member of the Unitarians in Ireland, which may explain Shelleys' interest. There were no Irish Catholics or any of the Irish radicals he had worked with in 1812 on the list.

47   *Poetical Works of Shelley,* 'Alastor', op cit, lines 75-77, p14.

48   P Foot, op cit, p209.

49   See R Holmes, op cit, p510.

50   Amelia Curran's (1775-1847) portrait of Claire is in Newstead Abbey in Nottingham, England, and that of William in the Pforzheimer Collection in the New York Public Library. Mary's portrait was acquired by Trelawny and disappeared after his death. Amelia's copy of a painting by Murillo (*Madonna*) was presented to Blackrock College, Dublin. According to the editors of Mary Shelley's *Journals* a miniature of Mary is held in a private Irish collection, though Miranda Seymour, *Mary Shelley* (London, 2000) believes that it may be of Mary, Shelley's sister, (p567). See J H Pollock's novel *The Moth and the Star* (Dublin, 1937) for a fictional account of an imagined romance between Shelley and Amelia Curran.

51   F L Jones, op cit, 2, p179.

52   The authorship by Lady Mount Cashell of three pamphlets in the Joly collection in the National Library in Dublin has been open to question, but Janet Todd, in her new book on Lady Mount Cashell, *Rebels in the Family: Ireland 1798*, (London, 2003) provides compelling evidence that Lady Mount Cashell was in fact the author. (1) *A few words in Favour of Ireland by way of Reply to a pamphlet called 'an Impartial View of the causes Leading this county to the necessity of a Union by No Lawyer'*, (Dublin, 1799); (2) *Reply to a Ministerial Pamphlet, entitled 'Considerations upon the state of Public Affairs in the year 1799'*, (Dublin, 1799); (3) *A Hint to the inhabitants of Ireland by a native*, (Dublin, 1800).

53   John Taaffe (1787-1862) was born in County Louth in Ireland and settled in Pisa in 1816. The best published account of Taaffe's life is that given by C L Cline in *Byron, Shelley and their Pisan Circle* (London, 1952).

54   J Taaffe, *Comment on Dante* (London, 1822).

55   See P Feldman and D Scott-Kilvert (eds), *The Journals of Mary W Shelley* (Oxford, 1987), 28/29 January 1820, p307, 20 February 1820, p309.

56   E McAleer, *The Sensitive Plant* (North Carolina, 1958), p138.

57   M Stocking (ed), *The Journals of Claire Clairmont* (Boston, 1968), 15 March 1820, pp119-178; M Shelley, *Journals*, vol 1, pp307-310.

58   B Bennett, (ed), *The Letters of Mary W Shelley* (Baltimore, 1980), 24 February 1820, vol 1, p135.

59   C Clairmont, *Journals*, 20 September 1820, pp173-174. Claire records borrowing Charles Vallancey, *A Grammar of the Iberno-Celtic or Irish Language* (Dublin, 1773), and Charlotte Brooke, *Reliques of Irish Poetry* (Dublin, 1789). Charlotte Brooke's (1740-1793) *Reliques* is a translation of 16 Irish poems, together with the originals and extensive background information. Her book established a genuinely Irish poetic tradition and answered the Ossianic fabrications of Macpherson in Scotland.

60   Claire Clairmont, *Journals*, 17 August 1820, p100. 'Begin Earl of Castlehaven's Memoirs'. James Touchet, *The Memoirs of James Lord Audley, Earl of Castleraven*, (London, 1680).

61   *Poetical Works of Shelley*, 'The Sensitive Plant', part 2, op cit, lines 5-6, p589.

CHAPTER EIGHT

The Two Souls of Ireland

> The Hour of Weak delusion's past
> The empty dream has flown:
> Our truest hope, we find at last,
> Is in ourselves alone.[1]

THE Anglo-Irish Ascendancy, through their control of Trinity College, the Royal Irish Academy and the Royal Dublin Society, dominated Irish cultural life at the beginning of the 19th century. Such a class was fearful of all artistic or political innovation. Therefore neoclassicism continued to be fashionable long after it was abandoned in England. An Irish Romantic literary tradition was slow to develop and had not the same cohesion as that in England. It developed in opposition to the status quo and was preoccupied almost by definition with republicanism and nationalism. It was 'intensely and undisguisedly political,'[2] even if some were political only by implication. In its first flowering it was preoccupied with the ruined and ancient landscape that gave witness to a dignified pre-conquest culture, as did the poetry and music of the old Gaelic society. Sydney Owenson, who was transformed into Lady Morgan after her marriage in 1812, was its most popular exponent. In *The Wild Irish Girl* (1806), a romantic and political fable set in an unknown year in the late 1700's, she introduced a different kind of Ireland to English readers, with a vision of a religiously and politically united Ireland. But even a liberal Whig such as Owenson felt it was still too dangerous to deal directly with the events surrounding the rebellion of 1798.

A distinct Irish literary culture in the English language developed behind the banner of the Catholic Association. This was a tradition that had to fight for its place in a debate on culture, identity and politics that continues to this day. Edna Longley in Belfast has long been opposed to the 'symptomatic yoking of "Irish literature" to nationalism'[3] by the likes of Seamus Deane and Brian Friel. She puts the case for a more inclusive literature, which takes account of the Protestant tradition. But in the early 1800s it was writers who espoused a nationalist culture who were the outsiders. Shelley's reputation in Ireland reflected the same factionalism that dominated politics – he was hated by the Protestant Ascendancy, tolerated by the Irish Whigs and championed by the Nationalists.

Shelley first came to attention in the *Dublin Magazine* in 1820, two years before his death. It accused Lord Byron of writing to 'poison the springs of social love and undermine the foundations of order and religion', and added:

> I need not waste time upon such men as Shelley, men who are too openly virulent to be dangerous; the wolf [Shelley] may be repelled from the fold while the serpent [Byron] glides in unsuspected and unnoticed.[4]

This was but a prelude to an attack of great length in the November issue:

> Now the fact is we think unfavourably of Mr Shelley; we think his talents unworthy devoted to evil purposes… It does not strike us as a task by any means difficult to colour the cold speculations of Godwin with the language of poetry…with Shelley atheism is a principle. We cannot of course consent to make our pages

instrumental in the circulation of the passages which justify these remarks.[5]

The article concluded with the safe lyrical poems, *The Cloud* and *To a Skylark,* and therefore, despite its hatred of Shelley, the *Dublin Magazine* had the distinction of being the first to publish his poetry in Ireland.

A minor renaissance in the 1830s saw an attempt by the more liberal sections of the establishment, on the back of a reforming British government, to reconcile political unionism with cultural nationalism. Writers from the unionist tradition now projected an image of a dignified Irishman who was not only very human but also very British. In this new climate the *National Magazine* felt the time had come for a review of Shelley's poetry freed from 'religious antipathy and personal offence' – 'we should forgive his madness' and 'appreciate his poetry'.[6] But the *Christian Examiner and Church of Ireland Gazette* was not in a forgiving mood. The official voice of the Protestant Ascendancy expressed the view 'of all who think seriously', that the works of Shelley the writer of 'that awful specimen of blasphemy, *Queen Mab*…should follow him to the tomb'.[7]

Despite the political gains of the 1830s a new generation of Irish nationalists had grown tired of O'Connell's compromises with the British Whig establishment. The Young Irelanders under the leadership of Thomas Davis espoused a militant policy of 'ourselves alone'. They set about transforming the Irish nation from 'a mob' dependent on the leadership and talents of O'Connell to one that relied on their own conscious activity to achieve dignity and individuality as Irish men and women. They attempted a definition of Irishness that was both cultural and political by a systematic process of education, based on popular and accessible publications. Their newspaper, the *Nation,* launched in 1842, was distributed through a network of clubs, reading rooms and societies based on the working class and artisans in the towns and country. The impact was astounding – by 1843 the circulation was 10,000, with an audience of over a quarter of a million, exemplified by the famous old print of the village labourers crowded around the cottage fireside to hear the *Nation* read out to them. They tried to infuse the non-sectarian spirit of 1798 into the 1840s. Ireland's rich and glorious past, or at least that part of it, which predated the religious battles of the 16th century, was appropriated to present a vision of a dignified and united Irish nation.

In November 1842 the *Dublin Evening Post*, which had championed Shelley's cause in 1812, reviewed a new edition of *Shelley's Works*. By now, the *Post* had settled down to pursue what would later be called a 'Castle Catholic' policy, under the editorship of F W Conway, who as MacCarthy revealed was in the pay of Dublin Castle. Conway used the review to attack Shelley's politics and the reputation of John Lawless:

> Shelley was an excellent kindly man; but he was what in Ireland we should call cracked. We have gotten a pamphlet of his written thirty years ago in this city – at once evidence of high generosity and of the most lamentable wildness and imbecility.[8]

The Young Irelanders could not let this pass and in a lengthy correspondence[9] Denis Florence MacCarthy and an unknown writing under the name of E V came to Shelley's defence. MacCarthy referred to the silence concerning Shelley's intervention in Irish politics:

> In reading all the scattered notices of Shelley, which the periodical literature of the last twenty years contains, I have been frequently struck with surprise at the total silence which all writers, friends and foe have observed on this point.[10]

And he went on to claim Shelley as a friend and supporter of the Irish people:

> I trust that the people of this country to whom was offered if not 'the first heir of his invention', at least the first production of his reasoning powers applied to political subjects will not be backward in raising a monument within their hearts, more endurable than marble or brass to the memory of that man.[11]

In an extended article over two issues of the *Nation* in 1845, MacCarthy presented the first rounded account of Shelley's early life. He accepted Shelley as a political writer, and his description of Shelley's understanding of the role of the poet was almost a model for the literary ambitions of the *Nation* itself:

> The poet…should be a teacher – he should impart knowledge to the ignorant, consolation to the afflicted, hope to the weary, in him the oppressed, that is nine-tenths of the human race should find their most powerful champion, and the oppressor his most invincible foe.[12]

While MacCarthy's own poetry has not worn to well,[13] he was not one to crudely apply political measuring rods to literature. For MacCarthy, poetry had to work on its own terms: poetic vision had to originate from within the poem rather than being dictated by some external political expediency. The first article was almost exclusively about Shelley's early life and ideas with long extracts from *The Address to the Irish People.* He concluded by saying that in the second instalment 'we shall present him to our readers in the still higher character of a poet'. A full page was given over to an assessment of his poetry with long quotations from his poems. This was the genesis of MacCarthy's biography, *Shelley's Early Life*, which was published in 1872, and laid the foundation for modern interpretations of Shelley's early life and politics.

MacCarthy did not have access to all the relevant Shelley material. The Shelley family stood sentinel over his reputation and took exception to almost every friend who ventured to record the Shelley they had known. The family had come to cherish a very definite and sanitised version of his life, which was by no means based on fact. As guardians of the Shelley archive, they were in a position to mould the Shelley legend to their own advantage. In 1883 Edward Dowden[14] was approached by the family to write the official life of Shelley.[15] He was given access to the family papers, but in return he was expected to deliver the official interpretation. A Protestant and professor of English at Trinity College Dublin, he was the essential Irish Victorian whose intellectual life was predominantly focused on English literary matters, with no understanding or sympathy for Irish nationalism or literature. Dowden was well chosen and a safe pair of hands, who duly turned in a perfumed performance. It was slated by Matthew Arnold, and Mark Twain, in his essay *In Defence of Harriet Shelley*, blasted it as 'a literary cakewalk',[16] much to the discomfort of Dowden. His innate conservatism, allied to the pressure from the Shelley family, led Dowden into compromise and evasion. Eight years earlier, in his essay on Walt Whitman, *The Poetry of Democracy*,[17] he allowed a far greater role for politics and ideas than he would later concede to Shelley. And in 1888, in a commentary on a manuscript copy of Shelley's *Philosophical View of Reform*,[18] his concluding paragraph, where he speculates on what would have happened if Shelley had lived, could easily serve as a valediction that Shelley would have been proud of:

> I do not think Shelley would have looked forth from his window disillusioned. A series of great events would probably have engaged his interest and aroused his imaginative ardour; first the liberation of Greece, then the emancipation of Catholics in Ireland, then the French Revolution of 1830, then the Reform Bill of 1832; and in 1832 Shelley would have reached his fortieth year, and his character would have gained the enduring ardour of manhood.[19]

The great revival of interest in Irish culture spans most of the 19th century. By the 1880s the debate on cultural identity became central to the argument for self determination. Ironically, the Irish literary renaissance that was to ally itself to a militant republican separatism at the beginning of the 20th century had its origins in Trinity College Dublin, the intellectual heart of the Protestant Ascendancy. Standish O'Grady, a radical Tory, published his *History of Ireland: Heroic Period* in 1878. His reworking of the Irish sagas is widely accepted as providing Yeats and the early revival movement with its store of imaginative material:

> Know, that I would accounted be
> True brother of a company
> That sang, to sweeten Ireland's wrong,
> Ballad and story, rann and song;[20]

O'Grady, in a challenge to the backwardness and isolation of the Protestant Ascendancy, published Shelley's *Refutation of Deism* in 1875. He presented it to the 'Youth of Ireland' as an antidote to the narrowness of Trinity College:

There is always something which we prefer to truth. Trinity College, of whose large and generous spirit we are all so proud, plainly postpones the interest of truth to those of religion. The course of philosophical study prescribed there, includes the best written defences of Theism and of Christianity, but does not contain a single hostile work.[21]

By the last quarter of the century the Protestant establishment had become a near irrelevancy in the unfolding debate on culture and politics. Undaunted, the sectarian and reactionary *Dublin University Magazine*, in what was to be almost a final gesture, continued the assault on Shelley, 'Whose writings are calculated to injure the youthful mind so deeply'.[22] From now on an assertive and confident Catholic church would arbitrate on what was morally acceptable in literature and art. For the Young Irelanders, Shelley's attack on religion had not been an issue. MacCarthy excused it as an 'unconscious libel on the religion of the people he addressed'.[23] But when the Catholic poet Francis Thompson, at the suggestion of Bishop Vaughan, submitted his essay on Shelley to the Catholic-controlled *Dublin Review* in 1889, it was censored and did not appear until after his death in 1908. Thompson's essay is a dewy-eyed piece asking us to 'peep over the wild mask of revolutionary metaphysics, and see the winsome face of the child'.[24] This harmless piece of nonsense did not escape the censure of Father George O'Neill, who took Thompson to task with Jesuitical preciseness in the *New Ireland Review*. He quoted Thompson as saying that there are 'but three passages to which exception can be taken' and replied:

Surely there are whole works to which exception can be taken… I have taken seriously the imperfection of substance veiled in the splendours of its imagery…the saintly and impulsive Father Faber once threw his edition of Shelley into the fire and never regretted it… Is it not a fact that the atheistic press-propagandism of our day had made itself the means of circulating *Queen Mab* by tens of thousands at the lowest popular price.[25]

Shelley would not be forgiven for his atheism by a church striving to impose a narrow sectarian morality on the emerging nationalist movement. Paradoxically, by the end of the 19th century, and for different reasons, the orthodox Protestant and Catholic tradition had arrived at a similar assessment of Shelley.

As Ireland moved towards independence, the literary revival played a central role in defining the growing sense of Irish identity. Many insisted that in Ireland there were two traditions, one Irish, one English, which could never be reconciled, and too much energy was wasted on promoting Anglo-Irish literary concerns. The time had come for Gaelic Ireland to assert itself. The issues surrounding Shelley and his poetry became submerged in that debate. Shelley disappeared from view in the literary controversies of the emerging state. From that time on his influence would operate at a more personal level.

In 1885 a meeting took place in Dublin between an ageing revolutionary and a young poet that changed the course of Irish literature. The revolutionary was John O'Leary, the former editor of the Fenian newspaper the *Irish People*, who in 1865 was sentenced to five years imprisonment and exiled for a further 15. The poet was William Butler Yeats, then an unknown 20 year old:

> The Irish Renaissance could have occurred without Yeats or
> O'Leary, but it would have been a different and poorer movement if
> they had not met… It found the writer in Yeats and the thinker in
> O'Leary.[26]

O'Leary had little time for the propagandist poetry of the Young Irelanders. He believed that Irish poetry should purge itself of politics and create a literature 'so essentially Irish, so reflective of the national imagination, that it would prepare the country spiritually for the coming day of political liberation'.[27] This was the task that Yeats set himself.

Like Shelley, Yeats hated didactic poetry, and what he called Shelley's 'vision of the divine order' was central to his role in the creation of a distinctive Irish literature. His very concept of a poet and of poetry was based on Shelley, and when he wrote that 'Shelley shaped my life'[28] he did not exaggerate. As a young man he imitated Shelley's style, and Shelley's theme of 'intellectual beauty' dominates his early work.

Shelley's astonishing influence is best illustrated in Yeats's essay, whose very title, *The Philosophy of Shelley's Poetry,*[29] reflected his attempt to uncover what he called 'the system of belief that lay behind the poems'.[30] Yeats wanted to be not only a great lyrical poet in the image of Shelley, but also an Irish Nationalist in an age of revolution. He tried to express himself 'by that sort of thought that leads straight to action'.[31] When he attempted to reconcile these two positions, he cited Shelley's theoretical *Defence of Poetry,* but not Shelley's career as a political activist. Nor did he proclaim Shelley's revolutionary activity in Dublin in 1812, or his Irish pamphlets or poems. Yeats ignored Shelley's attempt to create a unity between literary theory and political practice. Instead he looked to magical symbols and the classical past to locate the meaning in Shelley's poetry. After 1903, Yeats moved from an idealised view of the world to one that was more engaged with social and political reality. The more he celebrated Shelley as the representative of the spiritual world of 'intellectual beauty', the more his enthusiasm for Shelley declined. In order to remake himself and his poetry he had to repudiate his earlier work and the model on which it was based. But, in rejecting the one sided and unreal version of Shelley that he had created in favour of the reality of pre-revolutionary Ireland, he also retreated from the internationalism and the political insights that permeate Shelley's work. Having made Shelley the poet of an idealised world, there could be no place for the interventionist poetry of *The Mask of Anarchy* or *Swellfoot the Tyrant.* This left him with a distorted view of Shelley's world:

> Had he formed his style on, say, *The Mask of Anarchy* instead of *Alastor* or *Prometheus Unbound,* Yeats need not have broken with his predecessor; but in proving Shelley more than 'a crude revolutionist' Yeats had proved him something less as well.[32]

Yeats never recovered his early enthusiasm for Shelley, yet equally he never wavered in his appreciation of him as a visionary poet.[33]

Attitudes to Shelley were seldom formed on the basis of his poetry alone. A good case can be made for the proposition 'that the intellectual and aesthetic history of the Victorians could be written in terms of their response to Shelley'.[34] Therefore we should not be surprised at the influence of Shelley on the generation of Irish writers and activists who grew up during the literary revival and the political upheavals of the late 19th and early 20th century. George Moore, a painter and writer, whose reputation today is less than it should be,[35] was obsessed in his early life with Shelley. It was Shelley who led him into atheism: 'It pleased me to read *Queen Mab* and *Cain*, amid the priests and ignorance of a hateful Roman Catholic College'.[36]

In the works of James Joyce, Irish history is not so much described as taken for granted. However, Joyce could find no inspiration in a literature that looked for its theme and subject to a legendary Irish past. Joyce lived Irish history in a way that threatened to paralyse his very soul. He escaped by dedicating his life to art. In Shelley's *Defence of Poetry* Joyce found a role model for the writer's place in society. Timothy Webb draws attention to this passage from *Stephen Hero*, which mirrors Shelley's emphasis on the value of poetry in a materialistic age:

> Every age must look for its sanction to its poets and philosophers. The poet is the intense centre of the life of his age to which he stands in a relation than which none can be more vital. He alone is capable of absorbing in himself the life that surrounds him and of flinging it abroad again amid planetary music.[37]

All his works are littered with direct and indirect references to Shelley. In *Ulysses*, Joyce, like Shelley, keeps many strands of allegory running simultaneously. Leopold Bloom is Ulysses, but he is also cast in the role of Prometheus from Shelley's *Prometheus Unbound*. In the Scylla and Charybdis episode of *Ulysses* Joyce explores the role of art:

> The supreme question about a work of art is out of how deep a life does it spring. The painting of Gustave Moreau is the painting of ideas. The deepest poetry of Shelley, the words of Hamlet bring our mind into contact with the eternal wisdom, Plato's world of ideas. All the rest is the speculation of schoolboys.[38]

But there is little else to suggest that Joyce was either impressed by or even aware of the intellectual or political content of Shelley's poetry. Timothy Webb concludes that what Joyce valued most in Shelley was:

> ...neither the symbolic universe which Yeats charted with such

intuitive sympathy nor the philosophical subtlety and intellectual animation…the main emphasis in Joyce's response falls unequivocally on the music of the verse, the 'rhythms of extraordinary beauty' which Shelley shares with Mangan.[39]

Joyce's emphasis on Shelley as essentially the inspired singer of lyrics reflected the view of his English tutor at University College Dublin, Father George O'Neill. It was O'Neill who had criticised Francis Thompson in the *New Ireland Review* for his tolerance of Shelley's atheism, though he admired the lyrical quality of Shelley's poetry. Joyce was the great modernist, but the Romantic tradition or at least that element of it represented by Shelley, Keats and Byron flows through his work like an undercurrent, at a submerged but important level, particularly in its music and rhythm. This explains why *Ulysses* and *Finnegans Wake* work so well when read aloud. Joyce's exile in Italy, following in the footsteps of Shelley, was largely the inspiration for his play *Exiles,* and his visit to Shelley's grave in Rome leads directly to his short story *The Dead.*

Bernard Shaw and Oscar Wilde came from a different Irish tradition, one that focused primarily on the London stage. Wilde had an ambivalent attitude to Shelley. At one time he considered him 'merely a boy's poet'.[40] Yet his play *The Cardinal of Avignon,* is based on Shelley's drama *The Cenci,* and in his poem *The Garden of Eros* he hailed Keats and Shelley (the silver voice), as the torchbearers of intellectual life in an age of materialism:

Nay, When Keats died the muse still had left
One silver voice to sing his threnody.[41]

Bernard Shaw was in one sense the perfect Shelleyan: 'I read him, prose and verse from beginning to end'. As a young man in Ireland, under the influence of Shelley, he became a committed atheist. Therefore, imagine his surprise on finding that the Shelley Society in London represented the poet as 'a Church of England country gentleman whose pastime was writing sermons in verse'.[42] So shocking was Shaw's announcement at a society meeting that, like Shelley he was 'a socialist, an atheist, and a vegetarian' that two ladies immediately resigned. Shaw was no trimmer or respecter of sensibilities, like Shelley, he told the truth and made no attempt to hide the fact that he wrote for a purpose. Through his plays he introduced the realism of Ibsen to English audiences. He exposed the contradiction between the false morality of the ruling class and the reality of the world on which it was based. His work is full of Shelleyan characters – Marchbanks in *Candida,* the plot of *Mrs Warrens Profession,* a blend of Shelley's *The Cenci* and Pinero's *The Second Mrs Tanqueray.* In his essay *Shaming the Devil,* about Shelley, he poked fun at the country gentlemen who attended a meeting at Horsham in Sussex to celebrate the centenary of Shelley's birth in 1892:

> On all sides there went up the cry, 'We want our great Shelley, our darling Shelley, our best, noblest, highest of poets. We will not have it said that he was a Leveller, an Atheist, a foe of marriage, an advocate of incest'.[43]

He recounts how, that same evening, he attended a meeting in the East End of London,

that 'consisted for the most part of working men who took Shelley quite seriously' and was addressed by Mr G W Foote of the National Secular Society:

> Finally Mr Foote recited *Men of England,* which brought the meeting to an end amid thunders of applause. What would have happened had anyone recited it at Horsham is more than I can guess. Possibly the police would have been sent for.[44]

Almost alone in literary circles, Shaw defended the tradition of a radical Shelley in late Victorian England. But his defence is almost too one-sided! What is missing is the music and the lyricism. Shelley's poetry is sometimes reduced to economics and politics, just as in his Fabian lectures he was fond of suggesting that Keats in *Isabella* had condensed the opening chapter of Marx's *Capital* to a single stanza.

The Dublin that Sean O'Casey grew up in was not unlike the Dublin that Shelley had experienced in 1812. Nearly one third of the people lived in filth, ignorance and fear, an 'inferno of discontent' that left deep scars on the body and mind of the young O'Casey. There are many parallels between Shelley and O'Casey – their great lyrical quality, the refusal to compromise their art for the sake of political expediency, and their faith in the possibility of a better and more fulfilled life for all humanity. And not least was the failure of their friends and supporters to take their political commitment seriously. O'Casey's allies in America have spent the last 50 years trying to transform the humanism of his 'Red Star' into the 'Star of Bethlehem'.

James Larkin, who came to Dublin in 1907 on a 'divine mission of discontent', inspired O'Casey to use words as weapons in the fight against poverty and oppression. But, it was Shelley and Keats, Shakespeare and Dickens who prepared him for the task. O'Casey worked as a labourer with pick and shovel, and every week a few shillings were put aside to buy the books that meant so much to the self educated workingman of his time. O'Casey would sit down, with his copy of *Prometheus Unbound* and his *Chamber's Dictionary* side by side, and work his way through each verse until he understood it completely. He never for a moment hid his politics and he battled against the world with what he did best – writing plays, with the same fire that 'blazed within Shelley'. Whenever O'Casey wrote about socialism it was more likely that he would call on the idealism of Whitman or the compassion of Shelley than the works of Marx or Lenin. When he learned in the 1950s that the McCarthyite's in America had listed him as a subversive writer he replied:

> I am a subversive writer; always have been, and I hope, always will
> be. I take my place with the other subversive writers – Dickens,
> Milton, Shelley, Byron, Joyce, Shaw, and a shining host of others.[45]

O'Casey, though a lifelong supporter, never joined the Communist Party. His socialism was imbued with too much compassion and understanding to have survived the straitjacket of Communist Party dogma during the Stalinist era:

> I am a Shelleyan Communist, and a Dickensian one, and a Byronic
> one, and a Miltonic one, and a Whitmanian one, and like all those
> who thought big and beautifully, and who cared for others, as I am
> a Marxian one, too.[46]

O'Casey's work is steeped in the classical and romantic tradition from which he borrowed extensively, though at an unobtrusive level, and reproduced in a modern vernacular idiom. Right at the start of his career O'Casey identified himself with the 'champion' of Shelley's *Prometheus Unbound*, forever battling against oppression. His first Dublin play, *The Shadow of a Gunman,* is framed around a line from *Prometheus Unbound*, 'Ah me! alas, pain, pain ever, for ever',[47] and Jim Larkin, the champion of the Dublin working class, becomes 'Prometheus Hibernica' in O'Casey's autobiography. But more than anything it was Shelley's lyrical quality that became part of his own imagination and dominates his work. He gave a voice to the poor and the dispossessed in a way that nobody had done before. In *Juno and the Paycock*, Juno's lament for her dead son, executed as a traitor in the civil war, has a music and lyricism of extraordinary beauty:

> What was the pain I suffered, Johnny, bringing you into the world to carry you to the cradle to the pains I'll suffer carryin' you out o' the world to bring you to your grave! Mother o' God, Mother o' God, have pity on us all! Sacred Heart o' Jesus, take away our hearts o' stone, and give us hearts o' flesh! Take away this murdherin' hate, an' give us Thine own eternal love![48]

Much has been said of the beauty of these lines, which are reminiscent of Shelley's *Adonais*:

> Where wert thou, mighty mother, when he lay
> When thy Son lay, pierced by the shaft which flies
> In darkness?[49]

After O'Casey's death in 1964 his ashes were scattered beside the Shelley rose bed in the Garden of Remembrance at Golders Green Crematorium in London, a suitable place for one who loved and read Shelley all his life.

When James Larkin died in 1947, O'Casey's tribute appeared in the *Irish Times:* 'He fought for the loaf of bread as no man had ever fought; but, with the loaf of bread, he also brought the flask of wine and the book of verse'.[50] Larkin had that rare ability to move the heart of the masses. He spoke to the slum dweller as a human being, 'degraded, yet capable of nobility, capable even of music and literature'.[51] It was Shelley and Keats, Shakespeare and Omar Khayyam who infused his speeches with such power and eloquence. In the first issue of the *Irish Worker,*

Larkin declared, in a phrase taken almost directly from Wordsworth, that 'the *Irish Worker* will be a lamp to guide your feet in the hours of the impending struggle'.[52] In its 189 issues, in poetry and prose of remarkable quality, the *Irish Worker* kept its promise. Jim Connell, the County Meath born author of The Red Flag, was one of many whose poems graced its pages:

Workers of Ireland, why crouch ye like cravens?
Why clutch an existence of insult and want?
Why stand to be plucked by an army of ravens
Or hoodwinked for ever by twaddle and cant?[53]

Like many self educated writers Jim Connell was borrowing from the past, in this case Shelley's *Song to the Men of England*.[54] Though it was not one of Connell's better poems, he was trying, as all the great writers did, to mediate the tradition of the past through the experience of the present, which transforms them from imitation into works of originality and creativity. Much of Larkin's great ability to find the exact phrase or sentence that could electrify the moment was derived from the fact that he had immersed himself in the great writers of the past. John de Coursy Ireland told me that 'each night if Larkin was not out at a meeting he would retire to bed at 10 o'clock with a bundle of books; Keats and Shelley were his favourite, and announce that he would be finished them by morning'.[55] Speaking in Manchester in 1913, during the great lockout by the Dublin employers led by the Catholic businessman William Martin Murphy, Larkin responded to the criticism of the strike leaders by the Catholic church. Larkin displayed great courage in speaking out against the church and in a famous speech he declared:

They cannot terrify me with hell… Better to be in Hell with Dante and Davitt than to be in Heaven with Carson or Murphy, not forgetting our good friend the Earl of Aberdeen.[56]

Only someone steeped in the tradition of Shelley could have replied in that manner. In the preface to *Prometheus Unbound* Shelley accepted that his own poetry was influenced by the study of the past: 'I am willing to confess that I have imitated… For my part I had rather be damned with Plato and Lord Bacon, than go to heaven with Paley and

Malthus'.[57]

In Daniel Corkery's play *The Labour Leader,* Jim Larkin is the model for Davna, the strike leader. One of the strikers, Tim Murphy, mocks the suggestion that Davna be given a secretary:

And if ye give him a secretary his job will be to cut Davna off when he's giving us the history of Ireland in the tenth century, or giving us Shelley: 'Rise like lions after slumber'; 'Shake your manes like thunder'; 'Ye are many, they are few': He was a great lad, that Shelley, and he only a poor sheep of an Englishman and all. And what would we know about him only for Davna? Or about the Red Flag? Or about anything at all.[58]

The official trade union movement, which scorned and despised Larkin when he was alive, put him on a pedestal when he was safely dead. His statue, arms outstretched in that classic pose, stands in O'Connell Street in Dublin, only a few yards from where Shelley lived. His epitaph, carved on that statue – 'the great only appear great because we are on our knees, let us arise' – has many origins and not least is Shelley's *The Mask of Anarchy.* He loved poetry, so it is fitting that a poet should raise up a monument in the name of the poor and the dispossessed for whom 'he put a loaf on the table and a flower in the vase'. Austin Clarke's *Inscription for a Headstone* opens with the line, 'What Larkin bawled to hungry crowds' and concludes:

His name endures on our holiest page,
Scrawled in a rage by Dublin's poor.[59]

What was dynamic at the turn of the century had become stifling and conservative by the 1930s. The Celtic revival had nothing to offer in terms of form or content to a world heading towards the abyss. Even Yeats admitted as early as 1913 that:

Romantic Ireland's dead and gone
It's with O'Leary in the grave.[60]

Louis MacNeice acknowledged that a writer in the 20th century 'must have more of Shelley in him than of Spencer, or Herbert or Bunyan'.[61] The Irish literary world had become too internalised, too cut off from European trends, with far too little of Shelley in it. What outside influences there were, came from left intellectuals in Britain grouped around popular front organisations such as The Left Book Club. Edna Longley describes them as dispatching 'literary-political food-parcels' to the starved intellectuals in Ireland. They had plenty of content, but little substance. The 'well brought-up young men who discovered that people work in factories and mines, and wrote poems calling them Comrades from a distance',[62] had little to offer the likes of Sean O'Faolain or Kate O'Brien who were striving to create a literature relevant to their time and place. Kate O'Brien's characters struggle with passions and impulses at war with the world around them. O'Brien took the title *As Music and Splendour* and the theme from Shelley's *When the Lamp is Shattered* for her last novel.[63]

A few managed to reach out beyond the orthodoxies on offer – Brian Coffey, Louis MacNeice – as did Charlie Donnelly,[64] who died fighting in the Spanish Civil War at the age of 22. His work is little known, except for his dying words – 'even the olives are bleeding', which, for many, summarised the heartache and despair of fascism's victory in Spain. His small body of poems is a testament to his potential, and can stand comparison with the finest of that decade. He knew and loved the work of Keats and Shelley, Yeats and Joyce, and also, Rimbaud and Baudelaire. The poets influenced his politics, and his politics shaped his poetry. The tension between the public and private in poetry was intensified by the political and social crisis of the 1930s. The pressure 'to take sides' led many into propaganda and compromise. Donnelly was a dedicated member of the Irish Communist Party and it is to his credit that he never allowed his poetry to be dictated or compromised by party demands. His poetry is a fusion of the personal and the political. It is modern, tight and sparse in style, but with all the commitment, precision and passion of Shelley and Keats:

Your flag is public over granite. Gulls fly above it.
Whatever the issue of the battle is, your memory
Is public, for them to pull away with crooked hands,
Moist eyes. And village reputations will be built on
Inaccurate accounts of your campaign. Your name for orators,

Figure stone-struck beneath damp Dublin sky.[65]

In post-war Ireland, plagued by economic depression, unemployment and emigration, there was no place for a poetry that was outspoken, committed and European in its outlook. A narrow censorious morality forced the best to flee abroad and it was left to Patrick Kavanagh to speak for the rest:

Their intellectual life consisted in reading

Reynolds's News or the *Sunday Dispatch*

With sometimes an old almanac brought down from the ceiling

Or a school reader brown with the droppings of the thatch.[66]

It was not until the 1960s that a new generation, inspired by the struggles for freedom at home and abroad, accepted, as Michael Hartnet put it, that 'the act of poetry is a rebel act',[67] Both Desmond Egan and Michael Hartnet appropriated Shelley's *Ozymandias* to make powerful statements about imperialism and oppression. [68]

Shelley's great expression of his art, *A Defence of Poetry,* written in 1821, explored the effect of poetry upon society. He wrote it in response to Peacock's [69] assertion that poetry had become obsolescent, but in reality it is a summary of his views formulated over the years in his political pamphlets. It ends with the well known line, 'Poets are the unacknowledged legislators of the world'.[70] Shelley's concept of the role and function of poetry has altered over time. Of necessity it has been redefined according to new circumstances. But the core and spirit of his work is still valid and speaks to us today if we care to listen. Seamus Heaney, who set out his own values in *The Government of the Tongue* in 1988, writes within that tradition:

In one sense the efficacy of poetry is nil – no lyric ever stopped a tank. In another sense, it is unlimited. It is like the writing in the sand in the face of which accusers and accused are left speechless and renewed.[71]

This sense of purpose finds affirmation in Heaney's poem *The Unacknowledged Legislator's Dream,* which reaches back to Shelley's *A Defence of Poetry* and the preface to *Queen Mab* for reference points that connect the past with the present:

Archimedes thought he could move the world if he could
find the right place to position his lever. Billy Hunter
said Tarzan shook the world when he jumped down out of a tree.
I sink my crowbar in a chink I know under the masonry
of state and statute, I swing on a creeper of secrets into the Bastille.
My wronged people cheer from their cages. The guard-
dogs are unmuzzled, a soldier pivots a muzzle at
the butt of my ear, I am stood blindfolded with my hands
above my head until I seem to be swinging from a strappado.

The commandant motions me to be seated.
'I am honoured to add a poet to our list'. He is
amused and genuine. 'You'll be safer here, anyhow'.

In the cell, I wedge myself with outstretched arms
in the corner and heave, I jump on the concrete flags to
test them. Were those your eyes just now at the hatch?[72]

In the last decades of the 20th century Shelley's inspiration, in the
work of Seamus Heaney, Desmond Egan and many others became for a
while, an epitaph to the past and a monument to the future.

NOTES

1   J O'Hagan, 'Ourselves Alone', *Songs and Ballads of Young Ireland* (London, 1896), verse 2, lines 13-16, p37.

2   T Dunne, 'Haunted by History: Irish Romantic Writing 1800-1850', in R Porter and M Teich (eds), *Romanticism in National Context* (Cambridge, 1988), p68.

3   E Longley, *The Living Stream* (Newcastle, 1994), p23.

4   *Dublin Magazine*, vol 1, no 1, January 1820, p56.

5   Ibid, vol 2, no 11. November 1820, p393.

6   *National Magazine,* vol 1, no 3, September 1830, p285, (See also vol 2, no 9, March 1831, p278).

7   *Christian Examiner,* vol 1, no 65, November 1830, p880.

8   *Dublin Evening Post*, 17 November 1842.

9   Ibid, 17 November 1842, 24 November 1842, 6 December 1842, 8 December 1842, 13 December 1842, and 17 December 1842.

10   Ibid, 24 November 1842.

11   Ibid, 24 November 1842.

12   *Nation*, 13 December 1845, 27 December 1845.

13   MacCarthy published a dreadful poem, *Lines to the memory of Percy Bysshe Shelley*, in the *Weekly Dublin Satirist* of 10 October 1835, in which he had the humility to acknowledge in the closing two lines, 'This lowly lay of mine is made / An humble offering to thy shade'.

14   For details of Dowden see T Brown, 'Edward Dowden: Irish Victorian', in *Ireland's Literature* (Mullingar, 1988).

15   E Dowden, *The Life of Percy Bysshe Shelley,* op cit.

16   Quoted in R Smith, *The Shelley Legend* (New York, 1967), p257.

17   E Dowden, *Studies in Literature* (London, 1878), p468.

18   Leigh Hunt refused to publish it in 1820 for fear of prosecution. After his death it was suppressed by the Shelley family. Dowden had read a manuscript copy during his research and published his commentary in *Transcripts and Studies* (London, 1888). It was finally published in 1920.

19   E Dowden, *Transcripts and Studies*, op cit, p108.

20   W B Yeats, 'To Ireland in the Coming Times', *Collected Poems*, (London, 1950) lines 1-4, p56.

21   A Clive (Standish O'Grady), *Scintilla Shelleana* (Dublin, 1875), p6.

22   *Dublin University Magazine*, vol 39, June 1877, p776.

23   D F MacCarthy, op cit, p177.

24   F Thompson, *Shelley* (London, 1914), p45.

25   *New Ireland Review*, vol 31, May 1909, p169.

26   R Fallis, *The Irish Renaissance* (Dublin, 1978), pp4-5.

27   Ibid, p6.

28   W B Yeats, 'Prometheus Unbound', *Essay's by W B Yeats 1931-1936*, (Dublin, 1937), p61.

29   The first part was published in 1900. Both parts appeared in W B Yeats, *Ideas of Good and Evil* (London, 1903).

30   W B Yeats, 'The Philosophy of Shelley's Poetry', in *Essays and Introductions*, (New York, 1961), p66.

31   A Wade (ed), *The Letters of W B Yeats* (London, 1954), p379.

32   G Bornstein, *Yeats and Shelley* (Chicago, 1970), p122.

33   W B Yeats, *A Vision* (London, 1937).

34   M Allott. 'Attitudes to Shelley', in M Allott, (ed), *Essays on Shelley* (Liverpool, 1982), p9.

35   Adrian Frazier's new biography may help to restore Moore's reputation *George Moore* (New Haven, 2000). George Moore (1852-1933) was a painter and writer living in Paris who returned to Dublin in 1901 at Yeats's instigation to 'join the fight for the Irish language' and play his part in the literary revival movement.

36   G Moore, *Confessions of a Young Man* (London, 1961), p17.

37   J Joyce, *Stephen Hero* (London, 1975), p85.

38   J Joyce, *Ulysses* (London, 1968), p236.

39   T Webb, 'Planetary music' in W J McCormack and A Stead (eds), *James Joyce and Modern Culture* (London, 1982), p33.

40   Quoted in R Ellmann, *Oscar Wilde* (London, 1988), p252.

41   O Wilde, *Selected Poems* (London, 1911), p128. Threnody is an old fashioned word for a lament.

42   M Holroyd, *Bernard Shaw* (London, 1988), vol 1, p127.

43   B Shaw, 'Shaming the Devil about Shelley', in *Pen Portraits and Reviews*, (London, 1949), p241.

44   Ibid, p244.

45   D Krause, (ed), *The Letters of Sean O'Casey* (New York, 1980), vol 2, p512.

46   Ibid, p607.

47   S O'Casey, 'Shadow of a Gunman', in *Two Plays*, (London, 1925), act 1, p122.

48   S O'Casey, 'Juno and the Paycock', in *Two Plays*, op cit, act 3, p111.

49   *Poetical Works of Shelley*, op cit, verse 2, lines 10-12, p430.

50   D Krause, op cit, p442.

51   T Dorgan, 'Larkin through the Eyes of Writers', in D Nevin, (ed), *Lion of the Fold* (Dublin, 1998), p108.

52   *Irish Worker*, 27 May 1911. Wordsworth hoped that his paper *The Philanthropist*, 'Would put a lantern into each man's hand to guide him'. (See Chapter 3 p64).

53   *Irish Worker*, 15 June 1911.

54   *Poetical Works of Shelley*, op cit, p572.

55   John de Coursy Ireland, socialist and historian, lived with Larkin for a short time in 1934 and gave me this account in April 1999.

56   P Yeates, *Lockout, Dublin 1913* (Dublin, 2000), p150.

57   *Poetical Works of Shelley,* op cit, p207.

58   D Corkery, *The Labour Leader* (Dublin, 1920), act 1, p26.

59   A Clarke, 'Inscription for a Headstone', *Collected Poems* (Dublin, 1974), p202.

60   W B Yeats, 'September 1913', *Collected Poems*, op cit, lines 8-9, p120.

61   L MacNeice, *Varieties of Parable* (Cambridge, 1965), p52.

62   A Tate, '1937', quoted in J O'Connor, *Even the Olives are Bleeding* (Dublin, 1992), p43.

63   K O'Brien, *As Music and Splendour,* (London, 1958). See also A M Dalsimer, *Kate O'Brien: A critical study* (Dublin, 1990).

64   For details of Charlie Donnelly's life see J O'Connor, op cit.

65   J O'Connor , 'Poem', in *Even the Olives are Bleeding*, op cit, lines 7-12, p127.

66   P Kavanagh, 'The Great Hunger', *Selected Poems* (London, 1996), verse 10, lines 1-4, p18.

67   Quoted by B Kennelly on *RTE*, Radio 1, 23 July 2000.

68   D Egan, 'HMS Fishfingers: The Falklands' in O Komesu and M Sekine (eds), *Irish Writers and Politics,* (Gerrards Cross, 1989), p286; M Hartnet, 'Trapped in Shelley', *Collected Poems* (Methuen 2001), p195.

69   H Brett-Smith, (ed), *Peacock's Four ages of Poetry, Shelley's Defence of Poetry, Browning's Essay on Shelley* (Oxford, 1937).

70   Ibid p59.

71   S Heaney, *The Government of the Tongue* (London, 1988), p107.

72   S Heaney, 'The Unacknowledged Legislator's Dream', *North* (London, 1975), p56. In the preface to *Queen Mab* Shelley quotes Archimedes. 'Give me one firm spot on which to stand, and I will move the earth'. (*Poetical Works of Shelley,* op cit, p762).

CHAPTER NINE

A Paradise on Earth

All revolutions are interior
The displacement of spirit
By the arrival of fact.[1]

       JOHN Montague maintained that revolutions first happen in the imagination and only later are given flesh 'by the arrival of fact'. And this, in one sense, is what Shelley meant when he said that 'poets are the unacknowledged legislators of the world'.[2] Poetry, for Shelley, was not a programme of action it was 'an idealism', an imaginative picture of 'what ought to be, or might be'. His prose was much more concerned with immediate demands, what was possible or what may be. Nevertheless, there is a unity between his prose and his poetry, just as there is a continuity between his early and later work. Before he went to Ireland, poverty and oppression were abstractions. In Ireland they became a reality and that experience produced the indignation of *Queen Mab* and the commitment and anger that run through all of his best work:

Shelley himself repeatedly gives evidence that he wished not only to propose radical or ideal reforms, but also to suggest immediately attainable reforms in government. *A Proposal for Putting Reform to the Vote Throughout the Kingdom*, written in early 1817 is a link in the chain of such suggestions from the early *Address to the Irish People* to the much later and more comprehensive *Philosophical View of Reform*.[3]

He frequently returned to the imagery and ideals of his Irish pamphlets for inspiration. The influence of Godwin and the experience of the French Revolution had turned him against violence. In the *Address to the Irish People* he repeatedly spelt this out:

I agree with the Quakers so far as they disclaim violence and trust their cause solely to its own truth… If you descend to use the same weapons as your enemy, you put yourself on a level with him on that score… But appeal to the sacred principles of virtue and justice; then he is awed into nothing… Then firmly, yet quietly, resist. When one cheek is struck, turn the other to the insulting coward.[4]

In September 1819 Shelley was horrified to hear that the militia had attacked a peaceful demonstration in Manchester, killing 11 people and injuring many more. The events at Peterloo (as it became known) spurred Shelley into the most creative months of his life – a great outpouring of poetry and prose denouncing the actions of the British government. He was more excited over political matters than at any time since his first visit to Ireland, and in a torrent of indignation he sat down and wrote *The Mask of Anarchy*:

And these words shall then become
Like Oppression's thundered doom
Ringing through each heart and brain,
Heard again – again – again –

Rise like Lions after slumber
In unvanquishable number –
Shake your chains to earth like dew
Which in sleep had fallen on you –
Ye are many – they are few.[5]

Shelley's *The Mask of Anarchy* is one of the most powerful poems of protest ever written, but with all the contradictions and fears of a writer who ranged himself on the workers' side, yet somehow wanted to minimise the possibilities of violent working class retaliation. He calls on the workers, as he had in the *Address to the Irish People*, if attacked, to stand together 'with folded arms' as a great unarmed assembly against the tyrants – in effect to 'firmly, yet quietly resist' and shame the tyrants into conceding reform:

And if then the tyrants dare
Let them ride among you there,
Slash and stab, and maim, and hew, –
What they like, let them do.

With folded arms and steady eyes,
And little fear, and less surprise,
Look upon them as they slay
Till their rage has died away.[6]

It is here that the conflict between reform and revolution that troubled Shelley for most of his life is most visible. Passive resistance only works when it is so widespread as to stretch the government beyond its capabilities to strike back. And this was not the case in England in 1819, where a vicious government was intent on using whatever force was necessary to defeat the working class movement. In his poem on 1798, *Requiem for the Croppies,* Seamus Heaney outlines all too well the consequences that result from the difference in firepower available to the government and the rebels:

Until, on Vinegar Hill, the fatal conclave.
Terraced thousands died, shaking scythes at cannon.
The hillside blushed, soaked in our broken wave.
They buried us without shroud or coffin
And in August the barley grew up out of the grave.[7]

In situations of extreme repression a different form of resistance is necessary, one that goes beyond passive resistance or an armed conspiracy. Shelley, never really resolved this dilemma, in his political prose or in the openly political poems of 1819. But in *Prometheus Unbound* he found a solution to the problem. Reform, the poem concluded, is impossible without revolution, and the only power that cannot be contained is the people, organised, united, fighting for reforms, but ready for revolutionary action.

It was not only the events in England that excited Shelley – the Greek and Spanish revolutions rekindled his hopes for the future. But within a few short years the revolutionary wave had receded, the moment had passed and the old pessimism born out of isolation began to reassert itself. Two letters, one in December 1821 and the other in June 1822, indicate the shift in his mood:

There is no such thing as a rebellion in Ireland, or anything that looks like it. The people are indeed stung to madness by the oppression of the Irish system, and there is no such thing as getting rents or taxes even at the point of the bayonet throughout the southern provinces. But there are no regular bodies of men in opposition to the government, nor have the people any leaders. In England all bears for the moment the aspect of a sleeping Volcano.[8]

Six months later he was even more pessimistic:

England appears to be in a desperate condition, Ireland still worse, and no class of those who subsist on the public labour will be persuaded that their claims on it must be diminished. But the government must content itself with less in taxes, the landholder must submit to receive less rent, and the fundholder a diminished interest, – or they will all get nothing, or something worse [than] nothing: I once thought to study these affairs and write or act in them – I am glad that my good genius said refrain. I see little public virtue, and I foresee that the contest will be one of blood and gold two elements, which however much to my taste in my pockets and my veins, I have an objection to out of them.[9]

Within a month Shelley was dead, and it does appear as if at the end of his life he turned his back on his revolutionary principles. Much of his last uncompleted poem, *The Triumph of Life*, is so wrapped in gloom and despondency as to deny the meaning of its title. Ten years earlier the revolution seemed so close that he could almost touch it. Now times had changed, and the dead hand of reaction seemed to suffocate all the enthusiasm and energy of his youth.

Shelley was sometimes unsure, sometimes afraid of the prospect of revolution, and the fear that he was hitting at a void haunted him always. If he had fallen victim to it completely, he would no doubt have followed in the footsteps of Wordsworth and Coleridge and drifted to the right. But he never rejected his past or moved to the right. More often than not he worked his way through his gloom and isolation and reasserted his revolutionary principles. His poem *Ode to the West Wind*, written seven years after his departure from Ireland, is a magnificent example of this, and also illustrates the connection between the supposedly immature reformer and the mature poet. Here Shelley used an analogy taken from his *Proposals for an Association* to write an almost perfect assault on pessimism. In the *Proposals* Shelley was arguing against the Malthusian theory of over-population, which was used by the privileged classes to justify inequality. To demonstrate his contempt for such reasoning, Shelley used the following metaphor:

> We see in Winter that the foliage of the trees is gone, that they present to the view nothing but leafless branches, we see that the loveliness of the flower decays, though the root continues in the earth. What opinion should we form of that man who, when he walked in the freshness of the spring, beheld the fields enamelled with flowers and the foliage bursting from the buds, should find fault with this beautiful order and murmur his contemptible discontents because winter must come, and the landscape be robbed of its beauty for a while again?[10]

Shelley, in his poem, describes the 'West Wind' as a swirling chaos, blowing humanity first one way, then the other. He then reaches back to the theme of winter from his earlier work, and the seasons are transformed into a series of shifting symbols each connected with his ideas, his revolutionary inspiration and his feeling of hopelessness at putting them into effect:

> O wild West Wind, thou breath of Autumn's being,
> Thou, from whose unseen presence the leaves dead
> Are driven, like ghosts from an enchanter fleeing,
> Yellow, and black, and pale, and hectic red.
> Pestilence-stricken multitudes:[11]

But, as always with Shelley, hope shines through. It ends, as Paul Foot puts it:

> With a cry to the wind to lift the poet; to keep his ideas 'fierce and impetuous' as they had been in his youth; and to turn his poetry, which seemed dead, into a mighty agitation which would reach and awaken all humanity.[12]

> Drive my dead thoughts over the universe
> Like withered leaves to quicken a new birth!
> And, by the incantation of this verse,
>
> Scatter, as from an unextinguished hearth
> Ashes and sparks, my words among mankind!
> Be through my lips to unawakened earth
>
> The trumpet of a prophecy! O, Wind,
> If Winter comes, can spring be far behind?[13]

Shelley spent most of his intellectual life trying to come to terms with the failure of the French Revolution. In *Prometheus Unbound* he is tortured by the 'Furies' who remind him that the outcome of the French Revolution was inevitable because failure is deeply rooted in the human condition. In this difficult and dramatic poem he resolved that contradiction and the dilemma that the failure of the revolution posed for so many of his generation. But it is in the final line of, *Ode to the West Wind* that he most perfectly, if idealistically, presented the answer. He writes 'If Winter comes' not 'When Winter comes' – failure is not inevitable, and even if the forces of reaction do manage to reassert themselves, the masses can strike back – 'can Spring be far behind' – good will triumph over evil.

The same imagery is used in his incomplete and fragmentary verseplay from the same period, *Charles the First*. Here he used the analogy of winter against himself to set up a polemic about exploitation. The play opens with the great parade of the Inns of Court. An onlooker remarks that the pomp and riches on display are robbed from the poor:

Here is pomp that strips the houseless orphan,

Here is pride that breaks the desolate heart.

Here is health

Followed by grim disease, glory by shame,

Waste by lame famine, wealth by squalid want.[14]

A young man captivated by the pageantry tries to justify the 'wealth by squalid want' – what today is called in an almost perfect imitation of Shelley, 'private wealth, public squalor' – by arguing that it is part of the natural or divine law:

'Tis but

The anti-masque, and serves as discords do

In sweetest music. Who would love May flowers

If they succeeded not to Winter's flaw;

Or day unchanged by night; or joy itself

Without the touch of sorrow?[15]

Shelley constantly explored the nature of society and how it could be changed for the better. Sometimes he looked back to an idealised past, the ancient Greek and Roman world, as models for the future. At other times it was from the direct experience of the world around him. *The Address to the Irish People,* was Shelley's first complete statement of what his future ideal society would look like:

Can you conceive, O Irishmen! a happy state of society – conceive men of every way of thinking living together like brothers? The descendant of the greatest Prince would there be entitled to no more respect than the son of a peasant. There would be no pomp and no parade, but that which the rich now keep to themselves would then be distributed among the people. None would be in magnificence, but the superfluities then taken from the rich would be sufficient, when spread abroad, to make everyone comfortable. No lover would then be false to his mistress, no mistress would desert her lover. No friend would play false, no rents, no debts, no taxes, no frauds of any kind would disturb the general happiness.

Good as they would be, wise as they would be, they would be daily getting better and wiser. No beggars would exist, nor any of those wretched women who are now reduced to a state of the most horrible misery and vice by men whose wealth makes them villainous and hardened. No thieves or murderers, because poverty would never drive men to take away comforts from another, when he had enough for himself. Vice and misery, pomp and poverty, power and obedience, would then be banished altogether. It is for such a state as this, Irishmen that I exhort you to prepare.[16]

Seven years later in *Prometheus Unbound,* we have this wonderful poetic statement of a world freed from the spirit as well as the tyranny of the past. This does not differ in any substantial way from the 'state' that he exhorted Irishmen to prepare for, in the *Address to the Irish People*, as a young 19 year old eager to set the world to rights:

The loathsome mask has fallen, the man remains
Sceptreless, free, uncircumscribed, but man
Equal, unclassed, tribeless, and nationless,
Exempt from awe, worship, degree, the king
Over himself; just, gentle, wise: but man
Passionless? – no, yet free from guilt or pain,
Which were, for his will made or suffered them,[17]

In Shelley's writings it is always possible to find contradictory ideas. For every quote that proves his radicalism it is possible to find one to prove the opposite. But only a wilful misreading of his work would lead to the conclusion that he was anything other than a committed revolutionary. Unlike Southey, Wordsworth or Coleridge, he did not bend with the prevailing wind. Or, as Louis MacNeice put it when writing about the 1930s generation of poets who joined the Communist Party when it was fashionable to do so, and abandoned it when the political climate changed, as expeditiously as they had once embraced it:

But before you proclaim the millennium, my dear,
Consult the barometer –
This pose is perfect but maintained
For one day only.[18]

Shelley, isolated in Italy and far from the mass movement that could have provided an audience and a response to his poetry, wrote more and more for what Victor Serge in the 1940s, in relation to his own work and for the same reasons, called 'the desk drawer'.[19] Unwilling or unable to publish in the radical working class press, the reception of his poetry by future generations became crucial to his work. In his lifetime the editions of his work were pitiful, 100 copies of *Epipsychidion* and 250 copies of *The Cenci, Adonais* and *Queen Mab*, of which only 70 copies were circulated. Shelley estimated the total readership of *Prometheus Unbound* to be only five or six.[20] Despite the success of Byron this was not unique to Shelley, Keats's publisher records his delight at selling seven or eight copies of *Endymion* and the first edition of *Lyrical Ballads* was remaindered.[21] Shelley was depressed by the failure of *The Revolt of Islam*, a poem that had very few to praise it and none to love it, still feeling three years later that 'its date should be longer than a day'. Shelley's attempt to come to terms with this rejection is evident in his essay *A Defence of Poetry*: 'Even in modern times, no living poet ever arrived at the fullness of his fame…the jury which sits in judgement upon a poet…must be empanelled by time from the selectest of the wise of many generations'.[22]

Shelley had to wait 'many generations' for a favourable judgement by the literary establishment. In the first decade after his death his reputation and influence survived principally in radical working class circles. The Chartists felt that they were the future generation that Shelley was writing for. If we include Leigh Hunt, it is possible to say that Shelley would have been forgotten but for them[23] along with people like Richard Carlile, who as a young tin-plate worker of 25 borrowed £1 with which to start a career selling radical pamphlets, calmly calculating to spend eight or nine years in jail. In fact, he spent 10 between 1817 and 1834. Carlile's paper the *Republican* published Shelley's *Declaration of Rights* in September 1819, most likely with Shelley's support. William Clarke, a working class publisher, was prosecuted in 1821 by the Society for the Suppression of Vice for printing and selling a pirate edition of *Queen Mab*. He was fined £50 and forced to take it off the market.

Outraged by this censorship, Carlile challenged the authorities by immediately publishing his own edition. This was the first of four editions, all with the relevant notes translated, and all at a cheap price published during the 1820s. This was the kind of publication that Shelley required during his lifetime. But he was hampered by his dependence on upper-class reformers such as Leigh Hunt and his publisher Charles Ollier. Shelley in fact, made some contact with the radical press; in 1812 on Southey's recommendation he wrote to James Montgomery[24] about political pamphleteering, and in 1815 he assisted Cannon in publishing *The Refutation of Deism* and one third of *Queen Mab* in the *Theological Inquirer*. After 1815, he wrote works that were as radical in form and content – *The Mask of Anarchy, Swellfoot the Tyrant, Ballad of the Starving Mother* – as anything published at that time. Shelley unfortunately did not cultivate this tenuous relationship, and if in 1819 he had sent *Mask of Anarchy* to one of the Spencean[25] publications, instead of Leigh Hunt, it would have been published long before 1832.

Shelley drowned off the coast of Italy after his boat sank in a Mediterranean storm that blew up on the afternoon of 8 July 1822. Nearly a month went by before his death was reported in the British papers and, with few exceptions, they set about his reputation with a vengeance: 'Shelley, the writer of some infidel poetry, has been drowned; now he knows whether there is a God or no', proclaimed the *Courier*.[26] However, far more damage was done to Shelley's reputation by his friends and to greater effect. But before he could be adopted as a cultural icon his poetry had to be striped of its political and social content and reduced to a lyrical quality. This unholy alliance between those who loved him and those who despised him meant that the real Shelley was ignored or neglected. Shelley's grave in the Protestant Cemetery in Rome is covered with a simple tablet inscribed with a verse from Shakespeare's *The Tempest*:

Nothing of him that doth fade,
But doth suffer a sea-change
Into something rich and strange.

His friends set about the 'sea-change', transforming Shelley into something 'rich and strange', extracting the vitality and every trace of political or social thought from his work. Even Leigh Hunt carelessly stated that in the last years of his life Shelley repudiated his *Queen Mab* as a youthful indiscretion. The introduction by Isabel Quigly in the current Penguin edition of *Shelley: Selected Poems* best summarises the effect that the Shelley lovers have had on his work over the past 150 years: 'His faults were all the faults of an overabundant and undisciplined imagination. No poet better repays cutting; no great poet was ever less worth reading in his entirety'.[27] Over 100 editions of Shelley's selected works have appeared since his death in which there is no *Revolt of Islam*, no *Queen Mab*, no *Mask of Anarchy*, or *Swellfoot the Tyrant* – no ideas of any description. Instead, we are presented with the shorter poems or extracts without any context. Perhaps, it was for his friends rather than his enemies that Shelley wrote in the preface to *Prometheus Unbound*: 'Let the uncandid consider that they injure me less than their own hearts and minds by misrepresentation'.[28]

The hostile criticism in the early 1930s from the likes of F R Leavis and T S Eliot,[29] whose statements set the fashion in literary taste, left Shelley isolated and unloved. T S Eliot, in 1933, found him 'humourless and pedantic', not unexpected from a supporter of the establishment, but the left had turned against him as well. In the 1930s the Communist Party formed the popular front as an alliance of progressive forces for the defence of the Soviet Union and as a bulwark against fascism. The popular front in its various forms was dominated by the Communist Party and faithfully followed the political twists and turns of the Stalinist bureaucracy. Unfortunately this was reflected in literary circles where a crude party line dictated what people should, or should not read. Despite this, a new audience for radical and left wing writers emerged in the 1930s encouraged by the Left Book Club, the cheap Penguin sixpenny editions and publications such as *Poetry and the People*. They were not unlike the working class and Chartist audience, that had sustained Shelley's poetry 100 years previously. Unfortunately, the Communist Party destroyed its potential by reducing its output to slogans and rhetoric. Stephen Spender, whose membership of the Communist Party lasted a fashionable two weeks, and who, from this limited experience, managed to write three books on the subject, led the charge in exposing Shelley's political inadequacies. Shelley, according to Spender and his friends in the Left Book Club, lacked the true 'Marxist' vision – 'every problem he approaches seems unreal, every solution he offers, ineffectual'.[30]

To remove from poets their political ideas is almost as insulting as judging them solely on their politics. It took some time to rescue Shelley from the damage done by his friends and his enemies. Since the 1950s, Kenneth Cameron, Richard Holmes, Paul Foot, Geoffrey Matthews and many others have helped redress the distortions of the past. They started from an acceptance that Shelley was a political poet, but one whose politics happened in terms of poetry, within the poems, not as empty gestures to an ideology happening somewhere outside them. They developed an analysis, which presented a unity between his early and later work, his prose and his poetry, with no *a priori* separation of politics and poetry, while reading his work with a critical eye.

To rid life of its misery and evil was the ruling passion of Shelley's heart. He was a revolutionary through and through, but one whose life and work was full of uncertainty and contradiction. He was never afraid to face those contradictions, and neither should we, for it is how we arrive at our understanding of the complex world in which we live. The world that Shelley fought against is infinitely different today, yet the same, and today's largely unstructured challenge to capitalism needs to be infused with the same imaginative power that Shelley proclaimed. James Connolly said that 'no revolutionary movement is complete without a poetical expression' without which 'it is a dogma of a few, and not the faith of the multitude'.[31] Therefore, it is no coincidence that some of the best poetry of the past 30 years has emerged from the political struggle in the north of Ireland in the work Seamus Heaney, Paul Muldoon, Tom Paulin and Michael Longley. They do not write as part of a movement or in the same style, but as a group they reflect the convulsions of their time and place. There is not always an obvious connection between what they wrote and what went on in Northern Ireland. Their poems do not stand or fall on the themes of justice or oppression, but such themes are worthy of the wonderful lyrics in which they frame them. Seamus Heaney, particularly in his early poems, speaks 'about and for those whose voices are lost to history'.[32]

Poetry is more than the words on the page. It has a language and rhythm of its own which are distinct from prose that fixes the words and sentences in the mind. To decompose a poetical passage into prose and then call for a criticism upon it is to deny poetry its distinguishing feature. Louis MacNeice captured it beautifully when he said that, 'poet and reader both know, consciously or unconsciously the rest of the truth which lurks between the lines'.[33] We live in a world dominated by worn out clichés and sound-bites. It is because we need our writers to tell us the truth that we object to the propagandist and the second rate. Or, as Yeats put it, 'one never serves one's cause by putting one's head into a bag'.[34]

Tony Cliff, the Marxist writer and agitator, often said that 'the case for socialism takes less than two minutes to understand – a mere glance at the world and the way it is divided into rich and poor makes that case immediately'.[35] The revolutionary ideal does not need to be argued. It justifies itself, all we need is to give it voice. This Shelley did – he told the truth with all his doubts, uncertainties and personal difficulties. His poetry is 'the trumpet of a prophecy' that rings down the ages to give utterance to the inhumanity we see all around us, and the need for change. In 1812 in Dublin, a young 19 year old sat down to write his poem *To Liberty*:

And a Paradise on earth
From your fall shall date its birth,
And human life shall seem
Like a short and happy dream
Ere we wake in the daybeam of the skies.[36]

Almost 200 years later, Shelley's 'paradise on earth' has not yet come about, but he did well to dream it.

NOTES

1   J Montague, 'The Lure', *Collected Poems* (Loughcrew, 1995), verse 4, lines 15-17, p62.

2   R Duerkin, *Shelley, Political Writings*, op cit, p197.

3   Ibid, pXIV.

4   Appendix 3, p259.

5   *Poetical Works of Shelley*, op cit, lines 364-72, p338.

6   Ibid, lines 340-47, p338.

7   S Heaney, 'Requiem for the Croppies', *Door into the Dark* (London, 1972), lines 10-14, p12. The barley growing 'up out of the grave' is both a monument and a reference to the barley the insurgents carried in their pockets as food which germinated and grew over the battlefield the following summer.

8   F L Jones, op cit, 2, p370.

9   Ibid, 2, p441.

10   *Proposals*, Appendix 4, p299. In the preface to 'The Revolt of Islam', *Poetical Works of Shelley*, op cit, p34) Shelley develops the attack on Malthus first featured in the *Proposals* and he uses the metaphor of winter to the same effect in the poem (*Poetical Works of Shelley*, op cit, IX, XXV, lines 385-88, p128).

> This is the winter of the world; – and here
> We die, even as the winds of Autumn fade,
> Expiring in the frore and foggy air. –
> Behold! Spring comes.

The winter analogy was probably taken from the conclusion of Tom Paine's 'The Rights of Man' (see *The Thomas Paine Reader*, op cit, p363).

11   'Ode to the West Wind', *Poetical Works of Shelley*, op cit, lines 1-5, p577.

12   P Foot, op cit, p226.

13   'Ode to the West Wind', *Poetical Works of Shelley*, op cit, lines 63-70, p577.

14   'Charles the First', *Poetical Works of Shelley*, op cit, scene 1, lines 154-55, 162-64, p488.

15   'Charles the First', *Poetical Works of Shelley*, op cit, lines 175-79, p488.

16   Appendix 3, p268.

17   'Prometheus Unbound', *Poetical Works of Shelley*, op cit, act 3, scene 4, lines 193-99, p204.

18   L MacNeice, 'To a Communist', *Collected Poems* (London, 1979), lines, 5-8, p22.

19   Victor Serge (1890-1947) is best known as a novelist and for his autobiography *Memoirs of a Revolutionary.* He was a member of the Communist Party in Russia and a supporter of the Left Opposition. In 1936 he was expelled from Russia by Stalin, and became one of its most eloquent critics. He found it almost impossible to find a publisher for his work, but he continued to write for the 'bottom drawer'. He wrote for the future and has left a literary and political legacy that charts the political history of the first half of the 20th century.

20   F L Jones, op cit, 2, p388.

21   A Bennett, *Shelley and Contemporary Thought* (Baltimore, 1996), pp219-20.

22   P B Shelley, 'A Defence of Poetry', *Political Writings,* op cit, p171.

23   Newman Ivey White counted 140 items on Shelley published between 1823 and 1841 in working class or radical publications.

24   James Montgomery (1771-1854) was born in Ireland of missionary parents. He was editor of the *Sheffield Iris*, a weekly paper that advocated political and religious freedom. See F L Jones, op cit, 1, p215.

25   Followers of Thomas Spence (1750-1814), utopian socialists inspired by the ideas of the Levellers and the Diggers of the 17th century. Their newspaper, *Pigsmeat* (named as a response to Burke's 'Swinish Multitude') agitated for land expropria-tion, peasant co-operatives, women's rights, etc. See Thompson, op cit, pp161-62.

26   This famous quote is taken from the *Examiner* of 3 November 1822. *The Examiner* claimed that the passage was a quote from the *Courier* of 5 August 1822. In fact, the second sentence does not occur in the *Courier*'s obituary of Shelley.

27   E Quigley (ed), *Shelley: Selected Poems*, (London, 1985), p18.

28   *Poetical Works of Shelley,* op cit, p204.

29   See F R Leavis, *Revaluation* (Harmondsworth, 1964) and T S Eliot, *The Use of Poetry and The Use of Criticism* (London, 1933).

30   S Spender, *Forward from Liberalism* (London, 1937), p34.

31   Quoted in D Nevin, op cit, p488. James Connolly loved Shelley and frequently quoted him in his speeches and writings. The title of his pamphlet *The Axe to the Root* has a long history, from the bible to the anti slavery movement to Shelley's *Queen Mab* – 'Let the axe strike at the root', (*Poetical Works of Shelley,* op cit, canto IV, lines 82-3, p762).

32   H Vendler, *Seamus Heaney* (London, 1998), p13.

33   See E Longley, *Louis MacNeice* (London, 1988), pIX.

34   *United Irishman* 10 August 1903.

35   T Cliff, *A World to Win* (London, 2000), p250. Tony Cliff (1917-2000) was born in Palestine. He came to Britain in 1946 and was a founder member of the Socialist Workers Party in Britain. Among his many publications are biographies of Lenin and Trotsky.

36   P B Shelley, *The Esdaile Notebook*, op cit, lines 45-50, p58.

Poems

SHELLEY wrote four poems that deal directly with Ireland. Another six are concerned in part with Irish history and politics. These poems all date from the period 1809-1812, and clearly indicate Shelley's early interest in Irish affairs. Like nearly all his early work they deal with specific issues of a social or political nature, and demonstrate his anger at the suffering in the world around him. Shelley at this time was 'trying to find a form and an idiom that would…connect him with an audience among those segments of British society that, he thought, had both the interest and the power to initiate political change'.[1] In his later work, starting with *Queen Mab* in 1812-13, he developed a more philosophical and less specific world view. Ireland disappears as a subject in the poems and becomes integrated into a more comprehensive world view. Sometimes we have to look more carefully between the lines for these references to emerge. At a more obvious level, we can see the influence of Irish writers such as Tom Moore and Sydney Owenson in some of his later work – *Revolt of Islam, Adonais,* etc. Some, but not all of these references are included in the notes that follow each poem. The most exhaustive references are to be found in the Longman's Critical Edition – G Matthews (ed), *The Poems of Shelley*. The most accessible edition is the Oxford Standard Authors, which I have used throughout this book – *Poetical Works of Shelley* (Oxford, 1991). I have also used *The Esdaile Notebook* (Oxford, 1964) where appropiate for the early poems, as the text approximates what Shelley himself would have published in 1812.

The Irishman's Song

The stars may dissolve, and the fountain of light
May sink into ne'er ending chaos and night,
Our mansions must fall, and earth vanish away,
But thy courage O Erin! may never decay.
See! the wide wasting ruin extends all around,
Our ancestors' dwellings lie sunk on the ground,
Our foes ride in triumph throughout our domains,
And our mightiest heroes lie stretched on the plains.
Ah! dead is the harp which was wont to give pleasure,
Ah! sunk is our sweet country's rapturous measure,
But the war note is waked, and the clangour of spears,
The dread yell of Sloghan yet sounds in our ears.
Ah! where are the heroes! triumphant in death,
Convulsed they recline on the blood sprinkled heath,
Or the yelling ghosts ride on the blast that sweeps by,
And 'my countrymen! vengeance!' incessantly cry.

Note: Written in October 1809 and first published by Shelley in *Original Poetry* by
Victor and Cazire, (*Poetical Works of Shelley,* op cit, p849) in 1810. This is the first
indication of Shelley's interest in Irish politics. The influence of Tom Moore's *Irish
Melodies*, 10 vols. (London, 1808-1834) is obvious.

Line 12. 'Sloghan' is a Gaelic war cry, and the derivative of the modern word, slogan.

Line 13. Shelley rewrote this as the opening line of *Henry and Louisa*, in 1809: 'Where
are the Heroes? Sunk in death they lie' (*Esdaile Notebook,* p131).

On Robert Emmet's tomb

May the tempests of Winter that sweep o'er thy tomb
Disturb not a slumber so sacred as thine;
May the breezes of summer that breathe of perfume
Waft their balmiest dews to so hallowed a shrine.

May the foot of the tyrant, the coward, the slave,

Be palsied with dread where thine ashes repose,
Where that undying shamrock still blooms on thy grave
Which sprung when the dawnlight of Erin arose.

There oft have I marked the grey gravestones among,
Where thy relics distinguished in lowliness lay,
The peasant boy pensively lingering long
And silently weep as he passed away.

And how could he not pause if the blood of his sires
Ever wakened one generous throb in his heart?
How could he inherit a spark of their fires
If tearless and frigid he dared to depart?

Not the scrolls of a court could emblazon thy fame
Like the silence that reigns in the palace of thee,
Like the whispers that pass of thy dearly loved name,
Like the tears of the good, like the groans of the free.

No trump tells thy virtues – the grave where they rest
With thy dust shall remain unpolluted by fame,
Till thy foes, by the world and by fortune caresst
Shall pass like a mist from the light of thy name.

When the storm cloud that lowers o'er the daybeam is gone,
Unchanged, unextinguished its lifespring will shine,
When Erin has ceased with their memory to groan
She will smile thro' the tears of revival on thine.

Note: Shelley wrote this tribute to Emmet in 1812 (*Esdaile Notebook,* p60), just before or shortly after his departure from Dublin. Robert Emmet was buried in St Michan's Church after his execution in 1803. Also interred in the crypt are the Irish patriots who were executed during the 1798 rebellion – John and Henry Shears. The graveyard contains the remains of Oliver Bond and the Reverend W Jackson (See Claire Clairmont's *Journal* for the story of his death, 15 March 1820). Only a few of Emmet's poems have survived. 'Arbour Hill' (*The '98 Reader*, p180) was written in honour of the dead hero's of 1798. There is a marked resemblance to Shelley's poem on Emmet and its companion piece *The Tombs*:

No rising column marks this spot.
Where many a victim lies;
But oh! The blood which here has streamed,
To heaven for justice cries.

The Tombs

These are the tombs. O cold and silent Death,
Thy Kingdom and thy subjects here I see.
The record of thy victories
Is graven on every speaking stone
That marks what once was man.

These are the tombs. Am I, who sadly gaze
On the corruption and the skulls around,
To sum the mass of loathsomeness,
And to a mound of mouldering flesh
Say – 'thou wert human life'

In thee once throbbed the Patriot's beating heart,
In thee once lived the Poet's soaring soul,
The pulse of love, the calm of thought,
Courage and charity and truth
And high devotedness;

All that could sanctify the meanest deeds,
All that might give a manner and a form
To matter's speechless elements,
To every brute and morbid shape
Of this phantasmal world:

That the high sense which from the stern rebuke
Of Erin's victim-patriot's death-soul shone,
When blood and chains defiled the land,
Lives in the torn uprooted heart
His savage murderers burn.

Ah, no! else while these tombs before me stand
My soul would hate the coming of its hour,
Nor would the hopes of life and love
Be mingled with those fears of death
That chill the warmest heart.

Note: Written in Dublin in 1812 (*Esdaile*, p83) as a companion piece to the poem on Robert Emmet. The tombs are in the graveyard of St Michan's Church in Dublin, the burial place of some the leaders of the United Irishmen executed in 1798 (see note above).

Line 21. The 'stern rebuke' is Emmet's famous speech from the dock: 'Let no man write my epitaph' (see chapter 6, p121).

Line 23. 'When blood and chains defiled the land' refers to the atrocities committed by the British government during the rising of 1798.

The Ocean rolls between us

                    O thou Ocean,
Whose multitudinous billows ever lash
Erin's green isle, on whose shores
This venturous arm would plant the flag of liberty,
Roll on! and with each wave whose echoings die
Amid thy melancholy silentness
Shall die a moment too – one of those moments
Which part my friend and me.
                    I could stand
Upon thy shores, O Erin, and could count
The billows that, in their unceasing swell
Dash on thy beach, and every wave might seem
An instrument in Time the giant's grasp
To burst the barriers of eternity.
Proceed, thou giant, conquering and to conquer,
March on thy lonely way – The Nations fall
Beneath thy noiseless footstep – pyramids
That for millenniums have defied the blast

And laughed at lightnings thou dost crush to nought.
Yon monarch in his solitary pomp
Is but the fungus of a winter day
That thy light footstep presses into dust. –
Thou art a conqueror, Time! all things give way
Before thee, but the 'fixed and virtuous will',
The sacred sympathy of soul which was
When thou wert not, which shall be when thou perishest.

Note: This was part of a letter written in Dublin to Elizabeth Hitchener on 14 February 1812. In 1893 these lines were rendered into verse and appended to the fragment below (*Bear witness, Erin!*) from the same letter and published as a single poem *To Ireland* (*Poetical Works of Shelley*, p873). Geoffrey Matthews (*The Poems of Shelley*, vol 1, p208) and others have rightly questioned this connection and make the point that the two fragments have nothing in common, except for an Irish theme. Following this interpretation I have printed them as separate poetic fragments.

Lines 14-25. Shelley rewrote these lines and incorporated them into *Queen Mab* (*Poetical Works of Shelley*, verse 11, lines 23-37, p762).

In the same letter Shelley said that 'I find that I sometimes can write poetry when I feel', which is evident in a passage of blank verse that occurs in the fourth paragraph of *An address to the Irish People* (Appendix 3, p255).

Oh Ireland!

Thou emerald of the ocean, whose sons
Are generous and brave, whose daughters are
Honourable and frank and fair, thou art the isle
On whose green shores I have desired to see
The standard of liberty erected – a flag of fire –
A beacon at which the world shall light
The torch of Freedom!

Bear witness, Erin!

Bear witness, Erin! when thine injured isle
Sees summer on its verdant pastures smile,
Its cornfields waving in the winds that sweep
The billowy surface of thy circling deep –
Thou tree whose shadow o'er the Atlantic gave
Peace, wealth and beauty, to its friendly wave
               – its blossoms fade,
And blighted are the leaves that cast its shade,
Whilst the cold hand gathers its scanty fruit
Whose chillness struck a canker to its root.

Note: Written in Dublin and sent in a letter to Elizabeth Hitchener on 14 February 1812. First published in 1870 (*Poetical Works of Shelley*, p873) and titled *To Ireland* (see above for subsequent history). See Matthew's (*The Poems of Shelley*, vol 1, p211) Line 5. 'Thou tree' is the Tree of Liberty (see chapter 4, p77). The United Irishmen frequently carried branches as symbols of liberty or Tree of Liberty insignia on their uniforms.

Line 9. The 'cold hand' is the British government gathering in its 'scanty fruit' (taxes and tithes).

The following are extracts from poems that refer to Ireland or Irish matters, written between 1810 and 1813. A common theme is the contrast between the pomp of the monarch or despot with the terrible poverty and oppression of their subjects. Shelley points to the French and American revolutions, the United Irishmen and Robert Emmet as an example of what may happen if reforms are not granted.[2]

The Monarch's Funeral

To see this awful pomp of death
For one frail mass of mouldering clay,
When nobler men the tomb beneath
Have sunk unwept, unseen away.

For who was he, the uncoffined slain,
That fell in Erin's injured isle
Because his spirit dared disdain
To light his country's funeral pile?

Shall he not ever live in lays
The warmest that a Muse may sing
Whilst monumental marbles raise
The fame of a departed King?

May not the Muse's darling theme
Gather its glorious garland thence
Whilst some frail tombstone's Dotard dream
Fades with a monarch's impotence!

Note: Written in 1810, (*Esdaile Notebook*, lines 17-32, p68) in anticipation of the death and state funeral of George III. Shelley contrasts the marble monument raised to a despised king with the unmarked grave of Robert Emmet. While the marble will fade, Emmet will live on in the work of poets such as Robert Southey, *written immediately after reading the speech of Robert Emmet* and Thomas Moore's *Oh, breathe not his name.*[3] In *Robert Emmet in Poetry* (National Library of Ireland, Scrapbook) over 100 poems from newspapers and magazines are collected together.

The Spectral Horseman

What was the shriek that struck Fancy's ear
As it sate on the ruins of time that is past?
Hark! it floats on the fitful blast of the wind,
And breathes to the pale moon a funeral sigh.
It is the Benshie's moan on the storm,

Yet when the fierce swell of the tempest is raving,
And the whirlwinds howl in the caves of Inisfallen,
Still secure mid the wildest war of the sky,
The phantom courser scours the waste,
And his rider howls in the thunder's roar.

Than does the dragon, who, chained in the caverns
To eternity, curses the champion of Erin,
Moan and yell loud at the lone hour of midnight,
And twine his vast wreaths round the forms of the demons;
Then in agony roll his death-swimming eyeballs,
Though wildered by death, yet never to die!

Note: Written in 1810, and published in the same year in *Posthumous Fragments of Margaret Nicholson.* (Poetical Works of Shelley, op cit, lines 1-5, 34-38, 47-52, p866).
Line 5. Shelley uses the term the 'Benshie' in its Irish or Scottish context, 'a messenger of death'.
Line 35. 'Inisfallen' is a poetic name for Ireland.
Line 48. 'The champion of Erin' refers to the legendary Cuchullin who had to kill a dragon as part of his ordeal to become the Champion of Ulster (Ireland).

To Liberty

Regal pomp and pride
The Patriot falls in scorning,
The spot whereon he died
Should be the despot's warning.
The voice of blood shall on his crimes
call down Revenge!
And the spirits of the brave
Shall start from every grave
Whilst from her Atlantic throne
Freedom sanctifies the groan
That fans the glorious fires of its change.

Note: Date of composition is uncertain, but most likely this was written in the period of Shelley's visit to Ireland in 1812 (*Esdaile,* lines 21-30, p58). The contrast between the pomp of monarchy and the cry for revenge from the grave of the patriot is similar to most of the poems from that time.
Lines 28-30. These lines echo the sentiments in *To the Republicans of North America.* The 'Atlantic throne' is America where freedom took root and will cross the Atlantic to liberate Europe.

Falshood and Vice

Whilst Monarchs laughed upon their thrones
To hear a famished nation's groans,
And hugged the wealth, wrung from the woe
That makes their eyes and veins o'erflow,
Those thrones high built upon the heaps
Of bones where frenzied Famine sleeps,
Where slavery with her scourge of iron
Stained in mankind's unheeded gore,
And war's mad fiends the scene environ
Mingling with shrieks a drunken roar,
There Vice and Falshood took their stand
High raised above the unhappy land.

Note: Written in Dublin or just before Shelley left for Ireland (*Esdaile*, lines 1-12, p44). The 'famished nation' and the 'unhappy land' suggest Ireland and are similar to 'the wretched land' of Southey's *Curse of Kehama*,[4] which Shelley used in his advertisement for *A Poetical Essay* in 1811. The poem's inspiration appears to be Coleridge's *Fire, Famine and Slaughter*[5] in which William Pitt, the British prime minister, encourages the three apocalyptic sisters in their evil work in Ireland and England. *Falshood and Vice* was included in the notes to 'Queen Mab' (*Poetical Works of Shelley,* op cit, p802).

The Devils Walk

Fat – as the Death-birds on Erin's shore,
That glutted themselves in her dearest gore,
And flitted around Castlereagh,
When they snatched the Patriot's heart, that his grasp
Had torn from its widow's maniac clasp,
And fled at the dawn of the day.

Note: The Devil's Walk, (*Poetical Works of Shelley*, lines 57-62, p878) was written in the month prior to his departure for Ireland, and printed in Dublin as a broadsheet in March 1812. This political poem was based on the Southey/Coleridge ballad *The Devil's Thoughts* from 1799 and was Shelley's most direct attack on Castlereagh's murderous policy in Ireland.

Shelley returned to the same material and style in 1819 in *Peter Bell the Third* and *The Mask of Anarchy*. The imagery of the 'Death-birds' is one he used again in *Hellas*, (*Poetical Works of Shelley*, line 1025, p446) 'The death-bird descend to their feast' and in *Prometheus Unbound*, (Poetical Works of Shelley, act 1, lines 339-40, p204).

> The hope of torturing him smells like a heap
> Of corpses, to a death-bird after death.

Lines 60-61. After his execution Robert Emmet's 'Patriot's heart' was torn from his body and burnt. Emmet's lover, Sarah Curran, was denied his body for burial by the authorities. Shelley, following the tradition of Thomas Moore's poem *She is far from the Land*,[6] calls her his widow but they were never married.

To the Republicans of North America

Brothers! between you and me
Whirlwinds sweep and billows roar,
Yet in spirit oft I see
On the wild and winding shore
Freedom's bloodless banner wave,
Feel the pulses of the brave,
Unextinguished by the grave,
See them drenched in sacred gore,
Catch the patriot's gasping breath
Murmuring Liberty in death.

Shout aloud! let every slave
Crouching at corruption's throne
Start into a man, and brave
Racks and chains without a groan!
Let the castle's heartless glow
And the hovel's vice and woe

Fade like gaudy flowers that blow,
Weeds that peep and then are gone,
Whilst from misery's ashes risen
Love shall burst the Captive's prison.

Cotopaxi! bid the sound
Thro' thy sister mountains ring
Till each valley smile around
At the blissful welcoming.
And O! thou stern Ocean-deep,
Whose eternal billows sweep
Shores where thousands wake to weep
Whilst they curse some villain King,
On the winds that fan thy breast
Bear thou news of freedom's rest.

Earth's remotest bounds shall start,
Every despot's bloated cheek,
Pallid as his bloodless heart,
Frenzy, woe and dread shall speak . . .
Blood may fertilize the tree
Of new bursting Liberty.
Let the guiltiness then be
On the slaves that ruin wreak,
On the unnatural tyrant-brood
Slow to Peace and swift to blood.

Can the daystar dawn of love
Where the flag of war unfurled
Floats with crimson stain above
Such a desolated world . . .
Never! but to vengeance driven
When the patriot's spirit shriven
Seeks in death its native Heaven,
Then to speechless horror hurled.
Widowed Earth may balm the bier
Of its memory with a tear.

Note: Written in Dublin (*Esdaile Notebook*, p71) and, with the exception of the fourth verse, which was added later, was included in a letter to Elizabeth Hitchener on 14 February 1812. It is a tribute to the Mexican Revolution against Spanish colonialism. In 1810 Father Hidalgo gathered together a peasant army that captured several cities before he was defeated and executed by the Spanish in 1811. News of this defeat had not reached Shelley when he wrote the poem, for in the same letter he says: 'I have just written the following short tribute to its success'. Similar in many ways to his poems dedicated to Irish revolutionaries, Shelley places the Mexican Revolution in the same tradition as that of America, France and Ireland.

Lines 15-16. Shelley is referring to the Irish poor living in 'hovels' ruled by the British from a 'heartless' Dublin Castle.

Line 21. 'Cotopaxi' is a volcano in Ecuador, which Shelley uses as a metaphor for revolution.

Lines 27-29. This refers to the 'wind' that will bring news of a successful revolution to Ireland's shores.

Line 49. 'Widowed Earth' is a symbol for Sarah Curran, 'widowed' by the execution of Robert Emmet.

To a Balloon laden with Knowledge

A watch-light by the patriots lonely tomb,
A ray of courage to the oppressed and poor,
A spark, though gleaming on the hovels hearth,
Which through the tyrant's gilded domes shall roar,
A beacon in the darkness of the Earth,
A Sun which o'er the renovated scene
Shall dart like Truth where Falshood yet has been.

Note: Written in Devon in August 1812 (*Esdaile Notebook*, lines 8-14, p89). Shelley was using every means possible to distribute his broadsheets, even sending them aloft in balloons (see chapter 7, p132). The imagery of the 'patriots lonely tomb' standing as a 'ray of courage' and a beacon of truth that will speak of freedom to future generations also features in *On Robert Emmet's Tomb, The Tombs* and *Falshood and Vice*. See also *Ode to the West Wind* (*Poetical Works of Shelley*, lines 66-67, p577).

Scatter as from an unexpected hearth
Ashes and Sparks, my words upon mankind.

There are several other poems in which Shelley draws on Irish history and literature and in part on his experiences in Ireland. Richard Holmes suggests that in *Zeinab and Kathema* Shelley 'tried to relate the Irish social conditions more closely with his own political ambitions… Shelley turns Zeinab's career into an apocalyptic symbol of revolt, burning like a fiery comet through the darkness of society'.[7] *Peter Bell the Third* (1819), Shelley's satire on the apostasy of Wordsworth, opens with a dedication to Thomas Brown Esq (Tom Moore). Moore had just published *The Fudge Family*[8] to great literary and financial acclaim. Moore was attacking those writers who had professed radical political views in the 1790s and subsequently not only disowned their past, but went on to inform on their comrades of that era. Thomas Moore (1779-1852) is being somewhat disingenuous here. He was one of the first Catholics admitted to Trinity College Dublin after the act of 1793 relaxed the rules prohibiting Catholics. He was a friend of Robert Emmet's and a contributor to the *Press*, the paper of the United Irishmen. Moore never informed on his former friends, but while Emmet climbed the steps of the gallows, Moore quietly forgot his radical past and climbed the steps to social acceptance. Moore's *Irish Melodies* was a great favourite of Shelley's and his admiration for Moore was such, that he sent him copies of all his major poems.[9] In *Alastor* there are many similarities with Sydney Owenson's *The Missionary* with its encounter between a European missionary and a veiled eastern priestess. Owenson's influence is apparent in a number of other poems, *The Revolt of Islam, The Indian Serenade* and *Zeinab and Kathema*.[10] In *The Voyage* (1812) the terrible journey to and from Dublin was the inspiration for the first part of the poem. While in Dublin he became interested in the case of Redfern and the reference to the king suggests the arrest of Redfern by the subjects of George III, who controlled the press gang in Portugal:

> Yes! smooth-faced tyrants chartered by a Power
>
> Called King, who in the castellated keep
>
> Of miserable dotage, pace the quay[11]

In *Adonais*, Shelley's lament for the death of Keats, Tom Moore is sent as chief mourner from 'Ierne' (Ireland), who Shelley described as:

> In sorrow; from her wilds Ierne sent
>
> The sweetest lyrist of her saddest wrong,
>
> And Love taught Grief to fall like music from his tongue.[12]

Swellfoot the Tyrant (1820) is a satire on the attempt by King George IV (Swellfoot) and Castlereagh (Purganax) to charge his wife queen Caroline (Iona) with adultery. In act 1, the king complains that people in Ireland are continuing to feed themselves while 'taxes are withheld'. 'Allens rushy bog' is the Bog of Allen in the Irish Midlands:

> *Swellfoot:*   What! ye who grub
>
> With filthy snouts my red potatoes up
>
> In Allens rushy bog?[13]

Castlereagh who was Irish and therefore assumed to have a good turn of phrase – 'the gift o' the gab' – is asked to lecture the pigs (masses) on the guilt of the queen:

> You, Purganax, who have the gift o' the gab,
>
> Make them a solemn speech to this effect.[14]

Protesting her innocence, Iona and the Swinish Multitude pursue the evil Swellfoot and his ministers (Castlereagh, etc) across England. Iona, though vilified in England, claims she can walk freely in Ireland. 'Erin's laureate sings it' is a reference to the poem *Rich and Rare Were the Gems She Wore*[15] by Tom Moore, which tells the storey of a young lady adorned with jewels who undertook a journey from one end of Ireland to the other without being molested or robbed:

> Innocent Queens o'er white-hot ploughshares tread
>
> Unsinged, and ladies, Erin's laureate sings it,
>
> Decked with rare gems, and beauty rarer still,
>
> Walked from Killarney, to the Giants Causeway,
>
> Through rebels, smugglers, troops of yeomanry,

White-boys and Orange-boys, and constables,
Tithe-proctors, and excise people, uninjured![16]

In the next scene, Purganax and Swellfoot discuss the trial of the Lady P
– (the queen) and how they intend to discredit her. The blood which
the 'sad Genius of the Green Isle had fixed' on Purganax is that of the
United Irishmen executed by Castlereagh:

Purganax: I have rehearsed the entire scene
With an ox-bladder and some ditchwater,
On Lady P – ; it cannot fail. Your Majesty
In such a filthy business had better
Stand on one side, lest it should sprinkle you.
A spot or two on me would do no harm,
Nay, it might hide the blood, which the sad Genius
Of the Green Isle has fixed, as by a spell,
Upon my brow – which would stain all its seas,
But which those seas could never wash away![17]

Charles the First, Shelley's verse drama written between 1819 and 1822
is set in the reign of Charles I (1625-1649). The king sends Wentworth[18]
to subdue Ireland in the period leading up to the Confederate Catholic
rising of 1641. In public the king requests that this should be done wise-
ly and peacefully:

                You, Wentworth,
Shall be myself in Ireland, and shall add
Your wisdom, gentleness, and energy,
To what in me were wanting.

But privately, he demands that Ireland be subdued at any cost, by force
if necessary:

Be – as thou art within my heart and mind –
Another self, here and in Ireland:
Do what thou judgest well, take amplest licence,
And strike not even at questionable means.[19]

Wentworth (Earl of Stafford) played a vital part during the crisis in
England in 1641-2, not least because of his tactic of using Irish resources

and soldiers to back up the king:

    Stafford: The engine of parliaments
    Might be deferred until I can bring over
    The Irish regiments: they will serve to assure
    The issue of the war against the Scots.[20]

    I can only locate two translations of Shelley's poems into Irish, which are printed here in a limited extract. *An Néall* (*The Cloud*) by Conor Maguire was published in the *New Ireland Review* in 1909, which was also its first foreign translation. His object was to show that it was possible to translate lyrical poetry, what he termed 'word-painting', into Irish without using unfamiliar or archaic words. Father Pádraig de Brún's[21] translation of *Ode to the West Wind* (*Dán do'n Ghaoith Aniar*) published in the Sinn Féin newspaper in 1924 was far more important. His translations of the world's classics into Irish were a labour of love. This was a work of preservation and enrichment by an obscure but remarkable scholar.

An Néall

Bheirim fearthainn úr-mín do'n bhláth atá críon
 Ó'n sruth 's ó'n mhuir I gcéin;
Bheirim sgáth fionn-fhuar do shuain an duilleabhair
Áta sínte le teas faoi ghréin.
Ó mo sgeitheáin anuas seadh craithtear an drúcht
 A dhúisigheann na blátha go léir;
'S iad bréagtha chun suain ar bhrollach a rúin,
Le na damhsa thart ar an ghréin.
Sé mo shúiste an ghrán de shneachta bháin
A bhreacann na hacadh-reidh fúm;
Acht glanann mo dheór aríst an fheóir,
Sí an toirneach mo gháire neamh-bhuan.[22]

Dán do'n Ghaoith Aniar.

Déan cláirseach dhíom mar dheinis de'n bhforaois,
Má táimse féin 's a craobha súd ag feodh!
Nach geasfaidh tú do gháir thóirnighe le gaois

Go ceol orgáin dord íseal fómhair sa cheo,
Go binn is brónach. A spioraid áird, taisbeáin
Do neart im' anam féin, mair ann go deo!

Beir leat mo smaointe ar fuid ag domhain iomláin
Chun é d'aithbheochaint lem dhuilleabhar do sheirg.
Mo gheasa fághaim ort le draoidheacht mo dháin,

Mo Bhréithre a seideadh amách na ngríosaigh dheirg.
Ó'm theallach beo san oíche dubh is dall!
Bárr Buadh na saoirse atá 'na thost fé mheirg,

Seinn air trém' bhéal an tairngireacht gan feall:
Má's Geimhreadh, a ghaoth, atá ann, nach mbeidh Earrach ar ball?[23]

NOTES

1   W Keach, 'Young Shelley',
(http://www.rc.umd.edu/praxis/earlyshelley/keach/keach.hntl).

2   See also On an icicle that clung to the grass of a grave, *Poetical Works of Shelley,* op cit, verse 2 and 5, p869 for similar sentiments that may refer to Ireland, though it seems more likely that Shelley was referring to America.

3   R Southey, *Poems* p396 and T Moore, *Poetical Works* (London, 1915), p181.

4   See chapter 2, p28.

5   S T Coleridge, *Poetical Works* (Oxford, 1969), p237.

6   T Moore, op cit, p198.

7   RHolmes, op cit, p108.

8   T Moore, op cit, p456.

9   See F L Jones, op cit, vol 1 p44, p484n, p511n, p514n, p563, p580, p581n, p582, vol. 2, p24n, p118, p323, p348n, p351n, p368n, p412, p442, p480. See also Longman's Critical Edition, *Poems*, vol 1, p125, p146, p153, p230, p204, vol.2, p90, p91, p184, p191, p246.

10   See Percy B. Shelley, *Complete Poetical Works* (Boston, 1901), p591, p616, p619, p620 for details. See also Longman's Critical Edition, *Poems* vol 1, p153, p171, p470, vol. 2, p231, p248, p338.

11   P B Shelley, *The Esdaile Notebook*, op cit, lines 230-233, p98.

12   Ibid, lines 268-70, p430.

13   Ibid, act 1, scene 1, lines 23-5, p389.

14   Ibid, act 1, scene 1, lines 404-5, p389.

15   T Moore, op cit, p184.

16   *Poetical Works of Shelley,* op cit, act 2, scene 1, lines 172-178, p389.

17   Ibid, act 2, scene 2, lines 72-81, p389.

18   Thomas Wentworth was Lord Deputy of Ireland (1633-1639). Mrs Mason's library was a likely source of information for Shelley on this period in Ireland. We know from Claire Clairmont's *Journal* (17 August 1820) that she was reading the Earl of Castlehaven's *Memoirs of the Irish Wars* (London, 1680). Godwin also covers some of the same ground in *Mandeville* (London, 1817).

19   *Poetical Works of Shelley,* op cit, scene 2, lines 66-69, 196-199, p488.

20   Ibid, scene 2, lines 347-350, p488.

21   P de Brún (1889-1960). See *Studies* (Dublin, 1928), vol 17, p325 and *The Capuchin Annual* (Dublin, 1961), p371.

22   *New Ireland Review.* (Dublin, October 1909), vol.32, p76, *An Néall*, lines 1-12,

23   *Sinn Féin,* (16 February 1924), p6, *Dán do'n Ghaoith Aniar*, lines 57-70.

Selected Letters

ALL relevant letters, mostly in extracts, concerning Shelley and Ireland are included in this section. Shelley's letters are referenced by date and number to F L Jones (ed), *The Letters of Percy Bysshe Shelley*, 2 volumes (London, 1964). Harriet Shelley's letters are referenced by date and number to *Letters from Harriet Shelley to Catherine Nugent* (London, 1889). All other letters are referenced by date only to the F L Jones edition of Shelley's letters unless otherwise indicated.

Letter 49 (Extract):
Shelley, London, to Leigh Hunt, the *Examiner*, London. 2/03/1811.

The enclosed is an address[1] to the public, the proposal for a meeting, and shall be modified according to your judgement, if you will do me the honour to consider the point.

The ultimate intention of my aim is to induce a meeting of such enlightened unprejudiced members of the community, whose independent principles expose them to evils which might thus become alleviated, and to form a methodical society which should be organised so as to resist the coalition of the enemies of liberty which at present renders any expression of opinion on matters of policy dangerous to individuals. It has been for want of societies of this nature that corruption has attained the height at which we now behold it, nor can any of us bear in mind the very great influence, which some years since was gained by Illuminism without considering that a society of equal extent might establish rational liberty on as firm a basis as that which would have supported the visionary schemes of a completely-equalised community.

Letter 148 (Extract):

Shelley, Keswick, to Elizabeth Hitchener, Sussex. 10⁄12⁄1811

We design…to visit Ireland.[2] We are very near Port-Patric[3] – if you could extend your time could you not accompany us.

Letter 155 (Extract):

Shelley, Keswick, to Elizabeth Hitchener, Sussex. 26⁄12⁄1811

Southey hates the Irish, he speaks against Catholic Emancipation, & Parliamentary reform. In all these things we differ, & our differences were the subject of a long conversation.

Letter 160 (Extract):

Shelley, Keswick, to William Godwin, London. 16⁄01⁄1812

In a few days we set off to Dublin… Our journey has been settled some time. We go principally to forward as much as we can the Catholic Emancipation. Southey the Poet whose principles were pure & elevated once, is now the servile champion of every abuse and absurdity. I have had much conversation with him. He says `You will think as I do when you are as old'. I do not feel the least disposition to be Mr S's proselyte.

Letter 161 (Extract):

Shelley, Keswick, to Elizabeth Hitchener, Sussex. 16⁄01⁄1812

We have now serious thoughts of immediately going to Ireland. Southey's conversation has lost its charm, except it be the charm of horror, at so hateful a prostitution of talents. I hasten to go to Ireland. I am now writing an address to the poor Irish Catholics; part of it will be in the following strain. After describing their miseries, I select a passage which may give you some idea of my views.[4] 'Think of your children, and your childrens children, and take great care (for it all rests with you) that whilst one tyranny is destroyed another more fierce and terrible does not spring up – Take care of smoothfaced men who talk indeed of freedom, but who will cheat you into slavery – Can there be worse slavery than depending for the safety of your souls on another man? Is one man more favoured than another by God? No, if God makes any distinction they are favoured according to the good they do, not according to the rank or profession they hold – God loves a poor man as well as a priest. Jesus Christ has said as much, and has given him a soul as much to himself. The worship that a good Being must love is that of a simple affectionate heart that shews it's piety in good doings, and not in ceremonies confessions masses burials wonders and processions – Take care that you are not led away by these things. Doubt everything that leads you not to love and charity with all men, and think of the word heretic as of a word invented by some selfish knave for the ruin and misery of the world to answer his own paltry and narrow ambition'. You see my friend what I am about. I consider the state of Ireland [as] constituting a part of a great crisis in opinions. You shall see the pamphlet when it comes out; it will be cheaply printed, and in large sheets to be stuck about the walls of Dublin. I am eager and earnest to be there…

I had previously written to request the Duke of Norfolk to lend me £100. So if the Duke complies we shall be very rich. I shall likewise make money in Ireland. All the money I get shall be squeezed out of the rich; the poor cannot understand and would not buy my poems, therefore I shall print them expensively. My metaphysics[5] will be also printed expensively…the address to the Irish shall be printed very cheap, and I shall wilfully lose money by it. I shall distribute [it] throughout Ireland, either personally or by means of booksellers…we are not going to Ireland this week or next, but soon I hope.

Letter 162 (Extract):
Shelley, Keswick, to Elizabeth Hitchener, Sussex. 26⁄01⁄1812

All is now prepared for Ireland except the arrival of our £100[6] daily expected from Whitton the attorney… I have been busily engaged in an address to the Irish which will be printed as Paine's works were, and pasted on the walls of Dublin: my Poems will be printed there…

I have the vanity to think that you will be pleased with my address to the Irish; it is intended to familiarise to uneducated apprehensions ideas of liberty, benevolence peace and toleration. It is secretly intended also as a preliminary to other pamphlets to shake Catholicism at its basis, and to induce Quakerish and Socinian[7] principles of politics without objecting to the Christian Religion, which would do no good to the vulgar just now, and cast an odium over the other principles which are advanced.

Letter 163 (Extract):
Shelley, Keswick, to William Godwin, London. 26/01/1812

Your letter has reached me on the eve of our departure for Dublin. I cannot deny myself the pleasure of answering it altho' we shall probably have reached Ireland before an answer to this can arrive, – you do us a great and essential service by the enclosed introduction to Mr Curran, he is a man whose public character I have admired and respected…

I have been preparing an address to the Catholics of Ireland which however deficient may be its execution, I can by no means admit that it contains one sentiment which can harm the cause of liberty and happiness; it consists of the benevolent and tolerant deductions of Philosophy reduced into the simplest language, and such as those who by their uneducated poverty are most susceptible of evil impressions from Catholicism may clearly comprehend. I know it can do [no] harm; it cannot excite rebellion, as its main principle is to trust the success of a cause to the energy of its truth. It 'cannot widen the breach between the Kingdoms,' as it attempts to convey to the vulgar mind sentiments of universal philanthropy, and whatever impressions it may produce they can be no others but those of peace & harmony. it owns no religion but benevolence, no cause but virtue, no party but the world – I shall devote myself with unremitting zeal, so far as an uncertain state of health will permit towards forwarding the great ends of virtue and happiness in Ireland, regarding as I do the present state of that country's affairs, as an opportunity which if I thus disengaged permit to pass unoccupied I am unworthy of the character which I have assumed.

Letter 164 (Extract):

Shelley, Keswick, to Elizabeth Hitchener, Sussex. 29⁄01⁄1812

On Monday [3rd February] we depart for Ireland… Prospects appear fair but I have learned to doubt of the result of all human enterprises…

Have you no money. Write and say so – if not we can easily spare some, we shall have superfluity in Dublin… I must have no horrible forebodings. Everybody is not killed that goes to Dublin – perhaps many are now on the road for the very same purpose as that which we propose… Come, come to Ireland, arrange your affairs, give up school; it is a noble field, energies like your's ought to be unconfined – Write for what money you want.

[Added by Harriet]

then why will you not join us? I am well convinced that if you were in Ireland you might do as much good as Percy… I cannot wait till the Summer, you must come to us in Ireland. I am Irish, I claim kindred with them; I have done with the English, I have witnessed too much of John Bull and I am ashamed of him – till I am disappointed in the Brothers and Sisters of my affection I will claim kindred with those brave sons of the ocean and when I am deceived in them it will be enough…there seems to be sad work in Ireland but I hope Percy will escape all prosecutions.

Letter 166 (Extract):

Shelley, Dublin, to Elizabeth Hitchener, Sussex. 13⁄02⁄1812

Last night we arrived safe in this city. It was useless to have written to you before – now I have only time for a line to tell you of our safety. We were driven by a storm quite to the North of Ireland, and yesterday was the end of our journey thence.

Letter 167 (Extract):

Shelley, Dublin, to Elizabeth Hitchener, Sussex. 14⁄02⁄1812

At length however you are free from anxiety for our safety as here we have nothing to apprehend but a Government which will not assure yourself dare to be so barefacedly oppressive as to attack my address – it will breathe the spirit of peace, toleration and patience: In short in a few posts it will be sent to you – I shall continue to write to you as freely as from Keswick – whether our letters be inspected or not I cannot tell – if they are, this I know that their hatred to me will not thereby become stronger, or their conviction of my discontentedness clearer, as my name which will be prefixed to the address, will shew that my deeds are not deeds of darkness, nor my conceits those of mystery and fear. Dread nothing for me. The course of my conduct in Ireland, (as shall the entire course of my life) shall be marked by openness and sincerity. – The peace and toleration which I recommend can make no good men my enemies… We will meet you in Wales, and never part again. You shall not cross the Channel alone; it will not do. In compliance with Harriet's earnest solicitations I entreated you instantly to come, and join our circle. To resign your school, all everything for us, and the Irish cause. This could nor be done I now see plainly; consistently with the duties which you have imposed upon yourself, duties, which I ought to have respected, it could not be done. But the warmth of our hearts ran away with the coolness of our heads; forgive the fault of friendship. But summer will come – The ocean rolls between us. O thou Ocean, whose multitudinous billows ever lash Erin's green isle on whose shores this venturous arm would plant the flag of liberty, Roll on! and with each wave whose echoings die, amid thy melancholy silentness shall die a moment too – one of those moments which part my friend and me. I could stand upon thy shores O Erin and could count the billows that in their unceasing swell dash on thy beach, and every wave might seem an instrument in Time the giant's grasp, to burst the barriers of Eternity. Proceed thou giant conquering and to conquer. March on thy lonely way – the nations fall beneath thy noiseless footstep – pyramids that for millenniums have defied the blast, and laughed at lightnings thou dost crush to nought. Yon monarch in his solitary pomp, is but the fungus of a winter day that thy light footstep presses into dust – Thou art a conqueror Time! all things give way before thee but 'the fixed and virtuous will', the sacred sympathy of soul, which was when thou wert not, which shall be when thou perishest…[8]

Well do I know that economy is the greatest generosity; and altho' we cannot practise it so strictly in Dublin as I could wish, this will however be but short. Have you heard, a new republic is set up in Mexico. I have just written the following short tribute to its success [see Appendix 1, p199]...

My address will soon come out; it will be instantly followed by another, with downright proposals for instituting associations for bettering the condition of human kind. I even I, weak young poor as I am will attempt to organise them. The society of peace and love! Oh! that I [may] be a successful apostle of this only true religion, the religion of philanthropy – at all events I will have a debating society & see what will grow out of that…

In a few days I shall have more much more to tell you – Godwin has introduced me to Mr Curran. I took the letter this morning; he was not at home. I shall see him soon… You have not seen Tom Paine's works. Eliza [Westbrook] is going to employ herself in collecting the useful passages which we shall publish.

Letter 168 (Extract):
Shelley, Dublin, to Elizabeth Hitchener, Sussex. 18/02/1812
I send you the first sheet of my first address, as it comes out. The style of this, as you will perceive is adapted to the lowest comprehension that can read. It will be followed by another in my own natural style tho' in the same strain.

Letter 170 (Extract):
Shelley, Dublin, to William Godwin, London. 24/02/1812
A most tedious journey by sea and land has brought us to our destination; I have delayed a few days informing you of it because I inclose with this a little pamphlet[9] which I have just printed and thereby save a double expense. I have wilfully vulgarised the language of this pamphlet in order to reduce the remarks it contains to the taste and comprehension of the Irish peasantry who have been too long brutalised by vice and ignorance – I conceive that the benevolent passions of their breasts

are in some degree excited, and individual interest in some degree generalised by Catholic disqualifications and the oppressive influence of the Union Act: that some degree of indignation has arisen at the conduct of the prince which might lead to blind insurrections. A crisis like this ought not to be permitted to pass unoccupied or unimproved. I have another pamphlet in the press earnestly recommending to a different class, the institution of a Philanthropic Society. No unnatural unanimity can take place, if secessions of the minority on any question are invariably made. It might segregate into twenty different societies each coinciding generically, tho' differing specifically… I am exceedingly obliged by your letter of introduction to Mr Curran. His speeches had interested me before I had any idea of coming to Ireland. It seems that he was the only man who would engage on behalf of the prisoners during those times of horror of the Rebellions.[10] I have called upon him twice but have not found him at home. I hope that the motives which induce me to publish this early in life do not arise from any desire of distinguishing myself, any more than is consistent with, and subordinate to usefulness…

I will publish nothing that shall not conduce to virtue, and therefore my publications so far as they do influence shall influence to good. My views of society, and my hopes of it, meet with congenial ones in few breasts. But virtue and truth are congenial to many. I will employ no means but these for my object, and however visionary some may regard the ultimatum that I propose, if they act virtuously they will equally with myself forward its accomplishment. And my publications will present to the moralist and metaphysician a picture of a mind however uncultured and unpruned which had at the dawn of its knowledge taken a singular turn, and to leave out the early lineaments of its appearance would be to efface those which the attrition of the world had not deprived of right angled originality.

Letter 171:
Shelley, Dublin, to Hamilton Rowan, Dublin. 25/02/1812

Although I have not the pleasure of being personally known to you, I consider the motives which actuated me in writing the inclosed sufficiently introductory to authorise me in sending you some copies, and waiving ceremonials in a case where public benefit is concerned. Sir, although an Englishman, I feel for Ireland; and I have left the country in which the chance of birth placed me for the sole purpose of adding my little stock of usefulness to the fund which I hope that Ireland possesses to aid me in the unequal yet sacred combat in which she is engaged. In the course of a few days more I shall print another small pamphlet, which shall be sent to you. I have intentionally vulgarised the language of the inclosed. I have printed 1,500 copies, and am now distributing them throughout Dublin.

Letter 172 (Extract):
Shelley, Dublin, to Elizabeth Hitchener, Sussex. 27/02/1812

I have already sent 400 of my little pamphlets into the world, and they have excited a sensation of wonder in Dublin. 1,100 yet remain for distribution – Copies have been sent to 60 public houses, no prosecution is yet attempted. I do not see how it can be. Congratulate me my friend for everything proceeds well; I could not expect more rapid success. The persons with whom I have got acquainted, approve of my principles, & think the truths of the equality of man, the necessity of a reform and the probability of a revolution undeniable. But they differ from the mode of my enforcing these principles, & hold expediency to be necessary in politics in as much as it is employed in its utmost latitude by the enemies of innovation – I hope to convince them of the contrary of this…

I send a man[11] out every day to distribute copies, with instructions how and where to give them. His accounts correspond with the multitude of people who possess them. I stand at the balcony of our window, and watch till I see a man who looks likely. I throw a book to him. On Monday [2 March] my next book makes its appearance, this is addressed to a different class, recommending & proposing associations – I have in my mind a plan for proselytising the young men at Dublin College. Those who are not entirely given up to the grossness of dissipation are perhaps reclaimable; I know how much of good there is in human nature, spite of the overwhelming torrent of depravity which education unlooses. I see little instances of kindness and goodwill, almost everywhere, surely education, or impressions intentionally induced upon the mind might foster and encourage the good, as it might eradicate the evil. This 'Philanthropic Association' of ours is intended to unite both of these. Whilst you are with us in Wales I shall attempt to organise one there, which shall correspond with the Dublin one. Might I not extend them all over England and quietly revolutionise the country…

My youth is much against me here. Strange, that truth should not be judged by its inherent excellence independent of any reference to the utterer! – To improve on this advantage the servant gave out that I was only 15 years of age. The person who was told this of course did not believe it.

I have not yet seen Curran. I do not like him for accepting the office of Master of the Rolls. O'Connor brother to the Rebel Arthur is here, I have written to him. Do not fear what you say in your letters. I am resolved – Good principles are scarce here. The public papers are either oppositionist or ministerial; one is as contemptible and narrow as the other. I wish I could change this. I of course am hated by both of these parties. The remnant of United Irishmen whose wrongs make them hate England I have more hopes of. I have met with no determined Republicans, but I have found some who are DEMOCRATIFIABLE. I have met with some waverers between Xtianity and Deism.[12] – I shall attempt to make them reject all the bad, and take all the good of the Jewish Books. – I have often thought that the moral sayings of Jesus Christ might be very useful if selected from the mystery and immorality which surrounds them – it is a little work I have in contemplation.[13] We shall leave this place at the end of April.

[Added by Harriet]

I'm sure you would laugh were you to see us give the pamphlets. We throw them out of [the] window and give them to men that we pass in the streets; for myself I am ready to die of laughter when it is done and Percy looks so grave. Yesterday he put one into a woman's hood of a cloak. She knew nothing of it and we passed her. I could hardly get on my muscles were so irritated.

(Extract):
William Godwin, London, to Shelley, Dublin. 4/03/1812

In your last letter you say, 'I publish, because I will publish nothing that shall not conduce to virtue; and therefore my publications, so far as they do influence, shall influence to good'.

Oh! my friend, how shortsighted are the views which dictated that sentence! Every man, in every deliberate action of his life, imagines he sees a preponderance of good likely to result. This is the law of our nature, from which none of us can escape. You do not on this point generically differ from the human beings about you. Mr Burke and Tom Paine, when they wrote on the French Revolution, perhaps equally believed that the sentiments they supported were essentially conducive to the welfare of man…

In the pamphlet you have just sent me, your views and mine as to the improvement of mankind are decisively at issue. You profess the immediate object of your efforts to be 'the organisation of a society, whose institution shall serve as a bond to its members'. If I may be allowed to understand my book on *Political Justice,* its pervading principle is, that association is a most ill-chosen and ill-qualified mode of endeavouring to promote the political happiness of mankind. And I think of your pamphlet, however commendable and lovely are many of the sentiments it contains, that it will be either ineffective to its immediate object, or that it has no very remote tendency to light again the flames of rebellion and war. It is painful to me to differ so much from your views on the subject, but it is my duty to tell you that such is the case.

Does it not follow that you have read my writings very slightly? I wish, at least, you had known whether our views were in harmony or opposition.

Discussion, reading, inquiry, perpetual communication, these are my favourite methods for the improvement of mankind. but associations, organised societies, I firmly condemn…

Discussion and conversation on the best interests of society are excellent, as long as they are unfettered, and each man talks to his neighbour in the freedom of congenial intercourse, as he happens to meet with him in the customary haunts of men, or in the quiet and beneficent intercourse of each other's fireside.

I perfectly agree with you when you say that it is highly improving for a man, who is ever to write for the public, that he should write much while he is young. It improves him equally in the art of thinking and of expressing his thoughts.

But I see no necessary connection between writing and publishing; and, least of all, with one's name. The life of a thinking man, who does this, will be made up of a series of retractions. It is beautiful to correct our errors, to make each day a comment on the last, and to grow perpetually wiser; but all this need not be done before the public. It is commendable to wash one's face, but I will not wash mine in the saloon of the opera-house. A man may resolve, as you say, to present to the moralist and metaphysician a picture of all the successive turns and revolutions of his mind, and it is fit there should be some men that should do this. But such a man must be contented to sacrifice general usefulness, and confine himself to this. Such a man was Rousseau; but not such a man was Bacon, or Milton…

You confess that your thesis on atheism was not well judged or wise, though you still seek to shelter yourself under the allegation that it was harmless. I think the second chapter of your retractions is not far distant…

How did you manage with Curran? I hope you have seen him. I should not wonder, however, if your pamphlet has frightened him. You should have left my letter with your card the first time you called, and then it was his business to have sought you.

Letter 173 (Extract):
Shelley, Dublin, to William Godwin, London. 8/03/1812

I am not forgetful or unheeding of what you said of Associations. But *Political Justice* was first published in 1793; nearly twenty years have elapsed since the general diffusion of its doctrines. What has followed? Have men ceased to fight, has vice and misery vanished from the earth. – Have the fireside communications which it recommends taken place? – Out of the many who have read that inestimable book how many have been blinded by prejudice, how many in short have taken it up to gratify an ephemeral vanity and when the hour of its novelty had passed threw it aside and yielded with fashion to the arguments of Mr Malthus![14] I have at length proposed a Philanthropic Association, which I conceive not to be contradictory but strictly compatible with the principles of *Political Justice.* – The *Address* was principally designed to operate on the Irish 'mob'. Can they be in a worse state than at present? Intemperance and hard labour have reduced them to machines. The oyster that is washed and driven at the mercy of the tides appear to me an animal of almost equal elevation in the scale of intellectual being. – Is it impossible to awaken a moral sense in the breasts of these who appear so unfitted for the high destination of their nature? Might not an unadorned display of moral truth, suited to their comprehensions produce the best effects. – The state of society appears to me to be retrogressive; if there be any truth in the hopes which I so fondly cherish, then this cannot be. Yet even if it be stationary the eager activity of Philanthropists is demanded. – I think of the last twenty years with impatient scepticism as to the progress which the human mind has made during this period. I will own that I am eager that something should be done. But my Association – In some suggestions[15] respecting it, I have the following. 'That any number of persons who meet together for philanthropical purposes should ascertain by friendly discussion, those points of opinion wherein they differ, & those wherein they coincide. and should by subjecting them to rational analysis produce an unanimity founded on reason, and not the superficial agreement, too often exhibited at associations for mere party purposes; that the minority whose belief could not subscribe to the opinion of the majority on a division in any question of moment & interest should recede. Some associations might by refinement of secessions contain not more than three or four members'. I do not think a society such as this is incompatible with your chapter on associations, it proposes no violent or immediate measures, it's intentions are a facilitation of enquiry, and actually to carry into effect those confidential and private communications which you recommend. I send you with this the proposals, which will be followed by the 'suggestions.' – I had no conception of the depth of human misery until now. The poor of Dublin are assuredly the meanest & most miserable of all. In their narrow streets thousands seem huddled together – one mass of animated filth! With what eagerness do such scenes as these inspire me, how selfconfident too, do I feel in my assumption to teach the lessons of virtue to those who grind their fellow beings into worse than annihilation. These were the persons to whom in my fancy I had addressed myself; how quickly were my views on this subject changed! yet how deeply has this very change rooted the conviction on which I came hither. I do not think that my book can in the slightest degree tend to violence. The pains which I have taken even to tautology to insist on pacific measures, the necessity which every warrior and rebel must lay under to deny almost every passage of my book before he can become so, must at least exculpate me from tending to make him so. I shudder to think that for the very roof that covers me, for the bed whereon I lie, I am indebted to the selfishness of man. A remedy must somewhere have a beginning. Have I explained myself clearly? – Are we now at issue?

I have not seen Mr Curran. I have called repeatedly, left my address, and my pamphlet. I will see him before I leave Dublin. I send a newspaper, and the *Proposals*.

[PS] You will see the account of ME in the newspapers.[16] I am vain, but not so foolish as not to be rather piqued than gratified at the eulogia of a Journal.

Letter 174 (Extract):
Shelley, Dublin, to Elizabeth Hitchener, Sussex. 10/03/1812

An Irishman has been torn from his wife and family in Lisbon, because he was an expatriate and compelled to serve as a common soldier in the Portuguese army, by that monster of antipatriotic inhumanity Beresford[17] the idol of the belligerents. You will soon see a copy of his letter, & soon hear of my or Sir Francis Burdett's exertions in his favour. He shall be free; this nation shall awaken. It is attended with circumstances singularly characteristic of cowardice and tyranny. My blood boils to madness to think of it. A poor boy whom I found starving with his mother, in a hiding place of unutterable filth and misery, whom I rescued, and was about to teach to read, has been snatched on a charge of false and villainous effrontery to a magistrate of Hell, who gave him the alternative of the tender or of military servitude. He preferred neither yet was compelled to be a soldier. This has come to my knowledge this morning. I am resolved to prosecute this business to the very jaws of government, snatching (if possible) the poison from its fangs. – A widow woman with three infants were taken up by two constables. – I remonstrated, I pleaded – I was everything that my powers could make me. The landlady was overcome. The constable relented, and when I asked him if he had a heart, he said 'to be sure he had as well as another man, but – that he was called out to business of this nature sometimes twenty times in a night'. The woman's crime was stealing a penny loaf. She is however drunken, & nothing that I or anyone can do can save her from ultimate ruin and starvation. I am sick of this city & long to be with you and peace… I have not shown Harriet or Eliza your letter yet, they are walking with a Mr Lawless (a valuable man,) whilst I write this…

Send me the Sussex Papers. Insert or make them insert the account of me.[18] It may have a good effect on the minds of the people as a preparative. I send you two tonight. The Association proceeds slowly, and I fear will not be established. Prejudices are so violent in contradiction to my principles that more hate me as a freethinker, than love me as a votary of Freedom. You will see my letter next week to the Editor of the panegyrising paper.[19] – Some will call it violent. I have at least made a stir here, and set some men's minds afloat. I may succeed but I fear I shall not in the main object of associations. – Dublin is the most difficult of all. In Wales I fear not. In Lewes fear is ridiculous. I am certain – Your book-club is a beautiful idea, cherish the spirit and keep it alive…I am in hopes of getting a share in a management of a paper here. I have daily had numbers of people calling on me; none will do. The spirit of Bigotry is high.

[Added by Harriet]

Has Percy mentioned to you a very amiable man of the name of Lawless, he is very much attached to the cause yet dare not act. Percy has spoken to him of you & he wishes very much to know all about you, we have this Morning been introduced to his wife who is very near her confinement, she is a very nice woman tho' not equal to him… Send us the Paper in which you have inserted the *Address.*

Letter 175 (Extract):

Harriet Shelley, Dublin, to Elizabeth Hitchener, Sussex. 14/03/1812

…have you heard anything of this Habeas Corpus Act[20] being suspended? I have been very much alarmed at the intelligence, tho' I hope it is ill founded; if it is not where we shall be is not known, as from Percy's having made himself so busy in the cause of this poor Country, he has raised himself many enemies who would take advantage of such a time & instantly execute their vengeance upon him.

[Added by Shelley]

I do not like Lord Fingal or any of the Catholic aristocracy; their intolerance can be equalled by nothing but the hardy wickedness and falsehood of the Prince. My speech was misinterpreted. I spoke for more than an hour; the hisses with which they greeted me when I spoke of religion, tho' in terms of respect, were mixed with applause when I avowed my mission. The newspapers have only noted that which did not excite disapprobation – As to an Association my hopes daily grow fainter on the subject, as my perceptions of its necessity gain strength. I shall soon however have the command of a newspaper, with Mr Lawless of whom I shall tell more. – this will be a powerful engine of melioration. – Mr L tho' he regards my ultimate hopes as visionary, is willing to acquiesce in my means. He is a republican.

(Extract):

W Godwin, London, to Shelley, Dublin. 14/03/1812

I take up the pen again immediately on the receipt of yours, because I am desirous of making one more effort to save yourself and the Irish people from the calamities with which I see your mode of proceeding to be fraught. In the commencement of this letter you profess to 'acquiesce in my decisions,' and you go on with those measures which, with no sparing and equivocal voice, I have condemned. I smile, with a bitter smile, a smile of much pain, at the impotence of my expostulations on so momentous a topic, when I observe these inconsistencies. I have received nothing from you on this occasion but a letter and a newspaper. If you sent anything else – which I suspect from your saying, 'I send you with this the *Proposals*' – it has not reached me; and I mention this circumstance because, of course, 'I can only reason from what I know' – though I am as well assured as I can be of any moral truth whatever, that nothing that is behind can possibly vitiate and overturn the conclusions I came to in my last letter, and which I repeat in this.

You say in the extract contained in the *Weekly Messenger*, 'I propose an Association for the following purposes. first, of debating on the propriety of whatever measures may be agitated; and, secondly, for carrying, by united and individual exertion, such measures into effect when determined on'.

Can anything be plainer than this? Do you not here exhort persons, who you say 'are of scarcely greater elevation in the scale of intellectual being than the oyster. thousands huddled together, one mass of animated filth,' to take the redress of grievances into their own hands.

But if it were exactly the contrary, if you exhorted them to meet, having their hands carefully tied behind them before they came together, what would that avail? Would not the first strong sympathetic impulse which shot through the circle, like the electric fluid, cause them 'to break their cords, as a thread of tow is broken when it toucheth the fire?'

The people of Ireland have been for a series of years in a state of diseased activity; and, misjudging that you are, you talk of awakening them. They will rise up like Cadmus's seed of dragons teeth,[21] and their first act will be to destroy each other. You say, 'the pains you have taken, even to tautology, to insist on pacific measures must at least exculpate you from tending to make the Irish peasant a warrior and a rebel!' This is not the language of a philosopher, or a reasoner. If you are 'eager that something should be done,' you must take all the consequences of your efforts for that purpose. It behoves the friend of man to search into the hidden seeds of things, and to view events in their causes. He scarcely deserves the name, who plunges without consideration into a sea of important measures, and leaves the final result of all he begins to chance.

You have 'insisted on pacific measures, even to tautology, and therefore judge yourself exculpated'. But this is not so, I have made a main pillar of my doctrines of *Political Justice* – a hostility to associations. and yet I cannot but consider your fearful attempt at creating a chain of associations as growing, however indirectly and unfairly, out of my book. If you had never read my book, you would probably never have gone to Ireland upon the errand that has now led you thither. I shall ever regret this effect of my book; and I can only seek consolation in the belief that it has done more good to many other persons, and the hope that it may contribute, with other mightier and more important causes, to the melioration of future ages.

You say 'What has been done within the last twenty years?' Oh, that I could place, you on the pinnacle of ages, from which these twenty years would shrink to an invisible point!…

Shelley, you are preparing a scene of blood! If your associations take effect to any extensive degree, tremendous consequences will follow, and hundreds, by their calamities and premature fate, will expiate your error. And then what will it avail you to say, 'I warned them against this; when I put the seed into the ground, I laid my solemn injunctions upon it, that it should not germinate?'

If you wish to consider the sentiments which in the earnestness of my soul I have presented to you, you should consider my two letters as parts of the same discourse, and read them together. Do not be restrained by a false shame from retracting your steps; you cannot say, like Macbeth,

'I am in blood stepp'd in so far that should I wade no more, returning were as tedious as go o'er'.

Letter 176 (Extract):
Shelley, Dublin, to William Godwin, London. 18/03/1812

I have said that I acquiesce in your decisions, nor has my conduct militated with the assertion. I have withdrawn from circulation the publications wherein I erred & am preparing to quit Dublin. It is not because I think that such associations as I conceived would be deleterious, that I have withdrawn them. It is possible to festinate or retard the progress of human perfectibility, such associations as I would have recommended would be calculated to produce the former effect, the refinement of secessions would prevent a fictitious unanimity, as their publicity would render ineffectual any schemes of violent innovation.

I am not one of those whom pride will restrain from admitting my own short-sightedness, or confessing a conviction which wars with those previously avowed. My schemes of organising the ignorant I confess to be ill-timed. I cannot conceive that they were dangerous, as unqualified publicity was likewise enforced, moreover I do [not] see that a peasant would attentively read my *Address*, and arising from the perusal become imbued in sentiments of violence & bloodshed. It is indescribably painful to contemplate beings capable of soaring to the heights of science which Newton & Locke attained without attempting to awaken them from a state of lethargy so opposite. The part of this city called the Liberty[22] exhibits a spectacle of squalidness and misery such as might reasonably excite impatience in a cooler temperament than mine. But I submit. I shall address myself no more to the illiterate, I will look to events in which it will be impossible that I can share, and make myself the cause of an effect which will take place ages after I shall have mouldered into dust. I need not observe that this resolve requires Stoicism.[23] To return to the heartless bustle of ordinary life, to take interest in its uninteresting details – I cannot. Wholly to abstract our views from self undoubtedly requires unparalleled disinterestedness, there is not a completer abstraction than labouring for distant ages. My association scheme undoubtedly grew out of my notions of political justice, first generated by your book on that subject. I had not however read in vain of confidential discussions, & a recommendation for their general adoption, not in vain had I been warned against a fictitious unanimity. I have had the opportunity of witnessing the latter at public dinners. The peculiarity of my associations would have consisted in combining the adoption of the former with the rejection of the latter. Moreover I desired to sink the question of immediate grievance in the more general and remote consideration of a highly perfectible state of society. I desired to embrace the present opportunity for attempting to forward the accomplishment of that event, & my ultimate views looked to an establishment of those familiar parties for discussion which have not yet become general… We leave Dublin in three weeks…

Fear no more for any violence or hurtful measures in which I may be instrumental in Dublin. My mind is now by no means settled on the subject of associations. They appear to me in one point of view useful in another deleterious. I acquiesce in your decisions. I am neither haughty reserved or unpersuadable.

(Extract):
Harriet Shelley, Dublin, to E Hitchener, Sussex. 18/03/1812

As Percy has sent you such a large Box so full of inflammable matter, I think I may be allowed to send a little but not [of] such a nature as his. I sent you two letters in a newspaper, which I hope you received safe from the intrusion of Post masters. I sent one of the Pamphlets to my Father in a newspaper, which was opened and charged, but which was very trifling when compared to what you and Godwin paid.

I believe I have mentioned a new acquaintance of ours, a Mrs Nugent, who is sitting in the room now and talking to Percy about Virtue. You see how little I stand upon ceremony. I have seen her but twice before, and I find her a very agreeable, sensible woman. She has felt most severely the miseries of her country in which she has been a very active member. She visited all the Prisons in the time of the Rebellion to exhort the people to have courage and hope. She says it was a most dreadful task; but it was her duty, and she would not shrink from the performance of it. This excellent woman, with all her notions of Philanthropy and justice, is obliged to work for her subsistence – to work in a shop which is a furrier's; there she is every day confined to her needle. Is it not a thousand pities that such a woman should be so dependent upon others? She has visited us this evening for about three hours, and is now returned home. The evening is the only time she can get out in the week; but Sunday is her own, and then we are to see her. She told Percy that her country was her only love, when he asked her if she was married. She called herself Mrs I suppose on account of her age, as she looks rather old for a Miss She has never been out of her own country, and has no wish to leave it.

This is St. Patrick's night, and the Irish always get very tipsy on such a night as this. The Horse Guards are pacing the streets and will be so all the night, so fearful are they of disturbances, the poor people being very much that way inclined, as Provisions are very scarce in the southern counties. Poor Irish People, how much I feel for them. Do you know, such is their ignorance that when there is a drawing-room held they go from some distance to see the people who keep them starving to get their luxuries; they will crowd round the state carriages in great glee to see those within who have stripped them of their rights, and who wantonly revel in a profusion of ill-gotten luxury whilst so many of those harmless people are wanting Bread for their wives and children. What a spectacle! People talk of the fiery spirit of these distressed creatures, but that spirit is very much broken and ground down by the oppressors of this poor country. I may with truth say there are more Beggars in this city than any other in the world. They are so poor they have hardly a rag to cover their naked limbs, and such is their passion for drink that when you relieve them one day you see them in the same deplorable situation the next. Poor creatures, they live more on whiskey than anything, for meat is so dear they cannot afford to purchase any. If they had the means I do not know that they would, whiskey being so much cheaper and to their palates so much more desirable. Yet how often do we hear people say that Poverty is no evil. I think if they had experienced it they would soon alter their tone… Percy has sent you all his Pamphlets with the *Declaration of Rights*, which you will disperse to advantage. He has not many of his first *Address,* having taken great pains to circulate them through this city.

All thoughts of an Association are given up as impracticable. We shall leave this noisy town on the 7th of April, unless the Habeas Corpus Act should be suspended, and then we shall be obliged to leave here as soon as possible.

Letter 177 (Extract):
Shelley, Dublin, to Thomas Medwin, Sussex. 20/03/1812

I am now engaged with a literary friend in the publication of a voluminous History of Ireland, of which two hundred and fifty pages are already printed, and for the completion of which, I wish to raise two hundred and fifty pounds. I could obtain undeniable security for it at the end of eighteen months.

(Extract):
William Godwin, London, to Shelley, Dublin. 30/03/1812[24]

I received your last letter on the 24th instant, and the perusal gave me a very high degree of pleasure. The way in which my emotion of pleasure poured itself out was in writing a letter to Curran, stating that I supposed he had kept himself aloof from you on account of your pamphlet, and that at my importunity you had given up your project, and that that being the case, I trusted he would oblige me by seeking the man, whom, under different circumstances, he had probably thought himself bound to shun. This was the most expressive way I could think of, to convey to you the delight I felt in your conduct… I can now look upon you as a friend. Before, I knew not what might happen. It was like making an acquaintance with Robert Emmet, who, I believe, like yourself, was a man of a very pure mind, but respecting whom I could not have told, from day to day, what calamities he might bring upon his country; how effectually (like the bear in the fable) he might smash the nose of his mother to pieces, when he intended only to remove the noxious insect that tormented her – what premature and tragical fate he might bring down upon himself.

Letter 178 (Extract):
Shelley, Wales, to Elizabeth Hitchener, Sussex. 16/04/1812

We left Dublin, and arrived at Holyhead after a passage of wearisome length…have you ere this received our box & its contents. I paid the carriage as far as I could, that is across the channel, & I am positive that it did not come by the post… Your letter enjoined us to leave Dublin. We received it a short time before we had settled to depart. The Habeas Corpus has not been suspended, nor probably will they do it. We left Dublin because I had done all that I could do, if its effects were beneficial they were not greatly so, I am dissatisfied with my success, but not with the attempt; altho' the expense of our journey was considerable… If you think it will have any good effect, I will write a letter to the chairman or whatever you call him, of your book club, recommending some further organisation of the society. What think you of this. I have written some verses on Robert Emmet which you shall see, & which I will insert in my book of Poems… Harriet is now writing to Mrs Nugent, an excellent woman we discovered in Dublin, & of whom she will tell you.

Letter 181 (Extract):
Shelley, Wales, to William Godwin, London. 25/04/1812

We are no longer in Dublin! never did I behold in any other spot a contrast so striking as that which Grandeur & Misery form in that unfortunate country… Surely the inequality of rank is not felt so oppressively in England, surely something might be devised for Ireland, even consistent with the present state of politics, to meliorate its condition. Curran at length called on me. I dined twice at his house. Curran is certainly a man of great abilities, but it appears to me that he undervalues his powers, when he applies them to what is usually the subject of his conversation. I may not possess sufficient taste to relish humour, or his incessant comicality may weary that which I possess. He does not possess that mould of mind which I have been accustomed to contemplate with the highest feelings of respect & love. In short tho' Curran indubitably possesses a strong understanding, & a brilliant fancy, I should not have beheld him with the feelings of admiration which his first visit excited had he not been your intimate friend.

Letter 186 (Extract):
Shelley, Wales, to Elizabeth Hitchener, Sussex. 7/05/1812

Now my friend are we or are we not to sacrifice an attachment in which far more than you & I are immediately implicated, in which far more than these dear beings are remotely concerned; and to sacrifice to what? – To the world – to the swinish multitude, to the undiscriminating million, to such as burnt the House of Priestley, such as murdered Fitzgerald,[25] such as erect Barracks in Marylebonne, such as began & such as continue this liberticide war, such wretches as dragged Redfern to slavery or (equal in unprincipled cowardice)[26] the slaves who permit such things – for of these two classes is composed what may be called the world… I have only one copy (& that torn) with me of Redfern's letter. I enclose it. It is a horrible case.

Tell me in your next how your political affairs get on. Who are your agents? What have you done? Take care of letting any of the *Declaration of Rights* get into the hands of priests or aristocrats.

Letter 187 (Extract):
Shelley, Wales, to Catherine Nugent, Dublin. 7/05/1812

How unequally has the detestable system by which human beings govern their affairs distributed poverty & wealth! How much do you suffer from the distribution. Had you the millions which the Prince will possess how would England not be benefited! were he compelled to sit in Mr Newman's shop & sew fur on to satin in what would she be injured? – that this remark is not meant for flattery you will believe; no, your opinion of your own abilities is far too low… Redfern's letters have not yet been distributed, they were packed in a box which we left at Holyhead, but which we expect by the carrier tonight. Remember me to Reynolds, tell him I shall not be idle about Redfern,

& that as soon as I have done anything I will write to him.

Letter 4 (Extract):
Harriet Shelley, Wales, to Catherine Nugent, Dublin. 7/06/1812

What have you thought upon the murder of the Prime Minister?… It had been better if they had killed Lord Castlereagh. He really deserved it; but this poor Mr P[ercival] I believe was a very good private character. Do you not think it nonsense for all the little towns and villages to send petitions to the Prince upon the occasion. I suppose Ireland has not done anything half so silly. How do your poor countrymen go on? I hope things are not so scarce there as here… Do you ever see Mr Lawless? We hear from him sometimes. As to the poems I have no idea how and when they will come out. The printers are very slow in their operations.

Letter 5 (Extract):
Harriet Shelley, Devon, to Catherine Nugent, Dublin. 30/06/1812

I had hoped tho' we had left Nantgwillt that we should have been sure of a visit from you. However, I will say no more about it, as you must be the best judge of your own affairs, and I doubt not that were we to draw you from your own country that we should be the means, tho' innocently, of depriving many of your unfortunate countrymen of that relief you know so well how to bestow… We have still our Irishman Daniel, whom you may remember in Grafton Street. I am afraid we shall be obliged to part with him, as we do not find him that useful servant we expected he would have. Percy has some thoughts of sending him to Dublin, to see after his poems that are at the printers; but whether he will or not is impossible to say. We have not heard from Mr Lawless now for some time. I suppose his present employment (to my idea not very laudable) fills up his time so much that he cannot think of his absent friends. I hope this is not the case as I should be sorry, knowing him to be an Irishman, if it were true. I think he is a man of very great talent and abilities; but I am afraid that Mr Curran will never lend him a helping hand.

Letter 6 (Extract):

Harriet Shelley, Devon, to Catherine Nugent, Dublin. 4/08/1812

I thank you in Percy's name for your kind offer of service, though at the same time we cannot accept it. The case is this. His printer refuses to go on with his poems until he is paid. Now such a demand is seldom made, as printers are never paid till the profits arising from the work come in, and Percy agreed with him to this effect, and as long as we staid in Dublin he wore the mask which is now taken off. However I am in great hopes that Mr Lawless will get them from him. He is coming to London on business and then we shall see him. I wish to think well of him because he is your countryman, tho' there is too much 'the man of the world' about him. Perhaps he is different out of the city. If not, I shall still admire his talents, tho' I shall have no high opinion of him… Percy has sent you a defence of D I Eaton.[27] It must not be published; but you will give us your opinion of it…

Your being an Irishwoman must interest us in your happiness independently of our knowing the amiable qualities you possess. I have read Miss Owenson's *Missionary* and much do I admire the author. I am now reading her *Novice of St. Dominick*. I regret not having known her when I was in Dublin. Her *Patriotic Sketches* have won my heart. She speaks so feelingly of your dear country that I love her for that.

Letter 7 (Extract):

Harriet Shelley, Devon, to Catherine Nugent, Dublin. 11/08/1812

Your friend and our friend Bessey has been reading *Pieces of Irish History* and is so much enraged with the characters there mentioned that nothing will satisfy her desire of revenge but the printing and publishing of them… Percy thinks of printing it by subscription. 500 subscribers at seven shillings each will amply repay the printing and publishing. Percy intends to print some proposals for printing *Pieces of Irish History*, saying that every one whether Irish or English ought to read them. We depend upon you for many subscribers, as being upon the spot where so many of your exalted and brave countrymen suffered martyrdom. I should think there were very many would be glad to put their names to it. There must be many still smarting under the wounds they have seen, their brave companions suffer, and all from this hated country of mine. Good God, were I an Irishman or woman how I should hate the English – it is wonderful how the poor Irish people can tolerate them – but I am writing to one who from her example shows them how they ought to tolerate this barbarous nation of ours. Thank God we are not all alike, for I too can hate Lord Castlereagh as much as any Irishwoman. How does my heart's blood run cold at the idea of what he did in your unfortunate country. How is it that man is suffered to walk the streets in open daylight! Oh if I were to meet him I really think I could fly at him, and tear him to pieces!…

I cannot bear Curran; what use is he to your country? Was he active at the time of the union? No! if he had been, though his life had been the sacrifice, Ireland would have been saved. I have no patience with Curran. I shall convert Mr Lawless I hope from his idol. It is too sickening to hear him talk of Curran as he does. We are going to the valley of Llangothlin. It is much nearer to Ireland than we are here or even at Nangwylt. If we are there next summer I hope we shall see you. Bessy wishes very much to see you. Your last letter won her heart instantly. Reading *Pieces of Irish History* has made her so low-spirited.

[Added by Shelley]

We determine at any rate to publish the *Irish History*. It is a matter of doubt with me whether any bookseller will dare to put his name to it. This will be no obstacle. I shall print proposals for publishing by subscription, and if you could send us any names you would much benefit the Cause.

Letter 202 (Extract):
Shelley, Devon, to Thomas Hookham, London. 18/08/1812

I send you a copy of a work[28] which I have procured from America, & which I am exceedingly anxious should be published. It develops as you will perceive by the most superficial reading, the actual state of republicanised Ireland, & appears to me above all things calculated to remove the prejudices which have too long been cherished of that oppressed country, to strike the oppressors with dismay. I enclose also two pamphlets which I printed & distributed whilst in Ireland some months ago (no bookseller daring to publish them) – they were on that account attended with only partial success, & I request your opinion as to the probable result of publishing them with the annexed 'suggestions' in one pamphlet, with an explanatory preface, in London, – they would find their way to Dublin… I shall if possible prepare a vol. of essays moral & religious by November but all my MSS. now being in Dublin, & from peculiar circumstances not immediately obtainable, I do not know whether I can.

Letter 8 (Extract):
Harriet Shelley, London, to Catherine Nugent, Dublin. [October 1812]

Godwin is particularly fond of Curran, and I am to be introduced to Miss Curran on Sunday. How [came she to be] in England, can you solve this [problem]?…

Percy says he wishes you to go to Stockdale's, and get all his manuscript poems and other pieces. I am afraid you will be obliged to use a little manoeuvre to get them. In the first place you can say you wish to look at them, and then you may be able to stout them away from him. I leave it all to you, knowing you will do your best.

Letter 9 (Extract):
Harriet Shelley, Stratford, to Catherine Nugent, Dublin. 14/11/1812

Have you been able to get the poems from Stockdale? If not it cannot be helped, but do pray write to us, for we are quite uneasy at not hearing from you for so long a time… We are not very far from Ireland. If you could so manage it as to come to us in the Spring, you know not the happiness you would confer upon our little circle, which is now just as you beheld it in your own native air. I have got the Irish Melodies,[29] which I intend to study. If you know of any good Old Irish song I should esteem it a favor[30] to hear of it.

Letter 10 (Extract):

Harriet Shelley, Wales, to Catherine Nugent, Dublin. 16/01/1813

I am sorry to hear you have been so much engaged, as I cannot bear the idea of, a woman like yourself being obliged to do that which so many are better qualified to perform. I saw with very great sorrow the ruin of so many of your valuable manufactories. I knew how many of your unfortunate countrymen suffered all the miseries of famine before, and now there must be many more. That the wounds of thy beloved country may soon be healed for ever, is the first wish of an Englishwoman who only regrets her being born among those inhuman beings who have already caused so much misery wherever they turn their steps…

I admire your song much, and am determined to set it to some very plaintive tune. I have seen Miss Curran. she resides in England. What I saw of her I did not like. She said begging was a trade in Dublin. To tell you the truth she is not half such an Irishwoman as myself, and that is why I did not feel disposed to like her. Besides she is a coquette the most abominable thing in the world. I met her at Godwin's house, alas Godwin he too is changed, and filled with prejudices, and besides too he expects such universal homage from all persons younger than himself, that it is very disagreeable to be in company with him on that account, and he wanted Mr Shelley to join the Whig party and do just as they pleased, which made me very angry... with many thanks for your embassy to Stockdale, who will hear from Mr S soon.

(Extract):

Robert Leeson, Wales, to Shelley, Wales. 5/3/1813

Having heard from several quarters that you lie under a mistake relative to the manner in which I was put in possession of a pamphlet signed 'P B Shelley'… [it] was handed to me by John William's[31] with a remark that it contained matter dangerous to the State, and that you had been in the practise of haranguing 500 people at a time when in Ireland. So much for your friend.

Letter 229 (Extract):

Shelley, Dublin, to John Williams, Wales. 9/03/1813(?)

I write to tell you that we have safely arrived in Dublin… but so poor that, unless we find some friend, I know not what we shall do. I do not think that we can manage to live until the arrival of Mr Caldecott's expected loan. We are in a foreign country where our name even is scarcely known, and where no one will give us credit for a farthing.

(Extract):

Harriet Shelley, Dublin, to Thomas Hookham, London. 12/03/1813

Mr S promised you a recital of the horrible events that caused us to leave Wales… Mr S heard a noise proceeding from one of the parlours… I heard a pistol go off. I immediately ran down stairs, when I perceived that Bysshe's flannel gown had been shot through… Bysshe had sent Daniel to see what hour it was, when he heard a noise at the window. He went there, and a man thrust his arm through the glass and fired at him. Thank Heaven! the ball went through his gown and he remained unhurt…Mr Leeson had been heard to say that he was determined to drive us out of the country. He once happened to get hold of a little pamphlet which Mr S had printed in Dublin; this he sent up to Government In fact, he was for ever saying something against us.

Letter 233 (Extract):

Shelley, Dublin, To Thomas Hogg, London. 31/03/1813

We have just arrived in Dublin. had you remained here but one day, you would have seen us. We travelled night and day, from the receipt of your note… On Monday [29 March] evening we began travelling on Irish roads with Irish horses and chaise. We reached Cork at one the next day, took the mail, and today, Wednesday, at three o'clock arrived. We shall soon be with you in London; Eliza and our servant remain at Killarney.

You ought not to accuse me of reserve towards you. It is the inconceivable blindness and matter of fact stupidity of Lawless, that deserve your reprehension; but had you stayed one day longer, you would have heard the words of sincerity and friendship from my own lips.

Letter 234 (Extract):
Shelley, Dublin, To Thomas Hogg, London. 1/04/1813

I wrote yesterday before I had seen Lawless, under the one and only impression of disappointment at not meeting you here. That, however, shall speedily be remedied. I have raised a small sum of money, and tomorrow evening we embark for Holyhead.

I have been very much pleased at what Lawless has said of you. The first ten words he spoke entirely dissipated all the ill-humour I had cherished against him. He had done what I could not conceive any one, who dined with you, could have neglected. He had been open with you… I write from Lawless's. I am very much pleased and flattered by his account of you.

John Lawless, Dublin to Thomas Hogg, London. 3/05/1813

I take the liberty of troubling you with these few lines to be informed by you how our good friends the Shelley's are, from whom I have heard but once since they left this country. I did flatter myself with a letter from my friend long before this, and now begin to apprehend some serious cause for his not writing. I hope no such cause has interposed, and if not you will much oblige me by telling him how anxious both Mrs Lawless & I are to hear from him & Mrs Shelley. I suppose Miss Westbrook has long since arrived with you.

Letter 11 (Extract):
Harriet Shelley, London, to Catherine Nugent, Dublin. 21/05/1813

We have not got our boxes yet, that were sent from Cork to Bristol, and when we shall see them again is uncertain. Mr Ryan[32] dines with us to day. I give him meat, but we have all taken to the vegetable regimen again… Have you seen Mr Lawless? He wrote to us from prison a few weeks ago, but I do not suppose he was there, because Ryan knew nothing about it, and he is only just arrived from there… Mr Shelley continues perfectly well, and his poem of Queen Mab is begun, tho' it must not be published under pain of death, because it is too much against every existing establishment. It is to be privately distributed to his friends, and some copies sent over to America. Do you [know] any one that would wish for so dangerous a gift? If you do, tell me of them, and they shall not be forgotten.

Letter 12 (Extract):
Harriet Shelley, London, to Catherine Nugent, Dublin. 22/06/1813

I am sorry to hear that poor Lawless is confined. If he had taken his friends' advice all his debts would have been settled long ago; but pride, that bane of all human happiness unfortunately stopped and marred all his good prospects. Mr Ryan is still in London; but I expect to hear daily of his leaving us… Our Irish servant is going to leave. Poor fellow, he pines after his dear Ireland, and is at the same time very ill. He was never of any use to us; but so great was his attachment that we could not bear to send him away… What think you of Bonaparte? To most of the Irish he is a great favourite. I only wish we had peace. So long a war as this has been is indeed too dreadful to continue much longer.

Letter 15 (Extract):
Harriet Shelley, Cumberland, to Catherine Nugent, Dublin. 11/10/1813

Have you seen Daniel? We were obliged to discharge him, For his conduct was so unprincipled that it was impossible to have in our service any longer. Is Mr Lawless out of prison yet? Had he not taken us in as he did, Bysshe would have done something for him; but his behaviour was altogether so dishonest that Mr Shelley will not do anything for him at present. If he wished it he could not, for he is obliged to pay 3 for 1, which is so ruinous that he will only raise a sufficient [sum] to pay his [own] debts[33] … Some day, my dear friend, I hope you will come to England and pay us a visit.

Letter 17 (Extract):
Harriet Shelley, Edinburgh, to Catherine Nugent, Dublin. 23/11/1813

I am afraid Lawless has practised upon you, as he did upon us. Some time back he wrote to Mr S about Daniel, who lived with us, saying that we had not treated him well. Now the truth is this – we were very fond of this man. He appeared so much attached to us, so much honesty and simplicity, that we kept him tho' of no use whatever. For the whole time he stayed with us he never did anything. Afterwards he turned out very ungrateful and behaved so insolently that we were obliged to turn him away. That is the man Lawless wrote about; but do not think I am offended at what you say of him, as I know it proceeds from the goodness of your heart.

Harriet Shelley, London, to Mrs Newman, Dublin. 8/08/1814

It is so long since I have heard from my amiable friend, Mrs Nugent, that I begin to fear she has quitted this world of sorrow and pain. If she has, no human being will regret her loss more than myself. I must beg you to write by return of post and tell me all the particulars. If I am wrong in my conjectures, tell her to write, if only one line, to her most attached and faithful friend,

Letter 21 (Extract):
Harriet Shelley, London, to Catherine Nugent, Dublin. 11/12/1814

You will see us all in the spring; I am about to come to Ireland,[34] to get my boxes which are detained there. You shall then return with me to England, my dear friend, which you have often promised, and I will promise Mrs Newman not to keep you any longer than you wish to stay.

Letter 22 (Extract):
Harriet Shelley, London, to Catherine Nugent, Dublin. 24/01/1815

What will you do my dear Catherine? Now those Newmans retire you will not like to go to another house of business. The few years you have to live may surely be passed more pleasantly. Do make up your mind at once to come and stay with me. I will do everything to make you happy. For myself happiness is fled. I live for others. At nineteen I could descend a willing victim to the tomb… Your letters make me more happy. Tell me about Ireland. You know I love the green Isle and all its natives.

Letter 507 (Extract):

Shelley, Livorno, to Amelia Curran, Rome. 5/08/1819

A thousand thanks for your kind attention to my request.[35] I have considered the drawings, & neither of them, nor indeed perhaps, any attempt at Sculpture seems to me fit for the purpose. I strongly incline to prefer an unornamented pyramid of white marble as of the most durable form & the simplest appearance, but if you will permit, I will send you my decision soon. You have too much goodness not to excuse on such a subject the trouble which I give you – I will send at the same time the Inscription…

I have nearly finished my Cenci – which Mary likes. I wish very much to get a good engraving made of the picture in the Colonna Palace, & to have the plate by this autumn. How much time & money would a first-rate Roman artist demand for such a work – Dare I ask you to add to the amount of so many favours which must be so long unrepaid, that of charging yourself with such a kindness?

What we owe to you in possessing the picture,[36] is more than I can express – May I hope that some day will arrive on which it will be possible to find other expressions for it than words!

Letter 557 (Extract):

Shelley, Pisa, to Leigh Hunt, London. 5/04/1820

We see no one but an Irish lady and her husband,[37] who are settled here. She is everything that is amiable and wise, and he is very agreeable. You will think it my fate either to find or to imagine some lady of 45, very unprejudiced and philosophical, who has entered deeply into the best and selectest spirit of the age, with enchanting manners, and a disposition rather to like me, in every town that I inhabit. But certainly such this lady is.

Letter 617 (Extract):

Shelley, Pisa, to Claire Clairmont, Florence. 2/04/1821

Naples will be no place to visit at present, and you are much deceived by those who surround you if you imagine that the success of the

Austrians in that country has terminated the war in Italy… The Catholic Emancipation has passed the second reading by a majority of 11 in 497.[38] This will give the Government a momentary strength.

Letter 674 (Extract):
Shelley, Pisa, to Claire Clairmont, Florence. 31/12/1821

We have little new in politics. You will have heard of the amphibious state of things in France, and the establishment of the Ultra-Ministry by the preponderance afforded to that party by the coalition of the liberals with it. The Greeks are going on excellently, and those massacres at Smyrna and Constantinople import nothing to the stability of the cause. There is no such thing as a rebellion in Ireland, or anything that looks like it. The people are indeed stung to madness by the oppression of the Irish system, and there is no such thing as getting rents or taxes even at the point of the bayonet throughout the southern provinces. But there are no regular bodies of men in opposition to the government, nor have the people any leaders. In England all bears for the moment the aspect of a sleeping Volcano.

Letter 719 (Extract):
Shelley, Lerici, to Horace Smith, Versailles. 29/06/1822

England appears to be in a desperate condition, Ireland still worse, & no class of those who subsist on the public labour will be persuaded that their claims on it must be diminished. But the government must content itself with less in taxes, the landholder must submit to receive less rent, & the fundholder a diminished interest, – or they will all get nothing, or something worse [than] nothing. I once thought to study these affairs & write or act in them – I am glad that my good genius said refrain. I see little public virtue, & I foresee that the contest will be one of blood & gold two elements, which however much to my taste in my pockets & my veins, I have an objection to out of them.

(Extract):

Mary Shelley, London, to Thomas Crofton Croker, London. 30/10/1828[39]

I am writing a romance founded on the story of Perkin Warbeck – I have just brought him for the first time to Ireland – The antiquary is therefore of more use to me than the historian – After all I must rest satisfied with a very imperfect sketch, as never having been in Ireland and being very ignorant of its history I shall fall into a thousand mistakes – to diminish this number as much as possible, I have applied to you.

(Extract):

Mary Shelley, London, to A Berry, Sydney. 29/3/1847[40]

But it is fearful to think of Ireland and the million a month sent to her from England – and the unfortunate propensities of the people who, in the hopes of money from this country, can scarcely be induced to sow seed for the next harvest. All parties here shrink from the load of responsibility.

(Extract):

Mary Shelley, London, to A Berry, Sydney. 28/3/1848[41]

There is no doubt that a French propaganda is spread among all the nations – they are rousing the Irish and even exciting the English Chartists. Ireland is fortunate in having Lord Clarendon, a man of courage and wisdom – but will he be able to repress all the risings with which that country is menaced? – who can tell. One half of Ireland detests the other half – nor have the Irish any political grievance (for they have not the burthen of our taxes) except that the Catholics are forced to support the Protestant Church.

NOTES

1   The 'address' was not published by Hunt, but it seems to be the inspiration for his Irish Pamphlets.

2   This is the first mention of Shelley's intention to visit Ireland.

3   The Shelleys departed for Ireland from Whitehaven in Cumberland.

4   A revised version of this passage appears as the fourth paragraph of *An Address to the Irish People.*

5   They were never published in Shelley's lifetime. The essays that Shelley refers to are most likely those published in *Essays, Translations, and Fragments*, (London, 1839) as *Speculations on Metaphysics.*

6   This was not the £100 referred to in the letter above. Shelley's father had restored his allowance of £200 per annum.

7   Italian sect founded in the 16th century, which denied the divinity of Christ.

8   The section beginning 'The ocean rolls between us' was rendered into verse in 1883 and added to the lines 'Bear witness Erin' and published under the title *To Ireland.* Modern interpretation prints them separately (see Appendix 1, p194).

9   *An Address to the Irish People.*

10   John Philpot Curran defended the United Irishmen tried after the rebellion in 1798. Shelley seems to imply that Curran also defended those implicated in the 1803 rebellion, but Curran refused to defend Emmet or Russell.

11   Dan Healy, who joined the Shelley household, and went with them to Wales in April 1812.

12   X, an abbreviation for Christ as in Christianity. Today it is most commonly used in Xmas. Deism accepts the existence of God, but rejects revealed religion.

13   Shelley prepared this volume called *Biblical Extracts* for publication; but without success, and the manuscript is not now known to exist.

14   Thomas Malthus (1766-1834), *An Essay on the Principle of Population*, (London, 1798). Shelley, in his *Proposals for an Association of Philanthropists* argued against Malthus's theory of population (see Appendix 4, p298).

15   'Suggestions' which he intended to print up as rules for his proposed associations.

16   The article in the *Dublin Weekly Messenger* on 7/3/1812 (see chapter 5, p97).

17   William Beresford (1768-1854) was a marshal in the Portuguese Army (see chapter 6, p123 for details of Redfern).

18   The Sussex papers did not print an account of Shelley's activities in Dublin. They also refused to print the letter on Redfern on the grounds that it could only add to his problems.

19   The *Dublin Weekly Messenger,* which published the favourable article on Shelley. This letter was never published.

20   Habeas Corpus was not suspended until 1817.

21   In Greek mythology Cadmus killed the dragon and sowed its teeth, from which grew a number of armed men intent on killing him.

22   Inner city area near Christchurch Cathedral almost exclusively inhabited by the Catholic poor. Frederick Engels described the poverty of the area as 'among the most hideous and repulsive to be seen in the world'.

23   A Greek philosophy, which held that virtue was the highest good, and that passion and appetites should be subdued.

24   Shelley did not receive this letter until 11 June 1812, after his return to England.

25   Dr Joseph Priestley (1733-1804), scientist and philosopher whose house was burned down by a 'Church and King' mob in Birmingham in 1791. Lord Edward Fitzgerald (1763-1798), leader of the United Irishmen, was fatally wounded when captured just before the insurrection of 1798.

26   Shelley always had compassion for the poor and the oppressed, and placed the blame for their condition on the class divisions in society. In apportioning equal blame on the poor 'who permit such things', Shelley goes against his own principles.

27   D I Eaton was charged with sedition in London on 6 March 1812 for publishing Paine's *Age of Reason.* Shelley defended Eaton in a pamphlet published in July 1812, *A Letter to Lord Ellenborough.*

28   William MacNevin. *Pieces of Irish History* (New York, 1807).

29   Tom Moore (1779-1852). His *Irish Melodies* were issued as a series between 1807 and 1835.

30   Probably Harriet was using the American and republican spelling rather than the standard English one. It was politically symbolic to omit the 'u' from such words as 'labor', honor', 'favor' and 'valor' and use 'ize' rather than 'ise' at the end of words, see also *An Address to the Irish People* and *Proposals for an Association* where the republican spelling is used by Shelley in similar circumstances.

31   Shelley's friend John Williams from Tremadoc in Wales, where they settled after their return from Ireland.

32   Nearly all of Shelley's biographers such as White (*Shelley*, vol 1, pp674-675) and Cameron (*Shelley and his Circle*, vol 4, pp790-791) assume that the Mr Ryan mentioned in this letter is the person that Harriet is alleged to have had an affair with after their separation. They identify him as a Major Ryan in the British army. This seems to me a wrong assumption. A careful reading of letters 11 and 12 indicate that Catherine Nugent and John Lawless were on familiar terms with Mr Ryan. That a working class woman, a supporter of the United Irishmen, and an active campaigner for repeal of the union would be on familiar terms with a major in the British Army is unlikely. A more reasonable explanation is that Ryan was part of the radical circle that Shelley had met through Lawless and Nugent in Dublin, and was welcomed in London as a friend and former ally.

33   Shelley was borrowing money to be paid back at the rate of three pounds for every one borrowed on the attainment of his majority.

34   Harriet's intention of visiting Ireland was overshadowed by her separation from Shelley and she never did visit Ireland again, Her boxes were forwarded to her over a year later.

35   Amelia Curran was asked to help with the design of a monument for the Shelley's son William, who was buried in Rome. Shelley also requested a copy of the picture of Beatrice Cenci from the Colonna Palace in Rome.

36   Amelia's portrait of William Shelley, now in the New York Public Library, Pforzheimer Collection.

37   Lady Mount Cashell and George Tighe, who lived in Pisa under the name of Mr and Mrs Mason.

38   The bill was rejected by the House of Lords and Catholic Emancipation was not enacted into law until 1829.

39   *The Croker Correspondence*, National Library of Ireland. Mary Shelley's novel *The Fortunes of Perkin Warbeck* is set in the period immediately after the War of the Roses (1485). Reading the Irish chapters, it is obvious that Croker; a well known writer on Irish antiquity, was troubled to little purpose. In Mary Shelley's *Frankenstein* (vol3, chapters 3/4) Victor Frankenstein's boat is washed up in Ireland and is met by Daniel Nugent, probably an amalgam of Daniel Healy and Catherine Nugent, (London, 1998), pp148-158.

40   B Bennett, (ed), *Letters of Mary Shelley*, (Maryland, 1980), vol 3, p307. Mary is referring to the terrible famine of 1847, which decimated the country, killing over a million people and forcing at least the same number to emigrate. Her lack of compassion is all too evident in this letter.

41   Ibid, vol 3, p343. Lord Clarendon, was lord lieutenant of Ireland (1847-52). The 'French propaganda' refers to the bourgeois revolutions that swept Europe in 1848, which found expression in Ireland in the Young Ireland movement. Even before Shelley's death Mary had lost a lot of the revolutionary passion that initially had drawn them together. After his death the last flicker of political hope disappeared from Mary. As she got older, living in middle class isolation, she mover more and more to the right, as she admitted in a letter to Trelawny: 'I have no wish to ally myself to the Radicals – they are full of repulsion to me'. Her later romantic novels (*The Fortunes of Perkin Warbeck*, etc), written from financial necessity, are today mostly unreadable.

An Address to the Irish People
BY PERCY BYSSHE SHELLEY

ADVERTISEMENT

THE *lowest possible price is set on this publication, because it is the intention of the Author to awaken in the minds of the Irish poor, a knowledge of their real state, summarily pointing out the evils of that state, and suggesting rational means of remedy. Catholic Emancipation, and Repeal of the Union Act, (the latter, the most successful engine that England ever wielded over the misery of fallen Ireland) being treated of in the following address, as grievances which unanimity and resolution may remove, and associations conducted with peaceable firmness, being earnestly recommended, as means for embodying that unanimity and firmness, which must finally be successful.*

Dublin:

1812

Price – 5d.

Fellow men, I am not an Irishman, yet I can feel for you. I hope there are none among you who will read this address with prejudice or levity, because it is made by an Englishman; indeed, I believe there are not. The Irish are a brave nation. They have a heart of liberty in their breasts, but they are much mistaken if they fancy that a stranger cannot have as warm a one. Those are my brothers and my countrymen, who are unfortunate. I should like to know what there is in a man being an Englishman, a Spaniard, or a Frenchman, that makes him worse or better than he really is. He was born in one town, you in another, but that is no reason why he should not feel for you, desire your benefit, or be willing to give you some advice, which may make you more capable of knowing your own interest, or acting so as to secure it. There are many Englishmen who cry down the Irish, and think it answers their ends to revile all that belongs to Ireland; but it is not because these men are Englishmen that they maintain such opinions, but because they wish to get money, and titles, and power. They would act in this manner to whatever country they might belong, until mankind is much altered for the better, which reform, I hope, will one day be effected. I address you, then as my brothers and my fellow-men, for I should wish to see the Irishman who, if England was persecuted as Ireland is, who, if France was persecuted as Ireland is, who, if any set of men that helped to do a public service were prevented from enjoying its benefits as Irishmen are – I should like to see the man, I say, who would see these misfortunes, and not attempt to succour the sufferers when he could, just that I might tell him that he was no Irishman, but some bastard mongrel bred up in a court, or some coward fool who was a democrat to all above him, and an aristocrat to all below him. I think there are few true Irishmen who would not be ashamed of such a character, still fewer who possess it. I know that there are some, not among you my friends, but among your enemies, who seeing the title of this piece, will take it up with a sort of hope that it may recommend violent measures, and thereby disgrace the cause of freedom, that the warmth of a heart desirous that liberty should be possessed equally by all, will vent itself in abuse on the enemies of liberty, bad men who deserve the contempt of the good, and ought not to excite their indignation to the harm of their cause. But these men will be disappointed – I know the warm feeling of an Irishman sometimes carries him beyond the point of prudence. I do not desire to root out, but to moderate this honorable warmth. This will disappoint the pioneers of oppression and they will be sorry, that through this address nothing will occur which can be twisted into any other meaning but what is calculated to fill you with that moderation which they have not, and make you give them that toleration which they refuse to grant you. You profess the Roman Catholic religion which your fathers professed before you. Whether it is the best religion or not, I will not here inquire: all religions are good which make men good; and the way that a person ought to prove that his method of worshipping God is best, is for himself to be better than all other men. But we will consider what your religion was in old times and what it is now: you may say it is not a fair way for me to proceed as a Protestant, but I am not a Protestant, nor am I a Catholic, and therefore not being a follower of either of these religions, I am better able to judge between them. A Protestant is my brother, and a Catholic is my brother. I am happy when I can do either of them a service, and no pleasure is so great to me as that, which I should feel, if my advice could make men of any professions of faith, wiser, better, and happier.

The Roman Catholics once persecuted the Protestants, the Protestants now persecute the Roman Catholics – should we think that one is as bad as the other? No, you are not answerable for the faults of your fathers any more than the Protestants are good for the goodness of their fathers. I must judge of people as I see them; the Irish Catholics are badly used. I will not endeavour to hide from them their wretchedness; they would think that I mocked at them if I should make the attempt. The Irish Catholics now demand for themselves, and [proffer] to others unlimited toleration, and the sensible part among them, which I am willing to think constitutes a very large portion of their body, know that the gates of Heaven are open to people of every religion, provided they are good. But the Protestants, although they may think so in their hearts, which certainly, if they think at all they must, seem to act as if they thought that God was better pleased with them than with you; they trust the reins of earthly government only to the hands of their own sect; in spite of this, I never found one of them impudent enough to say, that a Roman Catholic, or a Quaker, or a Jew, or a Mahometan, if he was a virtuous man, and did all the good in his power, would go to Heaven a bit the slower for not subscribing to the thirty-nine articles – and if he should say so, how ridiculous in a foppish courtier not six feet high, to direct the spirit of universal harmony, in what manner to conduct the affairs of the universe!

The Protestants say that there was a time when the Roman Catholics burnt and murdered people of different sentiments, and that their religious tenets are now as they were then. This is all very true. You certainly worship God in the same way that you did when these barbarities took place, but is that any reason that you should now be barbarous. There is as much reason to suppose it, as to suppose that because a man's great-grandfather, who was a Jew, had been hung for sheep-stealing, that I, by believing the same religion as he did, must certainly commit the same crime. Let us then see what the Roman Catholic religion has been. No one knows much of the early times of the Christian religion, until about three hundred years after its beginning, two great churches, called the Roman and the Greek Churches, divided the opinions of men. They fought for a very long time, a great many words were wasted, and a great deal of blood shed. This as you may suppose, did no good. Each party however, thought they were doing God a service, and that he would reward them. If they had looked an inch before their noses, they might have found, that fighting and killing men, and cursing them and hating them, was the very worst way for getting into favor with a Being who is allowed by all to be best pleased with deeds of love and charity. At last, however, these two Religions entirely separated, and the Popes reigned like Kings and Bishops at Rome, in Italy. The inquisition was set up, and in the course of one year 30,000 people were burnt in Italy and Spain, for entertaining different opinions from those of the Pope and the Priests. There was an instance of shocking barbarity which the Roman Catholic Clergy committed in France by order of the Pope. The bigoted

Monks of that country, in cold blood, in one night massacred 80,000 Protestants;[1] this was done under the authority of the Pope, and there was only one Roman Catholic Bishop who had virtue enough to refuse to help. The vices of Monks and Nuns in their convents were in those times shameful, people thought that they might commit any sin, however monstrous, if they had money enough to prevail upon the Priests to absolve them; in truth, at that time the Priests shamefully imposed upon the people, they got all the power into their own hands, they persuaded them that a man could not be entrusted with the care of his own soul, and by cunningly obtaining possession of their secrets, they became more powerful than Kings, Princes, Dukes, Lords, or Ministers: This power made them bad men; for although rational people are very good in their natural state, there are now, and ever have been very few whose good dispositions despotic power does not destroy. I have now given a fair description of what your religion was; and Irishmen, my brothers! will you make your friend appear a liar, when he takes upon himself to say for you, that you are not now what the professors of the same faith were in times of yore. Do I speak false when I say that the inquisition is the object of your hatred? Am I a liar if I assert that an Irishman prizes liberty dearly, that he will preserve that right, and if he be wrong, does not dream that money given to a Priest, or the talking of another man erring like himself, can in the least influence the judgement of the eternal God? I am not a liar if I affirm in your name, that you believe a Protestant equally with yourself to be worthy of the Kingdom of Heaven, if he be equally virtuous; that you will treat men as brethren wherever you may find them, and that difference of opinion in religious matters shall not, does not in the least on your part, obstruct the most perfect harmony on every other subject. Ah! no, Irishmen, I am not a liar. I seek your confidence, not that I may betray it, but that I may teach you to be happy, and wise, and good. If you will not repose any trust in me I shall lament, but I will do everything in my power that is honorable, fair, and open, to gain it. Some teach you that others are heretics, that you alone are right; some teach that rectitude consists in religious opinions, without which no morality is good, some will tell you that you ought to divulge your secrets to one particular set of men; beware my friends how you trust those who speak in this way. They will, I doubt not, attempt to rescue you from your present miserable state, but they will prepare worse. It will be out of the frying-pan into the fire. Your present oppressors it is true, will then oppress you no longer, but you will feel the lash of a master a thousand times more blood-thirsty and cruel. Evil designing men will spring up who will prevent your thinking as you please, will burn you if you do not think as they do. There are always bad men who take advantage of hard times. The Monks and Priests of old were very bad men; take care no such abuse your confidence again. You are not blind to your present situation, you are villainously treated, you are badly used. That this slavery shall cease, I will venture to prophesy. Your enemies dare not to persecute you longer, the spirit of Ireland is bent, but it is not broken, and that they very well know. But I wish your views to embrace a wider scene, I wish you to think for your children and your children's children; to take great care (for it all rests with you) that whilst one tyranny is destroyed another more fierce and terrible does not spring up. Take care then of smooth-faced impostors, who talk indeed of freedom, but who will cheat you into slavery. Can there be worse slavery than the depending for the safety of your soul on the will of another man? Is one man more favored than another by God. No, certainly, they are all favored according to the good they do, and not according to the rank and profession they hold. God values a poor man as much as a Priest, and has given him a soul as much to himself; the worship that a kind Being must love, is that of a simple affectionate heart, that shews its piety in good works, and not in ceremonies, or confessions, or burials, or processions, or wonders. Take care then, that you are not led away. Doubt every thing that leads you not to charity, and think of the word 'heretic' as a word which some selfish knave invented for the ruin and misery of the world, to answer his own paltry and narrow ambition. Do not inquire if a man be a heretic, if he be a Quaker, or a Jew, or a Heathen; but if he be a virtuous man, if he loves liberty and truth, if he wish the happiness and peace of human kind. If a man be ever so much a believer and love not these things, he is a heartless hypocrite, a rascal, and a knave. Despise and hate him, as ye despise a tyrant and a villain. Oh! Ireland, thou emerald of the ocean, whose sons are generous and brave, whose daughters are honorable, and frank, and fair; thou art the isle on whose green shores I have desired to see the standard of liberty erected, a flag of fire, a beacon at which the world shall light the torch of Freedom!

We will now examine the Protestant Religion. Its origin is called the Reformation. It was undertaken by some bigoted men, who shewed how little they understood the spirit of Reform, by burning each other. You will observe that these men burnt each other, indeed they universally betrayed a taste for destroying, and vied with the chiefs of the Roman Catholic Religion in not only hating their enemies, but those men, who least of all were their enemies, or anybody's enemies. Now, do the Protestants, or do they not hold the same tenets as they did when Calvin burnt Servetus;[2] they swear that they do. We can have no better proof. Then with what face can the Protestants object to Catholic Emancipation, on the plea that Catholics once were barbarous, when their own establishment is liable to the very same objections, on the very same grounds? I think this is a specimen of bare-faced intoleration, which I had hoped would not have disgraced this age; this age, which is called the age of reason, of thought diffused, of virtue acknowledged, and its principles fixed. Oh! that it may be so. I have mentioned the Catholic and Protestant Religions more to shew that any objection to the toleration of the one forcibly applies to the nonpermission of the other, or rather to shew that there is no reason why both might not be tolerated, why every Religion, every form of thinking might not be tolerated. But why do I speak of *toleration?* This word seems to mean that there is some merit in the person who tolerates; he has this merit if it be one, of refraining to do an evil act, but he will share the merit with every other peaceable person who pursues his own business, and does not hinder another of his rights. It is not a merit to tolerate, but it is a crime to be intolerant: it is not a merit in me that I sit quietly at home without murdering any one, but it is a crime if I do so. Besides, no act of a National representation can make any thing wrong, which was not wrong before; it cannot change virtue and truth, and for a very plain reason: because they are unchangeable. An act passed in the British Parliament to take away the rights of Catholics to act in that assembly, does not really take them away. It prevents them from doing it by force. This is in such cases, the last and only efficacious way. But force is not the test of truth; they will never have recourse to violence who acknowledge no other rule of behaviour but virtue and justice.

The folly of persecuting men for their religion will appear if we examine it. Why do we persecute them? to make them believe as we do. Can anything be more barbarous or foolish. For although we may make them say they believe as we do, they will not in their hearts do any such thing, indeed they cannot; this devilish method can only make them false hypocrites. For what is belief? We cannot believe just what we like, but only what we think to be true; for you cannot alter a man's opinion by beating or burning, but by persuading him that what you think is right, and this can only be done by fair words and reason. It is ridiculous to call a man a heretic, because he thinks differently from you; he might as well call you one. In the same sense, the word orthodox is used; it signifies 'to think rightly' and what can be more vain and presumptuous in any man or any set of men, to put themselves so out of the ordinary course of things as to say – 'What we think is right, no other people throughout the world have opinions any thing like equal to ours'. Anything short of unlimited toleration, and complete charity with all men, on which you will recollect that Jesus Christ principally insisted, is wrong, and for this reason – what makes a man to be a good man? not his religion, or else there could be no good men in any religion but one, when yet we find that all ages, countries, and opinions have produced them. Virtue and wisdom always so far as they went produced liberty or happiness long before any of the religions now in the world were ever heard of. The only use of a religion that ever I could see, is, to make men wiser or better; so far as it does this, it is a good one. Now, if people are good, and yet have sentiments differing from you, then all the purposes are answered, which any reasonable man could want, and whether he thinks like you or not, is of too little consequence to employ means which must be disgusting and hateful to candid minds, nay they cannot approve of such means. For as I have before said, you cannot believe or disbelieve what you like – perhaps some of you may doubt this, but just try – I will take a common and familiar instance. Suppose you have a friend of whom you wish to think well, he commits a crime, which proves to you that he is a bad man. It is very painful to you to think ill of him, and you would still think well of him if you could. But, mark the word, you *cannot* think well of him, not even to secure your own peace of mind can you do so. You try, but your attempts are vain. This shews how little power a man has over his belief, or rather, that he cannot believe what he does not think true. And what shall we think now? What fools and tyrants must not those men be, who set up a particular religion, say that this religion alone is right, and that everyone who disbelieves it, ought to be deprived of certain rights which are really his, and which would be allowed him if he believed. Certainly, if you cannot help disbelief, it is not any fault in you. To take away a man's rights and privileges, to call him a heretic or to think worse of him, when at the same time you cannot help owning that he has committed no fault, is the grossest tyranny and intoleration. From what has been said, I think we may be justified in concluding that people of all religions ought to have an equal share in the state, that the words heretic and orthodox were invented by a vain villain, and have done a great deal of harm in the world, and that no person is answerable for his belief whose actions are virtuous and moral, that the religion is best whose members are the best men, and that no person can help either his belief or disbelief. Be in charity with all men. It does not therefore, signify what your Religion *was,* or what the Protestant Religion *was*, we must consider them as we find them. What are they *now?* Yours is not intolerant; indeed my friends I have ventured to pledge myself for you that it is not. You merely desire to go to Heaven in your own way, nor will you interrupt fellow travellers, although the road which you take, may not be that which they take. Believe me, that goodness of heart and purity of life are things of more value in the eye of the Spirit of Goodness, than idle earthly ceremonies, and things which have any thing but charity for their object.

And is it for the first or the last of these things that you or the Protestants contend. It is for the last. Prejudiced people indeed, are they who grudge to the happiness and comfort of your souls, things which can do harm to no one. They are not compelled to share in these rites. Irishmen; knowledge is more extended than in the early period of your religion, people have learned to think, and the more thought there is in the world, the more happiness and liberty will there be: Men begin now to think less of idle ceremonies and more of realities. From a long night have they risen, and they can perceive its darkness. I know no men of thought and learning who do not consider the Catholic idea of purgatory, much nearer the truth than the Protestant one of eternal damnation. Can you think that the Mahometans and the Indians who have done good deeds in this life, will not be rewarded in the next? The Protestants believe that they will be eternally damned – at least they swear that they do. I think they appear in a better light as perjurers, than believers in a falsehood so hurtful and uncharitable as this. I propose unlimited toleration, or rather the destruction, both of toleration and intoleration. The act permits certain people to worship God after such a manner, which, in fact, if not done, would as far as in it lay prevent God from hearing their address. Can we conceive anything more presumptuous, and at the same time more ridiculous, than a set of men granting a licence to God to receive the prayers of certain of his creatures. Oh Irishmen! I am interested in your cause; and it is not because you are Irishmen or Roman Catholics, that I feel with you and feel for you; but because you are men and sufferers. Were Ireland at this moment, peopled with Brahmins, this very same address would have been suggested by the same state of mind. You have suffered not merely for your religion, but [from]some other causes which I am equally desirous of remedying. The Union of England with Ireland has withdrawn the Protestant aristocracy, and gentry from their native country, and with these their friends and connections. Their resources are taken from this country, although they are dissipated in another; the very poor people are most infamously oppressed by the weight of burden which the superior ranks lay upon their shoulders. I am no less desirous of the reform of these evils (with many others) than for the Catholic Emancipation.

Perhaps you all agree with me on both these subjects; we now come to the method of doing these things. I agree with the Quakers so far as they disclaim violence, and trust their cause wholly and solely to its own truth. If you are convinced of the truth of your cause, trust wholly to its truth; if you are not convinced, give it up. In no case employ violence, the way to liberty and happiness is never to transgress the rules of virtue and justice. Liberty and happiness are founded upon virtue and justice, if you destroy the one, you destroy the other. However ill others may act, this will be no excuse for you if you follow their example; it ought rather to warn you from pursuing so bad a method. Depend upon it, Irishmen, your cause shall not be neglected. I will fondly hope, that the schemes for your happiness and liberty, as well as those for the happiness and liberty of the world, will not be wholly fruitless. One secure method of defeating them is violence on the side of the injured party. If you can descend to use the same weapons as your enemy, you put yourself on a level with him on this score, you must be convinced that he is on these grounds your superior. But appeal to the sacred principles of virtue and justice, then how is he awed into nothing! How does truth shew him in his real colours and place the cause of toleration and reform in the clearest light! I extend my view not only to you as Irishmen, but to all of every persuasion, of every country. Be calm, mild, deliberate, patient; recollect that you can in no measure more effectually forward the cause of reform than by employing your leisure time in reasoning, or the cultivation of your minds. Think and talk, and discuss. The only subjects you ought to propose, are those of happiness and liberty. Be free and be happy, but first be wise and good. For you are not all wise or good. You are a great and a brave nation, but you cannot yet be all wise or good. You may be at some time, and then Ireland will be an earthly Paradise. You know what is meant by a mob; it is an assembly of people who, without foresight or thought, collect themselves to disapprove of by force any measure which they dislike. An assembly like this can never do anything but harm, tumultuous proceedings must retard the period when thought and coolness will produce freedom and happiness, and that to the very people who make the mob, but if a number of human beings, after thinking of their own interests, meet together for any conversation on them, and employ resistance of the mind, not resistance of the body, these people are going the right way to work. But let no fiery passions carry them beyond this point, let them consider that in some sense, the whole welfare of their countrymen depends on their prudence, and that it becomes them to guard the welfare of others as their own. Associations for purposes of violence, are entitled to the strongest disapprobation of the real reformist. Always suspect that some knavish rascal is at the bottom of things of this kind, waiting to profit by the confusion. All secret associations are also bad. Are you men of deep designs, whose deeds love darkness better than light; dare you not say what you think before any man, can you not meet in the open face of day in conscious innocence? Oh, Irishmen ye can. Hidden arms, secret meetings, and designs violently to separate England from Ireland are all very bad, I do not mean to say the very end of them is bad; the object you have in view may be just enough, whilst the way you go about it is wrong, may be calculated to produce an opposite effect. Never do evil that good may come, always think of others as well as yourself, and cautiously look how your conduct may do good or evil, when you yourself shall be mouldering in the grave. Be fair, open, and you will be terrible to your enemies. A friend cannot defend you, much as he may feel for your sufferings, if you have recourse to methods of which virtue and justice disapprove. No cause is in itself so dear to liberty as yours. Much depends on you, far may your efforts spread, either hope or despair; do not then cover in darkness wrongs at which the face of day, and the tyrants who bask in its warmth ought to blush. Wherever has violence succeeded. The French Revolution, although undertaken with the best intentions, ended ill for the people, because violence was employed; the cause which they vindicated was that of truth, but they gave it the appearance of a lie, by using methods which will suit the purposes of liars as well as their own. Speak boldly and daringly what you think, an Irishman was never accused of cowardice, do not let it be thought possible that he is a coward. Let him say what he thinks, a lie is the basest and meanest employment of men, leave lies and secrets to courtiers and lordlings; be open, sincere, and single-hearted. Let it be seen that the Irish votaries of Freedom dare to speak what they think, let them resist oppression, not by force of arms, but by power of mind, and reliance on truth and justice. Will any be arraigned for libel – will imprisonment or death be the consequences of this mode of proceeding: Probably not – but if it were so? Is danger frightful to an Irishman who speaks for his own liberty, and the liberty of his wife and children: No, he will steadily persevere, and sooner shall pensioners cease to vote with their benefactors, than an Irishman swerve from the path of duty. But steadily persevere in the system above laid down; its benefits will speedily be manifested. Persecution may destroy some, but cannot destroy all, or nearly all; let it do its will, ye have appealed to truth and justice – shew the goodness of your religion by persisting in a reliance on these things, which must be the rules even of the Almighty's conduct. But before this can be done with any effect, habits of SOBRIETY, REGULARITY, and THOUGHT, must be entered into, and firmly resolved upon.

My warm-hearted friends, who meet together to talk of the distresses of your countrymen, until social chat induces you to drink rather freely, as ye have felt passionately, so reason coolly. Nothing hasty can be lasting; lay up the money with which you usually purchase drunkenness and ill-health, to relieve the pains of your fellow-sufferers. Let your children lisp of Freedom in the cradle – let your deathbed be the school for fresh exertions – let every street of the city, and field of the country be connected with thoughts which liberty has made holy. Be warm in your cause, yet rational, and charitable, and tolerant – never let the oppressor grind you into justifying his conduct by imitating his meanness.

Many circumstances, I will own, may excuse what is called rebellion, but no circumstances can ever make it good for your cause, and however honourable to your feelings, it will reflect no credit on your judgements. It will bind you more closely to the block of the oppressor, and your children's children, whilst they talk of your exploits, will feel that you have done them injury instead of benefit.

A crisis[3] is now arriving which shall decide your fate. The King of Great Britain has arrived at the evening of his days. He has objected to your emancipation; he has been inimical to you; but he will in a certain time be no more. The present Prince of Wales will then be king. It is said that he has promised to restore you to freedom: your real and natural right will, in that case, be no longer kept from you. I hope he has pledged himself to this act of justice, because there will then exist some obligation to bind him to do right. Kings are but too apt to think, little as they should do. They think everything in the world is made for them; when the truth is that it is only the vices of men that make such people necessary, and they have no other right of being kings but in virtue of the good they do. The benefit of the governed is the origin and meaning of government. The Prince of Wales has had every opportunity of knowing how he ought to act about Ireland and liberty. That great and good man, Charles Fox, who was your friend, and the friend of freedom, was the friend of the Prince of Wales. He never flattered or disguised his sentiments but spoke them *openly* on every occasion, and the Prince was the better for his instructive conversation. He saw the truth, and he believed it. Now I know not what to say; his staff is gone, and he leans upon a broken reed; his present advisers are not like Charles Fox,[4] they do not plan for liberty and safety, not for the happiness but for the glory of their country; and what, Irishmen, is the glory of a country divided from their happiness? It is a false light hung out by the enemies of freedom to lure the unthinking into their net. Men like these surround the Prince, and whether or no he has really promised to emancipate you, whether or no he will consider the promise of a Prince of Wales binding to a King of England, is yet a matter of doubt. We cannot at least be quite certain of it: on this you cannot certainly rely. But there are men who, wherever they find a tendency to freedom, go there to increase, support, and regulate that tendency. These men who join to a rational disdain of danger, a practice of speaking the truth, and defending the cause of the oppressed against the oppressor; these men see what is right and will pursue it. On such as these you may safely rely: they love you as they love their brothers; they feel for the unfortunate and never ask whether a man is an Englishman or an Irishman, a Catholic, a heretic, a Christian, or a heathen, before their hearts and their purses are opened to feel with their misfortunes and relieve their necessities: such are the men who will stand by you for ever. Depend then not upon, the promises of Princes, but upon those of virtuous and disinterested men: depend not upon force of arms or violence, but upon the force of the truth of the right which you have to share equally with others, the benefits and the evils of Government.

The crisis to which I allude as the period of your emancipation, is not the death of the present king, or any circumstance that has to do with kings, but something that is much more likely to do you good: it is the increase of virtue and wisdom which will lead people to find out that force and oppression is wrong and false; and this opinion, when it once gains ground, will prevent government from severity. It will restore those rights which government has taken away. Have nothing to do with force or violence, and things will safely and surely make their way to the right point. The Ministers have now in Parliament a very great majority, and the Ministers are against you. They maintain the falsehood that, were you in power you would [persecute] and burn, on the plea that you once did so. They maintain many other things of the same nature. They command the majority of the House of Commons, or rather the part of that assembly, who receive pensions from Government, or whose relatives receive them. These men of course are against you, because their employers are. But the sense of the country is not against you, the people of England are not against you – they feel warmly for you – in some respects they feel with you. The sense of the English and of their Governors is opposite – there must be an end of this; the goodness of a Government consists in the happiness of the Governed.[5] If the Governed are wretched and dissatisfied, the Government has failed in its end. It wants altering and mending. It will be mended, and a reform of English Government will produce good to the Irish – good to all human kind, excepting those whose happiness consists in others' sorrows, and it will be a fit punishment for these to be deprived of their devilish joy. This I consider as an event which is approaching, and which will make the beginning of our hopes for that period which may spread wisdom and virtue so wide as to leave no hole in which folly or villainy may hide themselves. I wish you, O Irishmen, to be as careful and thoughtful of your interests as are your real friends. Do not drink, do not play, do not spend any idle time, do not take everything that other people say for granted – there are numbers who will tell you lies to make their own fortunes. You cannot more certainly do good to your own cause, than by defeating the intentions of these men. Think, read, and talk; let your own condition and that of your wives and children fill your minds; disclaim all manner of alliance with violence, meet together if you will, but do not meet in a mob. If you think and read and talk with a real wish of benefiting the cause of truth and liberty, it will soon be seen how true a service you are rendering, and how sincere you are in your professions; but mobs and violence must be discarded. The certain degree of civil and religious liberty which the usage of the English Constitution allows, is such as the worst of men are entitled to, although you have it not; but that liberty which we may one day hope for, wisdom and virtue can alone give you a right to enjoy. This wisdom and this virtue I recommend on every account that you should *instantly begin* to practise. Lose not a day, not an hour, not a moment. Temperance, sobriety, charity, and independence will give you virtue; and reading, talking, thinking and searching, will give you wisdom; when you have those things you may defy the tyrant. It is not going often to chapel, crossing yourselves, or confessing, that will make you virtuous; many a rascal has attended regularly at Mass, and many a good man has never gone at all. It is not paying Priests, or believing in what they say that makes a good man, but it is doing good actions, or benefiting other people; this is the true way to be good, and the prayers, and confessions, and masses of him who does not these things, are good for nothing at all. Do your work regularly and quickly, when you have done, think, read, and talk; do not spend your money in idleness and drinking, which so far from doing good to your cause, will do it harm. If you have anything to spare from your wife and children, let it do some good to other people, and put them in a way of getting wisdom and virtue, as the pleasure that will come from these good acts, will be much better than the head-ache that comes from a drinking bout. And never quarrel between each other, be all of one mind as nearly as you can; do those things, and I will promise you liberty and happiness. But if, on the contrary of these things, you neglect to improve yourselves, continue to use the word heretic, and demand from others the toleration which you are unwilling to give; your friends and the friends of liberty will have reason to lament the deathblow of their hopes. I expect better things from you; it is for yourselves that I fear and hope. Many Englishmen are prejudiced against you, they sit by their own fire-sides and certain rumours, artfully spread are ever on the wing against you. But these people who think ill of you and of your nation, are often the very men who, if they had better information, would feel for you most keenly; wherefore are these reports spread, how do they begin? They originate from the warmth of the Irish character, which the friends of the Irish nation have hitherto encouraged rather than repressed; this leads them in those moments when their wrongs appear so clearly, to commit acts which justly excite displeasure. They begin therefore from yourselves, although falsehood and tyranny artfully magnify and multiply the cause of offence. – Give no offence.

I will for the present dismiss the subject of the Catholic Emancipation; a little reflection will convince you that my remarks are just. Be true to yourselves, and your enemies shall not triumph. I fear nothing, if charity and sobriety mark your proceedings. Everything is to be dreaded, you yourselves will be unworthy of even a restoration to your rights, if you disgrace the cause, which I hope is that of truth and liberty, by violence, if you refuse to others the toleration which you claim for yourselves. But this you will not do. I rely upon it Irishmen, that the warmth of your characters will be shewn as much in union with Englishmen and what are called heretics, who feel for you, and love you, as in avenging your wrongs, or forwarding their annihilation. It is the heart that glows and not the cheek. The firmness, sobriety, and consistence of your outward behaviour will not at all shew any hardness of heart, but will prove that you are determined in your cause, and are going the right way to work. I will repeat that virtue and wisdom are necessary to true happiness and liberty. The Catholic Emancipation I consider, is certain. I do not see that anything but violence and intolerance among yourselves can leave an excuse to your enemies for continuing your slavery. The other wrongs under which you labor will probably also soon be done away. You will be rendered equal to the people of England in their rights and privileges, and will be in all respects, so far as concerns the state, as happy. And now, Irishmen, another and a more wide prospect opens to my view. I cannot avoid, little as it may appear to have any thing to do with your present situation, to talk to you on the subject. It intimately concerns the well-being of your children, and your children's children, and will, perhaps more than anything, prove to you the advantage and necessity of being thoughtful, sober, and regular; of avoiding foolish and idle talk, and thinking of yourselves as of men who are able to be much wiser and happier than you now are; for habits like these, will not only conduce to the successful putting aside your present and immediate grievances, but will contain a seed, which in future times will spring up into the tree of liberty and bear the fruit of happiness.

There is no doubt but the world is going wrong, or rather that it is very capable of being much improved. What I mean by this improvement is, the inducement of a more equal and general diffusion of happiness and liberty. Many people are very rich and many are very poor. Which do you think are happiest? I can tell you that neither are happy, so far as their station is concerned. Nature never intended that there should be such a thing as a poor man or a rich one. Being put in an unnatural situation, they can neither of them be happy, so far as their situation is concerned. The poor man is born to obey the rich man, though they both come into the world equally helpless, and equally naked. But the poor man does the rich no service by obeying him – the rich man does the poor no good by commanding him. It would be much better if they could be prevailed upon to live equally, like brothers – they would ultimately both be happier. But this can be done neither to-day nor to-morrow, much as such a change is to be desired, it is quite impossible. Violence and folly in this, as in the other case, would only put off the period of its event. Mildness, sobriety, and reason, are the effectual methods of forwarding the ends of liberty and happiness.

Although we may see many things put in train, during our lifetime, we cannot hope to see the work of virtue and reason finished now; we can only lay the foundation for our posterity. Government is an evil, it is only the thoughtlessness and vices of men that make it a necessary evil. When all men are good and wise, Government will of itself decay, so long as men continue foolish and vicious, so long will Government, even such a Government as that of England, continue necessary in order to prevent the crimes of bad men. Society is produced by the wants, Government by the wickedness, and a state of just and happy equality by the improvement and reason of man. It is in vain to hope for any liberty and happiness, without reason and virtue – for where there is no virtue there will be crime, and where there is crime there must be Government. Before the restraints of Government are lessened, it is fit that we should lessen the necessity for them. Before Government is done away with, we must reform ourselves. It is this work which I would earnestly recommend to you, O Irishmen; REFORM YOURSELVES – and I do not recommend it to you particularly because I think that you most need it, but because I think that your hearts are warm and your feelings high, and you will perceive the necessity of doing it more than those of a colder and more distant nature.

I look with an eye of hope and pleasure on the present state of things, gloomy and incapable of improvement as they may appear to others. It delights me to see that men begin to think and to act for the good of others. Extensively as folly and selfishness has predominated in this age, it gives me hope and pleasure, at least, to see that many know what is right. Ignorance and vice commonly go together: he that would do good must be wise – a man cannot be truly wise who is not truly virtuous. Prudence and wisdom are very different things. The prudent man is he, who carefully consults for his own good: the wise man is he, who carefully consults for the good of others.

I look upon Catholic Emancipation, and the restoration of the liberties and happiness of Ireland, so far as they are compatible with the

English Constitution, as great and important events. I hope to see them soon. But if all ended here, it would give me little pleasure – I should still see thousands miserable and wicked, things would still be wrong. I regard, then, the accomplishment of these things as the road to a greater reform – that reform after which virtue and wisdom shall have conquered pain and vice. When no Government will be wanted but that of your neighbour's opinion. I look to these things with hope and pleasure, because I consider that they will certainly happen, and because men will not then be wicked and miserable. But I do not consider that they will or can immediately happen; their arrival will be gradual, and it all depends upon yourselves how soon or how late these great changes will happen. If all of you to-morrow were virtuous and wise, Government which to-day is a safeguard, would then become a tyranny. But I cannot expect a rapid change. Many are obstinate and determined in their vice, whose selfishness makes them think only of their own good, when in fact, the best way even to bring that about is to make others happy. I do not wish to see things changed now, because it cannot be done without violence, and we may assure ourselves that none of us are fit for any change however good, if we condescend to employ force in a cause which we think right. Force makes the side that employs it directly wrong, and as much as we may pity we cannot approve the headstrong and intolerant zeal of adherents.

Can you conceive, O Irishmen! a happy state of society – conceive men of every way of thinking living together like brothers. The descendant of the greatest Prince would there, be entitled to no more respect than the son of a peasant. There would be no pomp and no parade, but that which the rich now keep to themselves, would then be distributed among the people. None would be in magnificence, but the superfluities then taken from the rich would be sufficient when spread abroad, to make everyone comfortable. No lover would then be false to his mistress, no mistress would desert her lover. No friend would play false, no rents, no debts, no taxes, no frauds of any kind would disturb the general happiness: good as they would be, wise as they would be, they would be daily getting better and wiser. No beggars would exist, nor any of those wretched women, who are now reduced to a state of the most horrible misery and vice, by men whose wealth makes them villainous and hardened. No thieves or murderers, because poverty would never drive men to take away comforts from another, when he had enough for himself. Vice and misery, pomp and poverty, power and obedience, would then be banished altogether. It is for such a state as this, Irishmen, that I exhort you to prepare. 'A Camel shall as soon pass through the eye of a needle, as a rich man enter the Kingdom of Heaven'. This is not to be understood literally. Jesus Christ appears to me only to have meant that riches, have generally the effect of hardening and vitiating the heart; so has poverty. I think those people then are very silly, and cannot see one inch beyond their noses, who say that human nature is depraved; when at the same time wealth and poverty, those two great sources of crime, fall to the lot of a great majority of people; and when they see that people in moderate circumstances are always most wise and good. People say that poverty is no evil – they have never felt it, or they would not think so. That wealth is necessary to encourage the arts – but are not the arts very inferior things to virtue and happiness – the man would be very dead to all generous feelings who would rather see pretty pictures and statues than a million free and happy men.

It will be said, that my design is to make you dissatisfied with your present condition, and that I wish to raise a Rebellion. But how stupid and sottish must those men be, who think that violence and uneasiness of mind have anything to do with forwarding the views of peace, harmony, and happiness. They should know that nothing was so well-fitted to produce slavery, tyranny and vice, as the violence which is attributed to the friends of liberty, and which the real friends of liberty are the only persons who disdain. As to your being dissatisfied with your present condition, anything that I may say is certainly not likely to increase that dissatisfaction. I have advanced nothing concerning your situation, but its real case, but what may be proved to be true. I defy any one to point out a falsehood that I have uttered in the course of this address. It is impossible but the blindest among you must see that every thing is not right. This sight has often pressed some of the poorest among you to take something from the rich man's store by violence, to relieve his own necessities. I cannot justify, but I can pity him. I cannot pity the fruits of the rich man's intemperance, I suppose some are to be found who will justify him. This sight has often brought home to a day-labourer the truth which I wish to impress upon you, that all is not right. But I do not merely wish to convince you that [your] present state is bad, but that its alteration for the better, depends on your own exertions and resolutions.

But he has never found out the method of mending it, who does not first mend his own conduct and then prevail upon others to refrain from any vicious habits which they may have contracted – much less does the poor man suppose that wisdom as well as virtue is necessary, and that the employing his little time in reading and thinking, is really doing all that he has in his power to do towards the state, when pain and vice shall perish altogether.

I wish to impress upon your minds, that without virtue or wisdom there can be no liberty or happiness; and that temperance, sobriety, charity, and independence of soul, will give you virtue – as thinking, enquiring, reading, and talking, will give you wisdom. Without the first, the last is of little use, and without the last, the first is a dreadful curse to yourselves and others.

I have told you what I think upon this subject, because I wish to produce in your minds an awe and caution necessary, before the happy state of which I have spoken can be introduced. This cautious awe, is very different from the prudential fear, which leads you to consider yourself as the first object, as on the contrary it is full of that warm and ardent love for others that burns in your hearts, O Irishmen! and from which I have fondly hoped to light a flame that may illumine and invigorate the world!

I have said that the rich command, and the poor obey, and that money is only a kind of sign, which shews, that according to government the rich man has a right to command the poor man, or rather that the poor man being urged by having no money to get bread, is forced to work for the rich man, which amounts to the same thing. I have said that I think all this very wrong, and that I wish the whole business was altered. I have also said that we can expect little amendment in our own time, and that we must be contented to lay the foundation of liberty and happiness, by virtue and wisdom. This then, shall be my work; let this be yours, Irishmen. Never shall that glory fail, which I am anxious that you shall deserve. The glory of teaching to a world the first lessons of virtue and wisdom.

Let poor men still continue to work. I do not wish to hide from them a knowledge of their relative condition in society, I esteem it next [to] impossible to do so. Let the work of the labourer, of the artificer – let the work of every one, however employed, still be exerted in its accustomed way. The public communication of this truth, ought in no manner to impede the established usages of society; however, it is fitted in the end to do them away. For this reason it ought not to impede them, because if it did, a violent and unaccustomed and sudden sensation would take place in all ranks of men, which would bring on violence. and destroy the possibility of the event of that which in its own nature must be gradual, however rapid, and rational, however warm. It is founded on the reform of private men, and without individual amendment it is vain and foolish to expect the amendment of a state or government. I would advise them therefore, whose feelings this address may have succeeded in affecting (and surely those feelings which charitable and temperate remarks excite, can never be violent and intolerant), if they be, as I hope, those whom poverty has compelled to class themselves in the lower orders of society, that they will as usual attend to their business and the discharge of those public or private duties, which custom has ordained. Nothing can be more rash and thoughtless, than to shew in ourselves singular instances of any particular doctrine, before the general mass of the people are so convinced by the reasons of the doctrine, that it will be no longer singular. That reasons as well as feeling, may help the establishment of happiness and liberty, on the basis of wisdom and virtue, is our aim and intention. Let us not be led into any means which are unworthy of this end, nor, as so much depends upon yourselves, let us cease carefully to watch over our conduct, that when we talk of reform it be not objected to us, that reform ought to begin at home. In the interval that public or private duties and necessary labours allow, husband your time so, that you may do to others and yourselves the most real good. To improve your own minds is to join these two views: conversation and reading are the principal and chief methods of awakening the mind to knowledge and goodness. Reading or thought, will principally bestow the former of these – the benevolent exercise of the powers of the mind in communicating useful knowledge, will bestow a habit of the latter; both united will contribute so far as lies in your individual power to that great reform which will be perfect and finished, the moment everyone is virtuous and wise. Every folly refuted, every bad habit conquered, every good one confirmed, is so much gained in this great and excellent cause.

To begin to reform the Government, is immediately necessary, however good or bad individuals may be; it is the more necessary if they are eminently the latter, in some degree to palliate or do away the cause; as political institution has even the greatest influence on the human character, and is that alone which differences the Turk from the Irishman.

I write now not only with a view for Catholic Emancipation, but for universal emancipation; and this emancipation complete and unconditional, that shall comprehend every individual of whatever nation or principles, that shall fold in its embrace all that think and all that feel, the Catholic cause is subordinate, and its success preparatory to this great cause, which adheres to no sect but society, to no cause but that of universal happiness, to no party but the people. I desire Catholic Emancipation, but I desire not to stop here, and I hope there are few who having perused the preceding arguments will not concur with me in desiring a complete, a lasting, and a happy amendment. That all steps however good and salutary, which may be taken, all reforms consistent with the English constitution that may be effectuated can only be subordinate and preparatory to the great and lasting one which shall bring about the peace, the harmony, and the happiness of Ireland, England, Europe, the World. I offer merely an outline of that picture which your own hopes may gift with the colors of reality.

Government will not allow a peaceable and reasonable discussion of its principles by any association of men who assemble for that express purpose. But have not human beings a right to assemble to talk upon what subject they please; can anything be more evident than that, as government is only of use as it conduces to the happiness of the governed;[6] those who are governed have a right to talk on the efficacy of the safeguard employed for their benefit. Can any topic be more interesting or useful than one discussing how far the means of government, is or could be made in a higher degree effectual to producing the end. Although I deprecate violence, and the cause which depends for its influence on force, yet I can by no means think that assembling together merely to talk of how things go on, I can by no means think that societies formed for talking on any subject however government may dislike them, come in any way under the head of force or violence. I think that associations conducted in the spirit of sobriety, regularity, and thought, are one of the best and most efficient of those means which I would recommend for the production of happiness, liberty, and virtue.

Are you slaves, or are you men? If slaves, then crouch to the rod, and lick the feet of your oppressors, glory in your shame, it will become you if brutes to act according to your nature. But you are men; a real man is free, so far as circumstances will permit him. Then firmly, yet quietly resist. When one cheek is struck, turn the other to the insulting coward. You will be truly brave; you will resist and conquer. The discussion of any subject is a right, that you have brought into the world with your heart and tongue. Resign your heart's blood, before you part with this inestimable privilege of man. For it is fit that the governed should enquire into the proceedings of Government, which is of no use the moment it is conducted on any other principle but that of safety. You have much to think of. Is war necessary to your happiness and safety. The interests of the poor gain nothing from the wealth or extension of a nation's boundaries, they gain nothing from glory, a word that has often served as a cloak to the ambition or avarice of Statesmen. The barren victories of Spain, gained in behalf of a bigoted and tyrannical Government, are nothing to them. The conquests in India, by which

England has gained glory indeed, but a glory which is not more honourable than that of Buonaparte, are nothing to them. The poor purchase this glory and this wealth, at the expense of their blood, and labor, and happiness, and virtue. They die in battle for this infernal cause. Their labor supplies money and food for carrying it into effect, their happiness is destroyed by the oppression they undergo, their virtue is rooted out by the depravity and vice that prevail throughout the army, and which under the present system, is perfectly unavoidable. Who does not know that the quartering of a regiment on any town, will soon destroy the innocence and happiness of its inhabitants. The advocates for the happiness and liberty of the great mass of the people, who pay for war with their lives and labor, ought never to cease writing and speaking until nations see as they must feel, the folly of fighting and killing each other in uniform for nothing at all.[7] Ye have much to think of. The state of your representation in the House, which is called the collective representation of the country, demands your attention.

It is horrible that the lower classes must waste their lives and liberty to furnish means for their oppressors to oppress them yet more terribly. It is horrible that the poor must give in taxes what would save them and their families from hunger and cold; it is still more horrible that they should do this to furnish further means of their own abjectedness and misery; but what words can express the enormity of the abuse that prevents them from choosing representatives with authority to enquire into the manner in which their lives and labor, their happiness and innocence, is expended, and what advantages result from their expenditure which may counterbalance so horrible and monstrous an evil. There is an outcry raised against amendment; it is called innovation and condemned by many unthinking people who have a good fire and plenty to eat and drink; hard-hearted or thoughtless beings, how many are famishing whilst you deliberate, how many perish to contribute to your pleasures. I hope that there are none such as these native Irishmen, indeed I scarcely believe that there are.

Let the object of your associations (for I conceal not my approval of assemblies conducted with regularity, *peaceableness* and thought for any purpose) be the amendment of these abuses, it will have for its object universal Emancipation, liberty, happiness, and virtue. There is yet another subject, 'the Liberty of the Press'. The liberty of the press consists in a right to publish any opinion on any subject which the writer may entertain. The Attorney General in 1793 on the trial of Mr. Perry,[8] said, 'I never will dispute the right of any man fully to discuss topics respecting government, and honestly to point out what he may consider a proper remedy of grievances'. – 'The liberty of the Press is placed as a sentinel to alarm us when any attempt is made on our liberties'. It is this sentinel, O Irishmen, whom I now awaken! I create to myself a freedom which exists not. There is no liberty of the press, for the subjects of British government.

It is really ridiculous to hear people yet boasting of this inestimable blessing when they daily see it successfully muzzled and outraged by the lawyers of the crown, and by virtue of what are called ex-officio informations.[9] Blackstone[10] says, that 'if a person publishes what is improper, mischievous, or illegal, he must take the consequences of his own temerity;' and Lord Chief Baron Comyns[11] defines libel as 'a contumely, or reproach, published to the defamation of the Government, of a magistrate, or of a private person'. Now, I beseech you to consider the words, mischievous, improper, illegal, contumely, reproach, or defamation. May they not make that mischievous, or improper, which they please? Is not law with them, as clay in the potter's hand? Do not the words, contumely, reproach, or defamation, express all degrees and forces of disapprobation? It is impossible to express yourself displeased at certain proceedings of Government, or the individuals who conduct it, without uttering a reproach. We cannot honestly point out a proper remedy of grievances with safety, because the very mention of these grievances will be reproachful to the personages who countenance them; and therefore will come under a definition of libel. For the persons who thus directly or indirectly undergo reproach, will say for their own sakes, that the exposure of their corruption is mischievous and improper; therefore, the utterer of the reproach is a fit subject for three years' imprisonment. Is there anything like the Liberty of the Press in restrictions so positive yet pliant as these? The little freedom which we enjoy in this most important point, comes from the clemency of our rulers, or their fear lest public opinion, alarmed at the discovery of its enslaved state, should violently assert a right to extension and diffusion. Yet public opinion may not always be so formidable, rulers may not always be so merciful or so timid: At any rate, evils, and great evils, do result from the present system of intellectual slavery, and you have enough to think of if this grievance alone remained in the constitution of society. I will give but one instance of the present state of our Press.

A countryman of yours is now confined in an English gaol. His health, his fortune, his spirits, suffer from close confinement. The air which comes through the bars of a prison-grate does not invigorate the frame nor cheer the spirits. But Mr. Finnerty, much as he has lost, yet retains the fair name of truth and honor. He was imprisoned for persisting in the truth. His judge told him on his trial, that truth and falsehood were indifferent to the law, and that if he owned the publication any consideration, whether the facts that it related were well or ill-founded, was totally irrelevant. Such is the libel law. Such the liberty of the Press – there is enough to think of. The right of withholding your individual assent to war, the right of choosing delegates to represent you in the assembly of the nation, and that of freely opposing intellectual power to any measures of Government of which you may disapprove, are, in addition to the indifference with which the legislative and the executive power ought to rule their conduct towards professors of every religion, enough to think of.

I earnestly desire peace and harmony:– peace, that whatever wrongs you may have suffered, benevolence and a spirit of forgiveness should mark your conduct towards those who have persecuted you. Harmony, that among yourselves may be no divisions, that Protestants and Catholics unite in a common interest, and that whatever be the belief and principles of your countryman and fellow-sufferer, you desire to benefit his cause, at the same time that you vindicate your own; be strong and unbiased by selfishness or prejudice – for, Catholics, your religion has not been spotless, crimes in past ages have sullied it with a stain, which let it be your glory to remove. Nor Protestants, hath your religion always been characterized by the mildness of benevolence, which Jesus Christ recommended. Had it anything to do with the present subject I could account for the spirit of intolerance which marked both religions; I will, however, only adduce the fact, and earnestly exhort you to root out from your own minds everything which may lead to uncharitableness, and to reflect that yourselves, as well as your brethren may be deceived. Nothing on earth is infallible. The Priests that pretend to it are wicked and mischievous impostors; but it is an imposture which everyone, more or less, assumes, who encourages prejudice in his breast against those who differ from him in opinion, or who sets up his own religion as the only right and true one, when no one is so blind as [not] to see that every religion is right and true which makes men beneficent and sincere. I therefore, earnestly exhort both Protestants and Catholics to act in brotherhood and harmony, never forgetting, because the Catholics alone are heinously deprived of religious rights, that the Protestants and a certain rank of people, of every persuasion share with them all else that is terrible, galling and intolerable in the mass of political grievance.

In no case employ violence or falsehood. I cannot too often or too vividly endeavour to impress upon your minds, that these methods will produce nothing but wretchedness and slavery – that they will at the same time rivet the fetters with which ignorance and oppression bind you to abjectness, and deliver you over to a tyranny, which shall render you incapable of renewed efforts. Violence will immediately render your cause a bad one. If you believe in a Providential God, you must also believe that he is a good one; and it is not likely, a merciful God would befriend a bad cause. Insincerity is no less hurtful than violence; those who are in the habit of either would do well to reform themselves. A lying bravo will never promote the good of his country – he cannot be a good man. The courageous and sincere may, at the same time, successfully oppose corruption, by uniting their voice with that of others, or individually raise up intellectual opposition to counteract the abuses of Government and society. In order to benefit yourselves and your country to any extent, habits of sobriety, regularity, and thought are previously so necessary, that without these preliminaries, all that you have done falls to the ground. You have built on sand. Secure a good foundation, and you may erect a fabric to stand for ever – the glory and the envy of the world!

I have purposely avoided any lengthened discussion on those grievances to which your hearts are from custom, and the immediate interest of the circumstances, probably most alive at present. I have not however wholly neglected them. Most of all have I insisted on their instant palliation and ultimate removal; nor have I omitted a consideration of the means which I deem most effectual for the accomplishment of this great end. How far you will consider the former worthy of your adoption, so far shall I deem the latter probable and interesting to the lovers of human kind. And I have opened to your view a new scene – does not your heart bound at the bare possibility of your posterity possessing that liberty and happiness of which during our lives powerful exertions and habitual abstinence may give us a foretaste. Oh! if your hearts do not vibrate at such as this; then ye are dead and cold – ye are not men.

I now come to the application of my principles, the conclusion of my address; and O Irishmen, whatever conduct ye may feel yourselves bound to pursue, the path which duty points to, lies before me clear and unobscured. Dangers may lurk around it, but they are not the dangers which lie beneath the footsteps of the hypocrite or temporizer.

For I have not presented to you the picture of happiness on which my fancy doats as an uncertain meteor to mislead honorable enthusiasm, or blindfold the judgement which makes virtue useful. I have not proposed crude schemes which I should be incompetent to mature, or desired to excite in you any virulence against the abuses of political institution; where I have had occasion to point them out I have recommended moderation whilst yet I have earnestly insisted upon energy and perseverance; I have spoken of peace, yet declared that resistance is laudable; but the intellectual resistance which I recommend, I deem essential to the introduction of the millennium of virtue, whose period every one can, so far as he is concerned, forward by his own proper power. I have not attempted to shew that the Catholic claims or the claims of the people, to a full representation in Parliament, or any of those claims to real rights, which I have insisted upon as introductory to the ultimate claim of all, to universal happiness, freedom, and equality; I have not attempted, I say, to shew that these can be granted consistently with the spirit of the English Constitution: This is a point which I do not feel myself inclined to discuss, and which I consider foreign to my subject. But I have shewn that these claims have for their basis, truth and justice, which are immutable, and which in the ruin of Governments shall rise like a Phoenix from their ashes.[12]

Is any one inclined to dispute the possibility of a happy change in society? Do they say that the nature of man is corrupt, and that he was made for misery and wickedness? Be it so. Certain as are opposite conclusions, I will concede the truth of this for a moment. What are the means which I take for melioration? Violence, corruption, rapine, crime? Do I do evil, that good may come? I have recommended peace, philanthropy, wisdom. So far as my arguments influence, they will influence to these – and if there is any one *now* inclined to say, that 'private vices are public benefits,'[13] and that peace, philanthropy, and wisdom will, it once they gain ground, ruin the human race; he may revel in his happy dreams; though were I this man, I should envy Satan's Hell. The wisdom and charity of which I speak, are the *only* means which I will countenance, for the redress of your grievances and the grievances of the world. So far as they operate, I am willing to stand responsible for their *evil* effects. I expect to be accused of a desire for renewing in Ireland the scenes of revolutionary horror, which marked the struggles of France twenty years ago. But it is the renewal of that unfortunate era which I strongly deprecate, and which the tendency of this address is calculated to obviate. For can burthens be borne forever, and the slave crouch and cringe the while. Is misery and vice so consonant to man's nature that he will hug it to his heart? But when the wretched one in bondage beholds the emancipator near, will he not endure his misery awhile with hope and patience, then spring to his preserver's arms, and start into a man.

It is my intention to observe the effect on your minds, O Irishmen! which this address dictated by the fervency of my love and hope will produce. I have come to this country to spare no pains where expenditure may purchase your real benefit. The present is a crisis, which of all others is the most valuable for fixing the fluctuation of public feeling; as far as my poor efforts may have succeeded in fixing it to virtue, Irishmen, so far shall I esteem myself happy. I intend this address as introductory to another. The organisation of a society, whose institution shall serve as a bond to its members, for the purposes of virtue, happiness, liberty, and wisdom, by the means of intellectual opposition to grievances, would probably be useful. For the formation of such society, I avow myself anxious.

Adieu, my friends! May every Sun that shines on your green Island see the annihilation of an abuse, and the birth of an Embryon of melioration! Your own hearts – may they become the shrines of purity and freedom, and never may smoke to the Mammon of unrighteousness ascend from the unpolluted altar of their devotion!

No. 7, Sackville Street, Feb. 22.

POSTSCRIPT

I have now been a week in Dublin, during which time I have endeavoured to make myself more accurately acquainted with the state of the public mind, on those great topics of grievances which induced me to select Ireland as a theatre, the widest and fairest, for the operations of the determined friend of religious and political freedom.

The result of my observations has determined me to propose, an association for the purposes of restoring Ireland to the prosperity which she possessed before the Union Act; and the religious freedom, which the involuntariness of faith, ought to have taught all monopolists of Heaven long, long ago that every one had a right to possess.

For the purpose of obtaining the Emancipation of the Catholics from the penal laws that aggrieve them, and a Repeal of the Legislative Union Act; and grounding upon the remission of the church-craft and oppression which caused these grievances: *a plan of amendment and regeneration in the moral and political state of society, on a comprehensive and systematic philanthropy, which shall be sure, though slow in its projects; and as it is without the rapidity and danger of revolution, so will it be devoid of the time-servingness of temporising reform* – which in its deliberative capacity, having investigated the state of the government of England, shall oppose those parts of it, by intellectual force which will not bear the touch-stone of reason.

For information respecting the principles which I possess, and the nature and spirit of the association which I propose, I refer the reader to a small pamphlet, which I shall publish on the subject, in the course of a few days.

I have published the above address (written in England) in the cheapest possible form and have taken pains that the remarks which it contains should be intelligible to the most uneducated minds. Men are not slaves and brutes, because they are poor; it has been the policy of the thoughtless or wicked of the higher ranks, (as a proof of the decay, of which policy, I am happy to see the rapid success of a comparatively enlightened system of education) to conceal from the poor the truths which I have endeavoured to teach them. In doing so, I have but translated my thoughts into another language; and as language is only useful as it communicates ideas, I shall think my style so far good, as it is successful as a means to bring about the end which I desire, on any occasion, to accomplish.

A Limerick Paper,[14] which I suppose, professes to support certain *loyal* and *John Bullish* principles of freedom – has, in an essay for advocating the Liberty of the Press, the following clause: 'For lawless license of discussion never did we advocate, nor do we now'. What is lawless license of discussion? Is it not as indefinite as the words, *contumely, reproach, defamation,* that allow at present, such latitude to the outrages that are committed on the free expression of individual sentiment. Can they not see that what is rational will stand by its reason, and what is true stand by its truth, as all that is foolish will fall by its folly, and all that is false be controverted by its own falsehood. Liberty gains nothing by the reform of politicians of this stamp, any more than it gains from a change of Ministers in London. What at present, is contumely and defamation, would at the period of this Limerick amendment, be 'lawless license of discussion,' and such would be the mighty advantage, which this doughty champion of liberty proposes to effect.

I conclude, with the words of Lafayette,[15] a name endeared by its peerless bearer to every lover of the human race. 'For a nation to love Liberty it is sufficient that she knows it, to be free it is sufficient that she wills it'.

NOTES

1   The St. Bartholomew's Day massacre. On 24 August 1572 Catherine de Medici ordered a massacre of Protestants in Paris which spread throughout France and resulted in the deaths of at least 50,000.

2   Michael Servetus (1511-53), a Spanish theologian who denied the divinity of Christ. He escaped the Inquisition, but was later burnt as a heretic in Geneva on the basis of John Calvin's evidence.

3   The 'crisis' that Shelley refers to is the assumption of full regency powers by the Prince of Wales in February 1812 as a result of the insanity of George III, and its potential effect on Irish politics.

4   Charles Fox (1749-1806), Whig leader, a liberal in politics and a supporter of Catholic emancipation. He was the friend and confidant of the Prince of Wales. The 'broken reed' was the Tory politician, Lord Eldon (1751-1838).

5   From Tom Paine's 'Common Sense', *The Thomas Paine Reader*, op cit, p68. This section is taken almost complete from Paine.

6   These sentiments appear as articles 1 and 2 of Shelley's *Declaration of Rights*, (Appendix 5, p303).

7   See article 19 of the *Declaration of Rights*, (Appendix 5, p305).

8   James Perry, editor of the *Morning Chronicle,* was the defendant in two famous trials for seditious libel instigated by the government in 1793 and 1810. The

earlier case was of particular importance as it was the first test of Fox's Libel Act of 1792, whereby the jury as opposed to the judge decided on the question of libel. Perry was found not guilty, and in doing so the jury laid down a marker in support of 'the Liberty of the Press'.

9   The attorney-general was empowered to provide 'ex officio informations' against those who it considered had published libellous or seditious material against the state. Peter Finnerty was charged in this way in 1811, which precipitated a parliamentary motion for the repeal of the act.

10   Sir William Blackstone (1723-80), whose *Commentaries on the Laws of England*, (London, 1765-69) were considered the ultimate authority on English law.

11   Shelley is quoting from Sir John Comyns (d1740), *A Digest of the Laws of England* (London, 1792), vol 4, p713.

12   'The excellence of the Constitution of Great Britain appears to me to be its indefiniteness and versatility, whereby it may be unresistingly accommodated to the progression of wisdom and virtue. Such accommodation I desire; but I wish for the cause before the effect'. (Shelley's note)

13   Shelley is quoting from Bernard Mandeville, *The Fable of the Bees: or, Private Vices, Public Benefits* (London, 1714). (See also Chapter 9, p183).

14   *The Limerick Evening Post*. The article that Shelley is quoting from was reprinted in the *Freeman's Journal*, 18 February 1812, which is most likely Shelley's source.

15   Marquis de La Fayette (1757-1834) – born in France, he was a champion of religious freedom, trial by jury and the freedom of the press. He was a participant in both the American and French revolutions. Shelley most likely took the quote from Paine's 'Rights of Man', *Thomas Paine Reader*, op cit, p307.

Proposals for an Association of Philanthropists

who convinced of the inadequacy of the moral and Political State of Ireland to Produce Benefits which are nevertheless Attainable are Willing to Unite to Accomplish its Regeneration

I *propose an association which shall have for its immediate objects, Catholic Emancipation and the Repeal of the Act of Union between Great Britain and Ireland; and grounding on the removal of these grievances, an annihilation or palliation, of whatever moral or political evil, it may be within the compass of human power to assuage or eradicate.*

Man cannot make occasions, but he may seize those that offer.[1] None are more interesting to Philanthropy, than those which excite the benevolent, passions, that generalize and expand private into public feelings, and make the hearts of individuals vibrate not merely for themselves, their families, and their friends, but for posterity, *for a people*; till their country becomes the world and their family the sensitive creation.

A recollection of the absent, and a taking into consideration the interests of those unconnected with ourselves, is a principal source of that feeling which generates occasions, wherein a love for human kind may become eminently useful and active. Public topics of fear and hope, such as sympathize with general grievance, or hold out hopes of general amendment, are those on which the Philanthropist would dilate with the warmest feeling. Because these are accustomed to place individuals at a distance from self; for in proportion as he is absorbed in public feeling, so will a consideration of his proper benefit be generalized. In proportion as he feels with, or for, a nation or a world, so will man consider himself less as that centre, to which we are but too prone to believe that every line of human concern does, or ought to converge.

I should not here make the trite remark, that selfish motive biasses, brutalizes, and degrades the human mind, did it not thence follow that to seize those occasions wherein the opposite spirit predominates, is a duty which Philanthropy imperiously exacts of her votaries; that occasions like these are the proper ones for leading mankind to their own interest; by awakening in their minds a love for the interest of their fellows. A plant that grows in every soil, though too often it is choked by tares before its lovely blossoms are expanded. Virtue produces pleasure, it is as the cause to the effect; I feel pleasure in doing good to my friend, because I love him. I do not love him for the sake of that pleasure.

I regard the present state of the public mind in Ireland, to be one of those occasions, which the ardent votary of the religion of Philanthropy dare not leave unseized. I perceive that the public interest is excited, I perceive that individual interest has, in a certain degree, quitted individual concern to generalize itself with universal feeling. Be the Catholic Emancipation a thing of great or of small importance, be it a means of adding happiness to four millions of people, or a reform which will only give honor to a few of the higher ranks, yet a benevolent and disinterested feeling has gone abroad, and I am willing that it should never subside. I desire that means should be taken with energy and expedition, in this important yet fleeting crisis, to feed the unpolluted flame, at which nations and ages may light the torch of Liberty and Virtue!

It is my opinion that the claims of the Catholic inhabitants of Ireland, if gained to-morrow, would in a very small degree aggrandize their liberty and happiness. The disqualifications principally affect the higher orders of the Catholic persuasion, these would principally be benefited by their removal. Power and wealth do not benefit, but injure the cause of virtue and freedom. I am happy however, at the near approach of this emancipation, because I am inimical to all disqualifications for opinion. It gives me pleasure to see the approach of this enfranchisement, not for the good which it will bring with it, but because it is a sign of benefits approaching, a prophet of good about to come; and therefore do I sympathize with the inhabitants of Ireland, in this great cause; which, though in its own accomplishment, will add not one comfort to the cottager, will snatch not one from the dark dungeon, will root not out one vice, alleviate not one pang, yet it is the foreground of a picture, in the dimness of whose distance, I behold the lion lay down with the lamb and the infant play with the basilisk.[2] For it supposes the extermination of the eyeless monster bigotry, whose throne has tottered for two hundred years. I hear the teeth of the palsied beldame Superstition chatter, and I see her descending to the grave! Reason points to the open gates of the Temple of Religious Freedom, Philanthropy kneels at the altar of the common God! There, wealth and poverty, rank and abjectness, are names known but as memorials of past time: meteors which play over the loathsome pool of vice and misery, to warn the wanderer where dangers lie. Does a God rule this illimitable universe? Are you thankful for his beneficence – do you adore his wisdom – do you hang upon his altar the garland of your devotion? Curse not your brother, though he hath enwreathed with his flowers of a different hue; the purest religion is that of Charity, its loveliness begins to proselyte the hearts of men. The tree is to be judged of by its fruit. I regard the admission of the Catholic claims and the Repeal of the Union Act as blossoms of that fruit, which the Summer Sun of improved intellect and progressive virtue is destined to mature.

I will not pass unreflected on the Legislative Union of Great Britain and Ireland, nor will I speak of it as a grievance so tolerable or unimportant in its own nature as that of Catholic disqualification. The latter affects few, the former affects thousands. The one disqualifies the rich from power, the other impoverishes the peasant, adds beggary to the city, famine to the country, multiplies abjectedness, whilst misery and crime play into each other's hands, under its withering auspices. I esteem then, the annihilation of this second grievance to be something more than a mere sign of coming good. I esteem it to be in itself a substantial benefit. The aristocracy of Ireland (for much as I may disapprove other distinctions than those of virtue and talent, I consider it useless, hasty, and violent, not for the present to acquiesce in their continuance). The aristocracy of Ireland suck the veins of its inhabitants and consume the blood in England. I mean not to deny the unhappy truth, that there is much misery and vice in the world. I mean to say that Ireland shares largely of both. England has made her poor; and the poverty of a rich nation will make its people very desperate and wicked.

I look forward then, to the redress of both these grievances, or rather, I perceive the state of the public mind that precedes them as the crisis of beneficial innovation. The latter I consider to be the cause of the former, as I hope it will be the cause of more comprehensively beneficial amendments. It forms that occasion which should energetically and quickly be occupied. The voice of the whole human race; their crimes, their miseries, and their ignorance, invoke us to the task. For the miseries of the Irish poor, exacerbated by the Union of their country with England, are not peculiar to themselves. England, the whole civilized world, with few exceptions, is either sunk in disproportioned abjectness or raised to unnatural elevation. The Repeal of the Union Act will place Ireland on a level, so far as concerns the well-being of its poor, with her sister nation. Benevolent feeling has gone out in this country in favor of the happiness of its inhabitants – may this feeling be corroborated, methodized, and continued! May it never fail! But it will not be kept alive by each citizen sitting quietly by his own fire-side, and saying that things are going on well, because the rain does not beat on *him*, because *he* has books and leisure to read them, because *he* has money and is at liberty to accumulate luxuries to *himself*. Generous feeling dictates no such sayings. When the heart recurs to the thousands who have no liberty and no leisure, it must be rendered callous by long contemplation of wretchedness, if after such recurrence it can beat with contented evenness. Why do I talk thus. Is there anyone who doubts that the present state of politics and morals is wrong? They say shew us a safe method of improvement. There is no safer than the corroboration and propagation of generous and Philanthropic feeling, than the keeping continually alive a love for the human race, than the putting in train causes which shall have for their consequences virtue and freedom, and because I think that individuals acting singly, with whatever energy can never effect so much as a society, I propose that all those, whose views coincide with those that I have avowed, who perceive the state of the public mind in Ireland, who think the present a fit opportunity for attempting to fix its fluctuations at Philanthropy; who love all mankind, and are willing actively to engage in its cause, or passively to endure the persecutions of those who are inimical to its success; I propose to these to form an association for the purposes, first, of debating on the propriety of whatever measures may be agitated, and secondly, for carrying, by united or individual exertion, such measures into effect when determined on. That it should be an association for diffusing knowledge and virtue throughout the poorer classes of society in Ireland, for co-operating with any enlightened system of education; for discussing topics calculated to throw light on any methods of alleviation of moral and political evil, and as far as lays in its power, actively interesting itself in whatever occasion may arise for benefiting mankind.

When I mention Ireland, I do not mean to confine the influence of the association to this, or to any other country, but for the time being. Moreover, I would recommend, that this association should attempt to form others and to actuate them with a similar spirit, and I am thus indeterminate in my description of the association which I propose, because I conceive that an assembly of men meeting to do all the good that opportunity will permit them to do, must be in its nature as indefinite and varying as the instances of human vice and misery that precede, occasion, and call for its institution.

As political institution and its attendant evils constitute the majority of those grievances, which Philanthropists desire to remedy, it is probable that existing Governments will frequently become the topic of their discussion, the results of which may little coincide with the opinions which those who profit by the supineness of human belief, desire to impress upon the world. It is probable that this freedom may excite the odium of certain well-meaning people who pin their faith upon their grandmother's apron string. The minority in number are the majority in intellect and power. The former govern the latter, though it is by the sufferance of the latter that this originally delegated power is exercised. This power is become hereditary, and hath ceased to be necessarily united with intellect.

It is certain, therefore, that any questioning of established principles would excite the abhorrence and opposition of those who derived power and honour (such as it is) from their continuance.

As the association which I recommend would question those principles (however they may be hedged in with antiquity and precedent) which appeared ill adapted for the benefit of human kind; it would probably excite the odium of those in power. It would be obnoxious to the government, though nothing would be farther from the views of associated philanthropists than attempting to subvert establishments forcibly, or even hastily. Aristocracy would oppose it, whether oppositionists or ministerialists (for philanthropy is of no party,) because its ultimate views look to a subversion of all factitious distinctions, although from its immediate intentions I fear that aristocracy can have nothing to dread. The priesthood would oppose it, because a union of church and state; contrary to the principles and practice of Jesus, contrary to that equality which he fruitlessly endeavoured to teach mankind, is of all institutions that from the rust of antiquity are called venerable, the least qualified to stand free and cool reasoning, because it least conduces to the happiness of human kind: yet did either the minister, the peer, or the bishop, know their true interest, instead of that virulent opposition which some among them have made to freedom and philanthropy, they would rejoice and co-operate with the diffusion and corroboration of those principles that would remove a load of paltry equivocation, paltrier grandeur, and of wigs that crush into emptiness the brains below them from their shoulders; and by permitting them to reassume the degraded and vilified title of man would preclude the necessity of mystery and deception, would bestow on them a title more ennobling and a dignity which, though it would be without the gravity of an ape, would possess the ease and consistency of a man.

For the reasons above alleged, falsely, prejudicedly, and narrowly will those very persons whose ultimate benefit is included in the general good whose promotion is the essence of a philanthropic association, will they persecute those who have the best intentions towards them, malevolence towards none.

I do not, therefore, conceal that those who make the favour of government the sunshine of their moral day confide in the political creed makers of the hour, are willing to think things that are rusty and decayed venerable, and are uninquiringly satisfied with evils as these are, because they find them established and unquestioned as they do sunlight and air when they come into existence; that they had better not even think of philanthropy. I conceal not from them that the discountenance which government will shew to such an association as I am desirous to establish will come under their comprehensive definition of danger: that virtue and any assembly instituted under its auspices demands a voluntariness on the part of its devoted individuals to sacrifice personal to public benefit; and that it is possible that a party of beings associated for the purposes of disseminating virtuous principles, may, considering the ascendancy which long custom has conferred on opposite motives to action, meet with inconveniences that may amount to personal danger. These considerations, are, however, to the mind of the philanthropist as is a drop to an ocean; they serve by their possible existence as tests whereby to discover the really virtuous man from him who calls himself a patriot for dishonourable and selfish purposes. I propose then to such as think with me, a Philanthropic Association, in spite of the danger that may attend the attempt. I do not this beneath the shroud of mystery and darkness. I propose not an Association of Secrecy. Let it [be] open as the beam of day. Let it rival the sunbeam in its stainless purity, as in the extensiveness of its effulgence.

I disclaim all connection with insincerity and concealment. The latter implies the former, as much as the former stands in need of the latter. It is a very latitudinarian system of morality that permits its professor to employ bad means for any end whatever. Weapons which vice *can* use are unfit for the hands of virtue. Concealment implies falsehood; it is bad, and can therefore never be serviceable to the cause of philanthropy.

I propose, therefore, that the association shall be established and conducted in the open face of day, with the utmost possible publicity. It is only vice that hides itself in holes and corners whose effrontery shrinks from scrutiny, whose cowardice lets I *dare not* wait upon I would, like the poor cat in the adage. But the eye of virtue, eagle-like, darts through the undazzling beam of eternal truth, and from the undiminished fountain of its purity gathers wherewith to vivify and illuminate a universe.

I have hitherto abstained from inquiring whether the association which I recommend be or be not consistent with the English constitution. And here it is fit, briefly to consider what a constitution is.

Government can have no rights,[3] it is a delegation for the purpose of securing them to others. Man becomes a subject of government, not that he may be in a worse but that he may be in a better state than that of unorganized society. The strength of government is the happiness of the governed. All government existing for the happiness of others is just only so far as it exists by their consent, and useful only so far as it operates to their well-being. Constitution is to government what government is to law. Constitution may, in this view of the subject, be defined to be, not merely something constituted for the benefit of any nation or class of people, but something, constituted by themselves for their own benefit. The nations of England and Ireland have no constitution, because at no one time did the individuals that compose them constitute a system for the general benefit. If a system determined on by a very few, at a great length of time; if magna charta, the bill of rights, and other usages for whose influence the improved state of human knowledge is rather to be looked to, than any system which courtiers pretend to exist and perhaps believe to exist; a system whose spring of agency they represent as something secret, undiscoverable and awful as the law of nature. If these make a constitution, then England has one. But if (as I have endeavoured to shew they do not) a constitution is something else, then the speeches of kings or commissioners, the writings of courtiers, and the journals of parliament, which teem with its glory, are full of political cant; exhibit the skeleton of national freedom, and are fruitless attempts to hide evils in whose favor they cannot prove an alibi. As therefore, in the true sense of the expression, the spot of earth on which we live is destitute of constituted Government, it is impossible to offend against its principles, or to be with justice accused of wishing to subvert what has no real existence. If a man was accused of setting fire to a house, which house never existed, and from the nature of things could not have existed, it is impossible that a jury in their senses would find him guilty of arson. The English constitution then, could not be offended by the principles of virtue and freedom. In fact, the manner in which the Government of England has varied since its earliest establishment, proves that its present form is the result of a progressive accommodation to existing principles. It has been a continual struggle for liberty on the part of the people, and an uninterrupted attempt at tightening the reins of oppression and encouraging ignorance and imposture by the oligarchy to whom the first William parcelled out the property of the aborigines at the conquest of England by the Norman's. I hear much of its being a tree so long growing which to cut down is as bad as cutting down an oak where there are no more. But the best way, on topics similar to these, is to tell the plain truth, without the confusion and ornament of metaphor. I call expressions similar to these political cant, which like the songs of Rule Britannia and God save the king, are but abstracts of the caterpillar creed of courtiers, cut down to the taste and comprehension of a mob; the one to disguise to an alehouse politician the evils of that devilish practice of war, and the other to inspire among clubs of all descriptions a certain feeling which some call loyalty and others servility. A philanthropic association has nothing to fear from the English constitution, but it may expect danger from its government. So far however from thinking this an argument against its institution, establishment and augmentation, I am inclined to rest much of the weight of the cause which my duties call upon me to support, on the very fact that government forcibly interferes when the opposition that is made to its proceedings is professedly and undeniably nothing but intellectual. A good cause may be shewn to be good, violence instantly renders bad what might before have been good. 'Weapons that falsehood can use are unfit for the hands of truth'. Truth can reason, and falsehood cannot.

A political or religious system may burn and imprison those who investigate its principles; but it is an invariable proof of their falsehood and hollowness. Here then is another reason for the necessity of a Philanthropic Association, and I call upon any fair and rational opponent to controvert the argument which it contains; for there is no one who even calls himself a philanthropist that thinks personal danger or dishonour terrible in any other light than as it affects his usefulness.

Man has a heart to feel, a brain to think, and a tongue to utter. The laws of his moral as of his physical nature are immutable, as is everything of nature; nor can the ephemeral institutions of human society take away those rights, annihilate or strengthen the duties that have for their basis the imperishable relations of his constitution.

Though the parliament of England were to pass a thousand bills to inflict upon those who determined to utter their thoughts, a thousand penalties, it could not render that criminal which was in its nature innocent before the passing of such bill.

Man has a right to feel, to think, and to speak, nor can any acts of legislature destroy that right. He will feel, he must think, and he *ought* to give utterance to those thoughts and feelings with the readiest sincerity and the strictest candour. A man must have a right to do a thing before he can have a duty; this right must permit before his duty can enjoin him to any act. Any law is bad which attempts to make it criminal to do what the plain dictates within the breast of every man tells him that he ought to do.

The English Government permits a fanatic to assemble any number of persons to teach them the most extravagant and immoral systems of faith; but a few men meeting to consider its own principles are marked with its hatred, and pursued by its jealousy.

The religionist who agonizes the death-bed of the cottager, and by picturing the hell, which hearts black and narrow as his own alone could have invented, and which exists but in their cores, spreads the uncharitable doctrines which devote *heretics* to eternal torments, and represents heaven to be what earth is, a monopoly in the hands of certain favoured ones whose merit consists in slavishness, whose success is the reward of sycophancy. Thus much is permitted, but a public inquiry that involves any doubt of their rectitude into the principles of government is not permitted. When Jupiter and a countryman were one day walking out, conversing familiarly on the affairs of earth, the countryman listened to Jupiter's assertions on the subject for some time in acquiescence, at length happening to hint a doubt, Jupiter threatened him with his thunder; ah, ah, says the countryman, now Jupiter I know that you are wrong: you are always wrong when you appeal to your thunder. The essence of virtue is disinterestedness. Disinterestedness is the quality which preserves the character of virtue distinct from that of either innocence or vice. This, it will be said, is mere assertion. It is so: but it is an assertion, whose truth, I believe, the hearts of philanthropists are disinclined to deny. Those who have been convinced by their grandam of the doctrine of an original hereditary sin, or by the apostles of a degrading philosophy of the necessary and universal selfishness of man cannot be philanthropists. Now as an action, or a motive to action, is only virtuous so far as it is disinterested, or partakes (I adopt this mode of expression to suit the taste of some) of the nature of generalized self-love, then reward or punishment, attached even by omnipotence to any action, can in no way make it either good or bad.

It is no crime to act in contradiction to an English judge or an English legislator, but it is a crime to transgress the dictates of a monitor, which feels the spring of every motive, whose throne is the human sensorium, whose empire the human conduct. Conscience is a Government before which all others sink into nothingness; it surpasses, and where it can act supersedes, all other, as nature surpasses art, as God surpasses man.

In the preceding pages, during the course of an investigation of the possible objections which might be urged by Philanthropy, to an association such as I recommend, as I have rather sought to bring forward than conceal my principles, it will appear that they have their origin from the discoveries in the sciences of politics and morals, which preceded and occasioned the Revolutions of America and France. It is with openness that I confess, nay with pride I assert, that they are so. The names of Paine and Lafayette will outlive the poetic aristocracy of an expatriated Jesuit,[4] as the executive of a bigoted policy will die before the disgust at the sycophancy of their eulogists can subside.

It will be said, perhaps, that much as principles, such as these may appear marked on the outside with peace, liberty, and virtue, that their ultimate tendency is to a Revolution, which like that of France, will end in bloodshed, vice, and slavery. I must offer, therefore, my thoughts on that event, which so suddenly and so lamentably extinguished the overstrained hopes of liberty which it excited. I do not deny that the Revolution of France was occasioned by the literary labors of the Encyclopaedists.[5] When we see two events together, in certain cases, we speak of one as the cause, the other the effect. We have no other idea of cause and effect, but that which arises from necessary connection; it is therefore, still doubtful whether D'Alembert, Boulanger, Condorcet,[6] and other celebrated characters, were the causes of the overthrow of the ancient monarchy of France. Thus much is certain, that they contributed greatly to the extension and diffusion of knowledge, and that knowledge is incompatible with slavery. The French nation was bowed to the dust by ages of uninterrupted despotism. They were plundered and insulted by a succession of oligarchies, each more bloodthirsty and unrelenting than the foregoing. In a state like this, her soldiers learned to fight for Freedom on the plains of America, whilst at this very conjuncture, a ray of science burst through the clouds of bigotry that obscured the moral day of Europe. The French were in the lowest state of human degradation, and when the truth, unaccustomed to their ears, that they were men and equals was promulgated, they were the first to vent their indignation on the monopolizes of earth, because they were most glaringly defrauded of the immunities of nature.

Since the French were furthest removed by the sophistications of political institution from the genuine condition of human beings, they must have been most unfit for that happy state of equal law, which proceeds from consummated civilisation, and which demands habits of the strictest virtue before its introduction.

The murders during the period of the French Revolution, and the despotism which has since been established, prove that the doctrines of Philanthropy and Freedom, were but shallowly understood. Nor was it until after that period, that their principles became clearly to be explained, and unanswerably to be established.

Voltaire[7] was the flatterer of Kings, though in his heart he despised them: – so far has he been instrumental in the present slavery of his country. Rousseau[8] gave licence by his writings, to passions that only incapacitate and contract the human heart: – so far hath he prepared the necks of his fellow-beings for that yoke of galling and dishonorable servitude, which at this moment, it bears. Helvetius[9] and Condorcet established principles, but if they drew conclusions, their conclusions were unsystematical, and devoid of the luminousness and energy of method: – they were little understood in the Revolution. But this age of ours is not stationary. Philosophers have not developed the great principles of the human mind that conclusions from them should be unprofitable and impracticable. We are in a state of continually progressive improvement. Once truth that had been discovered can never die, but will prevent the revivification of its apportioned opposite falsehood. By promoting truth and discouraging its opposite, the means of Philanthropy are principally to be forwarded. Godwin wrote during the Revolution of France, and certainly his writings were totally devoid of influence, with regard to its purposes. Oh! that they had not! In the Revolution of France, were engaged men, whose names are inerasible from the records of Liberty. Their genius penetrated with a glance the gloom and glare which Church-craft and State-craft had spread before the imposture and villainy of their establishments. They saw the world – were they men? Yes! They felt for it! They risked their lives and happiness for its benefit! Had there been more of these men France would not now be a beacon to warn us of the hazard and horror of Revolutions, but a pattern of society, rapidly advancing to a state of perfection, and holding out an example for the gradual and peaceful regeneration of the world. I consider it to be one of the effects of a Philanthropic Association, to assist in the production of such men as these, in an extensive development of those germs of excellence, whose favorite soil is the cultured garden of the human mind.

Many well-meaning persons may think that the attainment of the good, which I propose as the ultimatum of Philanthropic exertion is visionary and inconsistent with human nature; they would tell me not to make people happy, for fear of overstocking the world, and to permit those who found dishes placed before them on the table of partial nature, to enjoy their superfluities in quietness, though millions of wretches crowded around but to pick a morsel,[10] which morsel was still refused to the prayers of agonising famine.

I cannot help thinking this an evil, nor help endeavouring, by the safest means that I can devise, to palliate at present, and in fine to eradicate this evil; war, vice, and misery are undeniably bad, they embrace all that we can conceive of temporal and eternal evil. Are we to be told that these are remedyless, because the earth would, in case of their remedy, be overstocked? That the rich are still to glut, that the ambitious are still to plan, that the fools whom these knaves mould are still to murder their brethren and call it glory, and that the poor are to pay with their blood, their labor, their happiness, and their innocence for the crimes and mistakes which the hereditary monopolists of earth commit? Rare sophism! How will the heartless rich hug thee to their bosoms and lull their conscience into slumber with the opiate of thy reconciling dogmas! But when the Philosopher and Philanthropist contemplates the universe, when he perceives existing evils that admit of amendment, and hears tell of other evils, which in the course of sixty centuries, may again derange the system of happiness, which the amendment is calculated to produce, does he submit to prolong a positive evil, because if that were eradicated, after a millennium of 6000 years (for such space of time would it take to people the earth) another evil would take place.

To how contemptible a degradation of grossest credulity will not prejudice lower the human mind! We see in Winter that the foliage of the trees is gone, that they present to the view nothing but leafless branches – we see that the loveliness of the flower decays, though the root continues in the earth. What opinion should we form of that man, who, when he walked in the freshness of the spring, beheld the fields enamelled with flowers, and the foliage bursting from the buds, should find fault with this beautiful order, and murmur his contemptible discontents because winter must come, and the landscape be robbed of its beauty for a while again?[11] Yet this man is Mr. Malthus. Do we not see that the laws of nature perpetually act by disorganisation and reproduction, each alternately becoming cause and effect. The [analogies] that we can draw from physical to moral topics are of all others the most striking.

Does anyone yet question the possibility of inducing radical reform of moral and political evil. Does he object from that impossibility to the Association which I propose, which I frankly confess to be one of the means whose instrumentality I would employ to attain this reform. Let them look to the methods which I use. Let me put my object out of their view and propose their own, how would they accomplish it? By diffusing virtue and knowledge, by promoting human happiness. Palsied be the hand, forever dumb be the tongue that would by one expression convey sentiments differing from these: I will use no bad means for any end whatever. Know then ye philanthropists, to whatever profession of faith, or whatever determination of principles, chance, reason, or education, may have conducted you, that the endeavours of the truly virtuous necessarily converge to one point, though it be hidden from them what point that is: they all labour for one end, and that controversies concerning the nature of that end, serve only to weaken the strength which for the interest of virtue should be consolidated.

The diffusion of true and virtuous principles (for in the first principles of morality *none* disagree) will produce the best of possible terminations.

I invite to an Association of Philanthropy those of whatever ultimate expectations, who will employ the same means that I employ; let their designs differ as much as they may from mine, I shall rejoice at their co-operation; because if the ultimatum of my hopes be founded on the unity of truth, I shall then have auxiliaries in its cause, and if it be false I shall rejoice that means are not neglected for forwarding that which is true.

The accumulation of evil which Ireland has for the last twenty years sustained, and considering the unremittingness of its pressure I may say patiently sustained; the melancholy prospect which the unforeseen conduct of the Regent of England holds out of its continuance, demands of every Irishman, whose pulses have not ceased to throb with the life-blood of his heart, that he should individually consult and unitedly determine on some measures for the liberty of his countrymen. That those measures should be pacific though resolute, that their movers should be calmly brave, and temperately unbending, though the whole heart and soul should go with the attempt, is the opinion which my principles command me to give.

And I am induced to call an Association, such as this occasion demands, an Association of philanthropy, because good men ought never to circumscribe their usefulness by any name which denotes their exclusive devotion to the accomplishment of its signification.

When I began the preceding remarks I conceived that on the removal of the restrictions from the Regent a ministry less inimical than the present to the interests of liberty would have been appointed. I am deceived and the disappointment of the hopes of freedom on this subject afford an additional argument towards the necessity of an Association.

I conclude these remarks which I have indited principally with a view of unveiling my principles with a proposal for an Association for the purposes of catholic emancipation, a repeal of the union act, and grounding upon the attainment of these objects a reform of whatever moral or political evil may be within its compass of human power to remedy.

Such as are favourably inclined towards the institution would highly gratify the proposer, if they would personally communicate with him on this important subject, by which means the plan might be matured, errors in the proposer's original system be detected, and a meeting for the purpose convened with that resolute expedition which the nature of the present crisis demands.

No. 7, Lower Sackville Street.

NOTES

1   From T Paine's 'The Rights of Man', *Thomas Paine Reader*, op cit, p240.

2   The legendary king of the serpents. It was reputed to be capable of 'looking anyone dead on whom it fixed its eyes'.

3   Shelley introduces his *Declaration of Rights* (Appendix 5, p303) with this point. In this section of the *Proposals* Shelley's position on 'rights' are based on Godwin's *Political Justice* and Paine's *Rights of Man.*

4   See *Memoires de Jacobinisme,* par l'Abbe Baruel. [Shelley's note]

5   A group of French Enlightenment philosophers and humanists whose *Encyclopédie*, (1751-80) was written to 'change the general way of thinking'. They were critics of religion and the monarchy, whose ideas laid the intellectual foundation for the French Revolution.

6   Jean le Rond D'Alembert (1717-83), Nicolas-Antoine Boulanger (1722-59) and Marquis de Condorcet (1743-94) were all contributors to the *Encyclopédie*, though only Condorcet was active in the revolution.

7   François-Marie Arouet de Voltaire (1649-1778), French philosopher and poet and sometimes 'flatterer' of kings and queens for personal advantage.

8   Jean-Jacques Rousseau (1712-1778), French philosopher and novelist. While Shelley was a critic of Rousseau in his early life, a position which was confirmed by Godwin in his letter of 4 March 1812 (Appendix 2, 219), he became more sympathetic and arrived at a more profound understanding of his work in later life.

9   Claude-Adrien Helvetius (1715-71), French philosopher who believed that political or social reform could only be brought about by universal education.

10   See Malthus on Population [Shelley's note]. Shelley uses the next two paragraphs to answer Malthus's *An Essay on the Principle of Population*, (London, 1798); for if Malthus is right then philanthropy is impossible.

11   Taken from Tom Paine's 'The Rights of Man', *Thomas Paine Reader*, op cit, p363. Shelley used this analogy again in his *Ode to the West Wind*, (see Chapter 9, p182).

Declaration of Rights

1

Government has no rights; it is a delegation from several individuals for the purpose of securing their own. It is therefore just, only so far as it exists by their consent, useful only so far as it operates to their well-being.

2

If these individuals think that the form of government which they, or their forefathers constituted is ill adapted to produce their happiness, they have a right to change it.

3

Government is devised for the security of rights. The rights of man are liberty, and an equal participation of the commonage of nature.

4

As the benefit of the governed, is, or ought to be the origin of government, no men can have any authority that does not expressly emanate from their will.

5

Though all governments are not so bad as that of Turkey, yet none are so good as they might be; the majority of every country have a right to perfect their government, the minority should not disturb them, they ought to secede, and form their own system in their own way.

6

All have a right to an equal share in the benefits, and burdens of Government. Any disabilities for opinion, imply by their existence, barefaced tyranny on the side of government, ignorant slavishness on the side of the governed.

7

The rights of man in the present state of society, are only to be secured by some degree of coercion to be exercised on their violator. The sufferer has a right that the degree of coercion employed be as slight as possible.

8

It may be considered as a plain proof of the hollowness of any proposition, if power be used to enforce instead of reason to persuade its admission. Government is never supported by fraud until it cannot be supported by reason.

9

No man has a right to disturb the public peace, by personally resisting the execution of a law however bad. He ought to acquiesce, using at the same time the utmost powers of his reason, to promote its repeal.

10

A man must have a right to act in a certain manner before it can be his duty. He may, before he ought.

11

A man has a right to think as his reason directs, it is a duty he owes to himself to think with freedom, that he may act from conviction.

12

A man has a right to unrestricted liberty of discussion, falsehood is a scorpion that will sting itself to death.

13

A man has not only a right to express his thoughts, but it is his duty to do so.

14

No law has a right to discourage the practice of truth. A man ought to speak the truth on every occasion, a duty can never be criminal, what is not criminal cannot be injurious.

15

Law cannot make what is in its nature virtuous or innocent, to be criminal, any more than it can make what is criminal to be innocent. Government cannot make a law, it can only pronounce that which was law before its organization, viz. the moral result of the imperishable relations of things.

16

The present generation cannot bind their posterity. The few cannot promise for the many.

17

No man has a right to do an evil thing that good may come.

18

Expediency is inadmissible in morals. Politics are only sound when conducted on principles of morality. They are, in fact, the morals of nations.

19

Man has no right to kill his brother, it is no excuse that he does so in uniform. He only adds the infamy of servitude to the crime of murder.

20

Man, whatever be his country, has the same rights in one place as another, the rights of universal citizenship.

21

The government of a country ought to be perfectly indifferent to every opinion. Religious differences, the bloodiest and most rancorous of all, spring from partiality.

22

A delegation of individuals for the purpose of securing their rights, can have no undelegated power of restraining the expression of their opinion.

23

Belief is involuntary; nothing involuntary is meritorious or reprehensible. A man ought not to be considered worse or better for his belief.

24

A Christian, a Deist, a Turk, and a Jew, have equal rights: they are men and brethren.

25

If a person's religious ideas correspond not with your own, love him nevertheless. How different would yours have been had the chance of birth placed you in Tartary or India!

26

Those who believe that Heaven is, what earth has been, a monopoly in the hands of a favoured few, would do well to reconsider their opinion: if they find that it came from their priest or their grandmother, they could not do better than reject it.

27

No man has a right to be respected for any other possessions, but those of virtue and talents. Titles are tinsel, power a corruptor, glory a bubble, and excessive wealth, a libel on its possessor.

28

No man has a right to monopolise more than he can enjoy; what the rich give to the poor, whilst millions are starving, is not a perfect favour, but an imperfect right.

29

Every man has a right to a certain degree of leisure and liberty, because it is his duty to attain a certain degree of knowledge. He may before he ought.

30

Sobriety of body and mind is necessary to those who would be free, because, without sobriety a high sense of philanthropy cannot actuate the heart, nor cool and determined courage, execute its dictates.

31

The only use of government is to repress the vices of man. If man were to day sinless, to-morrow he would have a right to demand that government and all its evils should cease.

Man! thou whose rights are here declared, be no longer forgetful of the loftiness of thy destination. Think of thy rights; of those possessions which will give thee virtue and wisdom, by which thou mayest arrive at happiness and freedom. They are declared to thee by one who knows thy dignity, for every hour does his heart swell with honourable pride in the contemplation of what thou mayest attain, by one who is not forgetful of thy degeneracy, for every moment brings home to him the bitter conviction of what thou art.

Awake! – arise! – or be for ever fallen.

BIBLIOGRAPHY

Newspapers and Periodicals.

Annual Register

Christian Examiner

Courier

Dublin Evening Post

Dublin Historical Record

Dublin Magazine

Dublin Political Review

Dublin University Magazine

Dublin Weekly Messenger

Eire-Ireland

Evening Herald

Fortnightly Review

Freeman's Journal

Hansard

Hibernian Journal

Irish Review

Irish Times

Irish Worker

Labour History News

Left Review

Modern Language Notes

Nation

Nation (New York)

National Magazine

New Ireland Review

North British Review

Patriot

Political Register

Saothar

Saunders Newsletter

Shelley Memorial Association Bulletin

Sinn Féin

United Irishman

University Review

Walker's Hibernian Magazine

Weekly Dublin Satirist

Books: Selected primary and secondary sources

Allott, M (ed), *Essays on Shelley* (Liverpool, 1982)

Aveling, Edward and Marx, Eleanor, *Shelley's Socialism* (London, 1975)

Arnold, Matthew, *The Essential Matthew Arnold* (London, 1949)

Bardon, J, *A History of Ulster* (Belfast, 1992)

Barry, Michael, *The Romance of Sarah Curran* (Fermoy, 1985)

Bennett, Andrew, *Shelley and Contemporary Thought* (Baltimore, 1996)

Bennett, Betty and Curran, Stuart (eds), *Shelley: Poet and Legislator of the World* (Baltimore, 1996)

Blunden, Edward, *Leigh Hunt* (London, 1930)

Blunden, Edward, *Shelley* (London, 1946)

Boas, Louise Schutz, *Harriet Shelley: Five Long Years* (London, 1962)

Bornstein, George, *Yeats and Shelley* (Chicago, 1970)

Boyce, D. George, *Nineteenth-Century Ireland* (Dublin, 1990)

Brailsford, H N, *Shelley, Godwin, and Their Circle* (London, 1913)

Breen, Jennifer (ed), *Women Romantic Poets 1785-1832* (London, 1995)

Brett-Smith, H, *The Four Ages of Poetry* (Oxford, 1937)

Brown, Philip, *The French Revolution in English History* (London, 1918)

Brown, Terence, *Louis MacNeice: Sceptical Vision* (Dublin, 1985)

Brown, Terence, *Ireland's Literature* (Mullingar, 1988)

Burke, Edmund, *Reflections on the French Revolution* (London, 1935)

Burke, J, *The Speeches of Edmund Burke* (Dublin, 1867)

Burns, Robert, *The Poetical Works* (London, 1950)

Byron, Lord, *Selected Prose* (London, nd)

Cameron, Kenneth, *The Young Shelley (*New York, 1950)

Cameron, Kenneth, *Shelley: The Golden Years (*Massachusetts, 1974)

Cameron, Kenneth, and Reiman, Donald (eds), *Shelley and his Circle 1773-1822*, 8 volumes (Massachusetts, 1961-1986)

Carswell, Catherine, *Robert Burns* (London, 1933)

Castlereagh, Lord (ed), *Memoirs and Correspondence of Viscount Castlereagh* Londonderry, 3rd Marquess of, 12 vols (London, 1848-1854)

Clairmont, Claire, *The Journals of Claire Clairmont*, Stocking, M (ed) (Boston, 1968)

Clarke, Austin, *Collected Poems (*Dublin, 1974)

Cliff, Tony, *A World to Win* (London, 2000)

Cliff, Tony, *Trotsky* 4 volumes (London, 1993)

Clifford, Brendan (ed), *The Veto Controversy* (Belfast, 1985)

Clive, Arthur (Standish O'Grady) *Scintilla Shelleana* (Dublin, 1875)

Coleridge, Samuel Taylor, *The Notebooks of S T Coleridge,* K Coburn and M Christensen (eds), 4 volumes (London, 1957-73)

Coleridge, Samuel Taylor, *Biographia Literaria* (London, 1997)

Coleridge, Samuel Taylor, William Keach (ed), *Collected Poems* (London, 1997)

Connolly, James, *Collected Works*, 2 volumes (Dublin, 1988)

Coombs, Heather, *The Age of Shelley and Keats* (Glasgow, 1978)

Cosgrave, A (ed), *Dublin Through the Ages* (Dublin, 1988)

Costello, Peter, *James Joyce: The Years of Growth* (London, 1996)

Cullen, Mary (ed), *1798: 200 Years of Resonance* (Dublin, 1998)

Curran, John Philpot, *Speeches of the Rt Hon John Philpot Curran* (Dublin, 1808)

Dalsimer, A M, *Kate O'Brien: A Critical Study* (Dublin 1990)

Dalsimer, A M, *The Unappeaseable Shadow: Shelley's influence on Yeats* (NY 1990)

Darvall, F, *Popular Disturbances and Public Order in Regency England* (London, 1934)

Davies, R T, and Beatty, B G (eds), *Literature of the Romantic Period*, (Liverpool, 1980)

Dickson, David (ed), *The Gorgeous Mask: Dublin 1700-1850* (Dublin, 1987)

Dickson, David, Keogh, Daire, and Whelan, Kevin (eds), *The United Irishmen* (Dublin, 1993)

Dooley, Dolores, *Equality in Community* (Cork, 1996)

Dowden, Edward, *The Life of Percy Bysshe Shelley*, 2 volumes (London, 1886)

Dowden, Edward, *Southey* (London, 1879)

Dowden, Edward, *Transcripts and Studies* (London, 1888)

Dowden, Edward, *Studies in Literature 1789-1877* (London, 1878)

Drennan, William, *A Letter to the Right Honourable James Fox* (Dublin, 1806)

Duerkin, Roland (ed), *Shelley's Political Writings* (New York, 1970)

Elwin, Malcolm, *The First Romantics* (London, 1947)

Elliot, Marianne, *Wolfe Tone* (London, 1989)

Elliot, Marianne, *Partners in Revolution* (London, 1982)

Ellmann, Richard, *Oscar Wilde* (London, 1988)

Ellmann, Richard, *James Joyce* (New York, 1965)

Emmet, Robert, *Speech from the Dock* (Dublin, 1978)

Fallis, Richard, *The Irish Renaissance* (Dublin, 1978)

Farrell, James T, *On Irish Themes* (Philadelphia, 1982)

Fennessy, R R, *Burke, Paine, and The Rights of Man* (La Haye, 1963)

Foot, Paul, *Red Shelley* (London, 1980)

Foot, Paul (ed), *Shelley's Revolutionary Year* (London, 1990)

Ford, Boris (ed), *From Blake to Byron* (London, 1957)

Foster, Roy, *Paddy & Mr Punch* (London, 1995)

Frazier, Adrian, *George Moore* (New Haven, 2000)

Godwin, William, *Memoirs of Mary Wollstonecraft* (London, 1928)

Godwin, William, *Caleb Williams* (London, 1988)

Godwin, William, *Enquiry concerning Political Justice* (London, 1976)

Godwin, William, *Uncollected Writings* (Florida, 1968)

Grylls, Rosalie G, *William Godwin and his World* (London, 1953)

Gwynn, Denis, *The Struggle for Catholic Emancipation* (London, 1928)

Gwynn, Denis, *Daniel O'Connell the Irish Liberator* (London, nd)

Gwynn, Stephen, *The Masters of English Literature* (London, 1938)

Hale, Leslie, *John Philpot Curran* (London, 1958)

Hames, J H, *Arthur O'Conner, United Irishman* (Cork 2001)

Hazlitt, William, *Spirit of the Age* (London, 1964)

Heaney, Seamus, *The Government of the Tongue* (London, 1988)

Heaney, Seamus, *North* (London, 1975)

Heaney, Seamus, *Door into the Dark* (London, 1972)

Hobsbawm, Eric, *The Age of Revolution* (London, 1977)

Hobsbawm, Eric, and Ranger, Terence (eds), *The Invention of Tradition* (Cambridge, 1984)

Hogg, Thomas Jefferson, *The Life of Percy Bysshe Shelley*, 2 volumes (London, 1906)

Holmes, Richard, *Coleridge: Early Visions* (London, 1989)

Holmes, Richard, *Coleridge: Darker Reflections* (London, 1998)

Holmes, Richard, *Footsteps* (London, 1986)

Holmes, Richard, *Shelley: The Pursuit* (London, 1974)

Holmes, Richard, *Shelley on Love* (London, 1996)

Holroyd, Michael, *Bernard Shaw*, 5 volumess (London, 1988-1993)

Hough, Graham, *The Romantic Poets* (London, 1968)

Houston, A, *Daniel O'Connell: His Early Life, and Journal 1795-1802* (London, 1906)

Hunt, Leigh, *Autobiography* (London, 1861)

Ingpen, Roger, *Shelley in England* (London, 1917)

Jackson, A, *Ireland Her Own* (London, 1947)

Joyce, James, *Exiles* (London, 1962)

Joyce, James, *Ulysses* (London, 1968)

Kavanagh, Patrick, *Selected Poems* (London, 1996)

Keach, William, *Young Shelley* (Internet: Romantic Circles Praxis Series)

Keane, John, *Tom Paine: A Political Life* (London, 1995)

Keats, John, *Poetical Works* (London, 1940)

Kennelly, Brendan, *Shelley in Dublin* (Dun Laoire, 1974)

King-Hele, Desmond, *Shelley: His Thought and Work* (London, 1971)

Klaus, H G (ed), *Strong Words Brave Deeds* (Dublin, 1994)

Komesu, Okifumi, and Sekine, Masuru (eds), *Irish Writers and Politics* (Gerrards Cross, 1989)

Larkin, Emmet, *James Larkin* (London, 1977)

Lawless, John, *A Compendium of the History of Ireland* (Dublin, 1814)

Leavis, F R, *Revaluation* (London, 1964)

Leerson, Joseph, *Remembrance and Imagination* (Cork, 1998)

Legouis, Emile, *The Early Life of William Wordsworth* (London, 1921)

Linebaugh, P and Rediker, M, *The Many-Headed Hydra* (Boston 2000)

Longley, Edna, *The Living Stream* (Newcastle, 1994)

Longley, Edna, *Louis MacNeice* (London, 1988)

Madden, Richard, *The United Irishmen*, 4 volumes (London, 1857-60)

Mansergh, N, *Britain and Ireland* (London, 1942)

Marx, K, and Engels, F, *Collected Works*, 50 volumes in progress (Moscow, 1975-)

Matthews, G M, *Shelley* (London, 1970)

Maume, Patrick, *Daniel Corkery and the search for Irish Ireland* (Belfast, 1993)

McAleer, Edward, *The Sensitive Plant* (Chapel Hill, 1958)

McCormack, W J, *From Burke to Beckett* (Cork, 1994)

McCormack, W J, *The Battle of the Books* (Mullingar, 1986)

McCormack, W J, and Stead, A (ed), *James Joyce and Modern Culture* (London, 1982)

McDowell, R B, *Ireland in the Age of Imperialism and Revolution* (London, 1979)

McDowell, R B, *Irish Public Opinion: 1750-1800* (London, 1944)

McDowell, R B, *Social Life in Ireland: 1800-1845* (Dublin, 1957)

McLaughlin, Thomas, *Contesting Ireland* (Dublin, 1999)

MacCarthy, Denis F, *Shelley's Early Life* (London, 1872)

MacNeice, Louis, *Collected Poems* (London, 1979)

MacNeice, Louis, *Varieties of Parable* (Cambridge, 1965)

MacNevin, W, *Pieces of Irish History* (New York, 1807)

Medwin, Thomas, *The life of Percy Bysshe Shelley* (London, 1913)

Mendilow, J, *The Romantic Tradition in British Political Thought* (Beckenham, 1986)

Mitchel, John, *The History of Ireland* (Glasgow, nd)

Montague, John, *Collected Poems* (Loughcrew, 1995)

Moore, George, *Confessions of a Young Man* (London, 1961)

Moore, Thomas, *Letter to Roman Catholics of Dublin* (Dublin, 1810)

Moore, Thomas, *Corruption and Intolerance* (London, 1808)

Moore, Thomas, *Poetical Works* (London,1915)

Moorman, Mary, *Wordsworth: The Early Years* (London, 1968)

Moorman, Mary, *Wordsworth: The Later Years* (London, 1968)

Morley, John, *Burke* (London, 1879)

Motion, Andrew, *Keats* (London, 1997)

Nevin, Donal (ed), *James Larkin: The Lion in the Fold* (Dublin, 1998)

Nichol, John, *Byron* (London, 1908)

Norman, Sylva, *Flight of the Skylark* (London, 1954)

O'Brien, Conor Cruise, *The Great Melody: A Biography of Edmund Burke* (London, 1993)

O'Casey, Sean, *Autobiography,* 6 vols (London, 1939-1954)

O'Casey, Sean, *Two Plays* (London, 1925)

O'Casey, Sean, *The Letters of Sean O'Casey* (ed), Krause, David, 4 volumes (New York, 1980-1992)

O'Connell, John, *The Selected Speeches of Daniel O'Connell,* 2 volumes (Dublin, 1868)

O'Connell, Maurice (ed), *Daniel O'Connell: Political Pioneer* (Dublin, 1991)

O'Connor, Emmet, *A Labour History of Ireland* (Dublin, 1992)

O'Connor, Joe, *Even the Olives are Bleeding* (Dublin, 1992)

O'Farrell, Padraic (ed), *The '98 Reader* (Dublin, 1998)

O'Farrell, Fergus, *Daniel O'Connell* (Dublin, 1981)

O'Hagan, John, *Songs and Ballads of Young Ireland* (London, 1896)

O'Neill, Michael, *Shelley: A Literary Life* (London, 1989)

Opie, Amelia, *Adeline Mowbray* (Oxford, 1999)

O'Toole, Fintan, *A Traitor's Kiss* (London, 1998)

O'Tuathaigh, Gearoid, *Ireland Before the Famine* (Dublin, 1972)

Paine, Thomas, *The Thomas Paine Reader* (London, 1987)

Paulin, Tom, *The Day-Star of Liberty* (London, 1998)

Peacock, T, *Memoirs of Shelley* (London, 1970)

Peacock, William, *Selected English Essays* (London, 1926)

Peck, Walter, *Shelley: His Life and Work*, 2 volumes (Boston, 1927)

Phillips, Charles, *Recollections of Curran* (London, 1818)

Poirteir, Cathal (ed), *The Great Irish Rebellion of 1798* (Cork, 1998)

Pollard, H, *The Secret Societies of Ireland* (Kilkenny, 1998)

Pollock, J H, *The Moth and the Star* (Dublin, 1937)

Porter, R and Teich, M (eds), *Romanticism in National Context* (Cambridge, 1988)

Rafroidi, Patrick, *Irish Literature in English: The Romantic Period*, 2 volumes (Gerrards Cross, 1980)

Read, Herbert, *Selected Writings* (London, 1963)

Reiman, Donald, *Percy Bysshe Shelley* (New York, 1969)

Roberts, Michael, *The Whig Party 1807-1812* (London, 1965)

Salt, Henry, *Shelley's Principles* (London, nd)

Scott, Winifr(ed), *Jefferson Hogg* (London, 1951)

Shaw, Bernard, *The Diaries, 1885-1897* (ed), Weintraub, Stanley, 2 volumes (Pennsylvania, 1986)

Shaw, Bernard, *Pen Portraits and Reviews* (London, 1949)

Shaw, Bernard, *Collected Letters* (ed), Laurence, Dan H, 4 volumes (London, 1965-1988)

Shelley, Lady, *Shelley Memorials: From Authentic Sources* (London, 1875)

Shelley, Mary, *Frankenstein* (London, 1998)

Shelley, Mary, *Maurice* (London, 1998)

Shelley, Percy Bysshe, *The Complete Poetical Works* (London, 1991)

Shelley, Percy Bysshe, *The Poems of Shelly,* 2 volumes (ed), G Matthews (London 1989, 2000)

Shelley, Percy Bysshe, *The Esdaile Notebook* (London, 1964)

Shelley, Percy Bysshe, *Selected Poems* (ed), Quigley, Isabel (London, 1985)

Shelley, Percy Bysshe, *The Complete Poetical Works* (Boston, 1901)

Shelley, Percy Bysshe, *Selections from Shelley* (London, nd)

Shelley, Percy Bysshe, *St Irvyne* (London, 1822)

Shelley, Percy Bysshe, *The Letters of P B Shelley*, Jones, F L, (ed), 2 volumes (London, 1964)

Sloan, Barry, *The Pioneers of Anglo-Irish Fiction: 1800-1850* (Gerrards Cross, nd)

Smith, Olivia, *The Politics of Language 1791-1819* (Oxford, 1984)

Smith, Robert, *The Shelley Legend* (New York, 1967)

Somerville-Large, Peter, *Dublin* (London, 1981)

Southey, C C, *Life and Correspondence of Robert Southey*, 4 volumes (London, 1849)

Spark, Murial, *Mary Shelley* (London, 1988)

Spender, Stephen, *Forward from Liberalism* (London, 1937)

Storey, Mark (ed), *Poetry and Ireland since 1800* (London, 1988)

Symonds, J, *Shelley* (London, 1884)

Taylor, Philip (ed), *The Industrial Revolution in Britain* (Massachusetts, 1958)

Thompson, E P, *The Making of the English Working Class* (London, 1964)

Thompson, Francis, *Shelley* (London, 1914)

Thomson, George, *Marxism and Poetry* (New York, 1946)

Thomson, George, *Island Home: The Blasket Heritage* (Dingle, 1998)

Todd, F M, *Politics and the Poet: A Study of Wordsworth* (London, 1957)

Todd, Janet (ed), *A Wollstonecraft Anthology* (Cambridge, 1989)

Todd, Janet, *Rebels in the family: Ireland 1798* (London, 2003).

Todd, Janet, *Mary Wollstonecraft: A Revolutionary Life* (London, 2000).

Tomalin, Claire, *Mary Wollstonecraft* (London, 1992)

Tone, Theobald Wolfe, *The Life of Theobald Wolfe Tone*, 2 volumes (Washington, 1826)

Townsend, Molly, *Not by Bullets and Bayonets* (London, 1983)

Trelawny, Edward, *Recollections of the last days of Shelley and Byron* (London, 1923)

Trory, Ernie, *Cradled into Poetry* (Hove, 1991)

Vance, Norman, *Irish Literature: A Social History* (Oxford, 1990)

Vendler, Helen, *Seamus Heaney* (London, 1998)

Webb, Timothy, *Shelley: A Voice Not Understood* (Manchester, 1977)

Whelan, Kevin, *The Tree of Liberty* (Cork, 1996)

White, Newman Ivey, *Shelley*, 2 volumes (New York, 1940)

Wilde, Oscar, *Selected Poems* (London, 1911)

Williams, Raymond, *Culture and Society 1780-1950* (London, 1961)

Williams, Raymond, *The Long Revolution* (London, 1975)

Wilmot, Catherine, *An Irish Peer on the Continent* (London, 1920)

Wollstonecraft, Mary, *A Vindication of the Rights of Women* (London, 1992)

Woodcock, George, *William Godwin* (London, 1946)

Woodward, Llewellyn, *The Age of Reform 1815-1870* (Oxford, 1962)

Wordsworth, William, *The Poetical Works of Wordsworth* (London, 1946)

Wordsworth, William, and Coleridge, S T, *Lyrical Ballads* (London, 1931)

Wright, N, *An Historical Guide to Ancient and Modern Dublin* (London, 1829)

Yeates, Padraig, *Lockout: Dublin 1913* (Dublin, 2000)

Yeats, W B, *Selected Criticism (*London, 1964)

Yeats, W B, *Collected Poems* (London, 1950)

Yeats, W B, *Essay's by W B Yeats 1931-1936* (Dublin, 1937)

Other Sources

The Scully Papers (Dublin, 1988)

Wilson's Dublin Directory of 1812 (Dublin, 1812)

Bradshaw's Irish Collection (Cambridge, 1916)

Alfred Webb, 'Harriet Shelley and Catherine Nugent', *Nation* (Issue 48, 1889)

'98 Centenary Cttee Publications, no1, *The Storey of William Orr* (Dublin, 1898)

Pollard, M, *A Dictionary of the Dublin Book Trade: 1500-1800* (London, 2000)

National Library of Ireland

British Museum Library

New York Public Library, Pforzheimer Collection

Public Records Office, London

National Archives, Dublin

Trinity College, Dublin

Royal Irish Academy, Dublin

INDEX

Paul O'Brien was born in Dublin in 1946 and has been an active socialist for over 30 years. In that time he has written on the relationship between literature, history and politics in many newspapers and magazines.

REDWORDS

www.redwords.org.uk